CITIES IN TF...
The challenge for developing countries

Highlights from a workshop of representatives of international aid agencies and governments in developing countries to consider the new urban policy statements of the World Bank, the United Nations Development Programme and the United Nations Centre for Human Settlements, November 1991.

EDITED BY
NIGEL HARRIS
Development Planning Unit
University College London

Overseas Development Administration
Development Planning Unit

© Development Planning Unit,
University College London, 1992

This book is copyright under the Berne Convention.
No reproduction without permission.
All rights reserved.

First published in 1992 by UCL Press

UCL Press Limited
University College London
Gower Street
London WC1E 6BT

The name of University College London (UCL) is a registered
trade mark used by UCL Press with the consent of the owner.

ISBN: 1-85728-029-6 HB, 1-85728-030-X PB

A CIP catalogue record for this book
is available from the British Library.

Typeset in Palacio (Palatino).
Printed and bound by
Biddles Ltd, King's Lynn and Guildford, England.

Contents

	Page
Foreword *The Right Honourable, the Baroness Chalker of Wallasey* MINISTER FOR OVERSEAS DEVELOPMENT	v
Glossary of terms and acronyms	vii
Acknowledgements	viii
Introduction *Nigel Harris* DEVELOPMENT PLANNING UNIT	ix
Opening address *Tim Lankester* PERMANENT SECRETARY OVERSEAS DEVELOPMENT ADMINISTRATION	1

PART I The discussion

1 The new agendas *Michael Cohen* *Shabbir Cheema* Discussion and summing up	9
2 Country experience Discussion Response *Michael Cohen* Discussion resumed	43

Comment *Michael Cohen*
Summing up *Shabbir Cheema* and *Mark Hildebrand*

3 Urban development strategies 69
Experience from the past
Opening *Kenneth Watts*
Problems and issues of implementation *Nigel Harris*
Discussion and summing up

4 Issues of urban management 93
Opening *Mark Hildebrand* and *Patrick McAuslan*
Discussion
Summing up *Mark Hildebrand* and *Patrick McAuslan*
Final statement *Michael Cohen* and *Shabbir Cheema*
Final address *Al Van Huyck*

PART II Policy experience

5 National urban development policies and strategies: a review of country experience *Kenneth Watts*   123

6 Productivity and poverty in the cities of the developing countries *Nigel Harris*   173

APPENDICES

1 Summary   199
Urban policy and economic development: an agenda for the 1990s
World Bank Policy Paper, 1991
Cities, people and poverty: urban development co-operation for the 1990s
UNDP Strategy Paper, 1991

2 Workshop programme   219

3 Participants   221

Index   225

Foreword
The Right Honourable, the Baroness
LYNDA CHALKER
Minister for Overseas Development

Developing countries are urbanizing rapidly. Over the next generation the number of people living in the urban areas of developing countries is projected to increase by 2.4 billion. By the year 2000 there will be 22 mega-cities, those with populations of over 8 million, in the developing world.

Urbanization on such a scale poses new problems and new challenges and requires reappraisal of development priorities. It was for this reason that the Overseas Development Administration was pleased to join the Development Planning Unit of University College London in sponsoring an international workshop in London in November 1991 to discuss new thinking and approaches to urban development.

The workshop was well attended by senior representatives of donor agencies and also by experts from cities and governments in the developing world. This volume includes a summary of the presentations and of the discussions at that workshop. I hope that its publication will assist in the design and implementation of policies and programmes to tackle what will become one of the most critical development issues in the years ahead.

Acknowledgements

A great debt is owed to the team which has put together this record. Four members of the DPU staff – Babar Mumtaz, Sheilah Meikle, Julio Dávila and Geoffrey Payne – took the initial record. Susan Thomas and others made the transcription of the main speeches from the video record. Véronique Goëssant supervized the project and turned it into a book. Many thanks to Kenneth Watts for his work as an editorial adviser on the publication of this book. UCL Press has been most helpful in organizing a very rapid publication schedule.

We are also most grateful for ODA's strong support for the workshop, the active participation of members of ODA staff and the financial support without which this record could not have been produced.

April 1992   NH

Glossary of terms and acronyms

Agenda 21 — the programme of action on the environment to be presented to UNCED (see below)
AID — see USAID below
ANC — African National Congress, South Africa
AsDB — Asian Development Bank
bilateral — aid, capital or technical assistance, extended by one government to another
bilaterals — aid donors which are national governments
CBOs — community-based organizations
conditionality — the extension of aid, loans, grants or technical assistance, on specified conditions with which the recipient must conform
GDI — gross domestic investment
GDP — gross domestic product
GTZ — Deutsche Gesellschaft für Technische Zusammenarbeit, the main aid agency of the German Federal Republic
Habitat — cf. UNCHS below
IMF — International Monetary Fund
multilateral — aid, capital or technical assistance, extended by an international organization
NGOs — non-governmental organizations, voluntary or charitable organizations, sometimes including but not invariably CBOs (but always excluding private companies)
NUDS — National Urban Development Strategy, Indonesia
NUPS — National Urban Policy Study, Egypt
ODA — Overseas Development Administration, Foreign and Commonwealth Office, Government of the United Kingdom
OECD — Organization for Economic Cooperation and Development

UMP	Urban Management Programme, a joint programme of research and aid organized and financed by the UNDP, the World Bank and UNCHS
UNCED	United Nations Conference on the Environment and Development, also known as the Earth Summit, Rio de Janeiro, June 1–12, 1992
UNDP	United Nations Development Programme
UNGA	United Nations General Assembly
UNICEF	United Nations International Children's Emergency Fund
UNOV	United Nations Office at Vienna
USAID	United States Agency for International Development
UNCHS	United Nations Centre for Human Settlements (Habitat), Nairobi

Introduction
NIGEL HARRIS
Professor of Development Planning
Development Planning Unit

The world's urban inhabitants numbered about 25 million in 1800 (or 3 per cent of the population of the world). By the 1980s, city dwellers had reached 1.8 billion (1,800 million) or 40 per cent of a much larger total. Until the turn of this century, only Britain had an urban majority; now all developed countries do, and a majority of developing countries should have made the same transition by early in the next century. The 100 years since 1900 will have encompassed this remarkable world demographic transition.

The speed of urbanization in developing countries today is not faster than normal, but the numbers involved are unprecedented. Inhabitants of towns and cities increased from 300 million in 1950 to the 1.8 billion of the 1980s; if UN projections are right, there could be 4 billion by 2020. In sub-Saharan Africa where the level of urbanization is still low (25-27 per cent), expected growth in the next thirty years could produce urban populations of great size – 179 million in Nigeria, 58 million in Zaire, 47 million in Tanzania and 42 million in Kenya[1].

The patterns of urbanization have changed from the past. Many more people are going to live in larger cities. In the developing world of 1950, there were 31 cities of one million or more people, and five of 4 million or more; by 1985, the equivalent figures were 146 and 28; projected for 2025 are 486 and 114. In sub-Saharan Africa, the share of the urban population living in cities of half a million or more people grew from 7 to 41 per cent in the thirty years before 1980.

The largest cities are, with a few exceptions, not growing especially quickly (small cities are, and so become large ones), but their

---

1 For a more extended discussion, see my "Urbanisation, economic development and policy in developing countries", *Habitat International* **14**, no.4, 1990, pp.3-42, and an earlier version, "Urbanisation and economic development: territorial specialization and policy", Chapter 2 in my *City, class and trade: social and economic change in the Third World*, DPU/I. B. Tauris, London, 1991, pp.12-64.

inhabitants are spreading out over much larger metropolitan regions (so as population size increases, densities decline). The regions absorb smaller cities and towns. The population in part follows the movement of medium and large manufacturing plants along major highways, leaving small scale industries in the old cities.

Much of the growth of city population now comes from the natural increase of the urbanites, exaggerated because of their relative youth. However, inmigration remains important in China and sub-Saharan Africa. In general the experience of migrants is – contrary to popular opinion – not bad. They do improve the standard of living of themselves and their families, and there is no correlation between being a migrant and being unemployed, badly housed or poor, etc.

This rapid process of urbanization has become notorious for the scale of problems which it seems to entail. The most striking feature of this is the vast spread of squatter settlements and shanty towns, ill supplied, if at all, with basic amenities. Rapid environmental deterioration, giant traffic jams, violence and crime, urban sprawl eating into the countryside, these are some of the most striking visible features of the growth of large cities in developing countries. Understandably, people feel there must be some alternative way to modernize society without such a scale of tangible misery for so many; there must be forms of public intervention which will make possible reasonable and decent lives for the inhabitants of cities without impoverishing those who are often even poorer, in the countryside. It is from here that policy reactions begin.

Governments and policies

Throughout the history of urbanization since the industrial revolution, cities have tended to excite great fears in the minds of authorities and the better off classes of society. The horror of the nineteenth century city was mixed with feelings that such a great concentration of the poor, without roots in the land or society, must surely threaten sooner or later to overwhelm the propertied minority, engulfing society and civilization in anarchy. In Victorian England, the future Conservative leader, Disraeli, linked the romantic world of his early life as a novelist, horrified – as indeed was simultaneously Friedrich Engels – at the new urban form embodied in Manchester, to his later efforts to root the urban working classes in city cultivation, the allotment movement, and provide them with some minimum level of social facilities. The

INTRODUCTION

emphasis upon the need to live in some relationship to the rural and to cultivation was a tradition which later flowed into Ebenezer Howard's conception of the garden city and the foundations of British Town and Country Planning. Nature, it was thought, would bind up the wounds inflicted by urban industrialism.

On the other side, it was precisely the fact that supposedly social bonds were burned off the industrial proletariat in the factory – Prometheus tore off his chains – that inspired Marx with hopes of the creation of a rational and free society, liberated from the nightmarish inheritance of the past. The nightmare was primarily embodied in the superstitions, the fantasies and conservatism of rural life, a pillar of support for reaction, for keeping society poor and enslaved.

The majority suffered, usually quietly, between these two positions, more familiar with the negative fantasies of the rulers than the positive hopes of the revolutionaries. But the upper classes were not exclusively preoccupied with defending property and social order. The argument usually went with a rural mercantilist bias that the only proper producers of wealth in society were cultivators, yeomen and farmers, but they were constantly robbed of their birthright by the greed of the urban classes. Horror and unjust exploitation were mixed in the famous description of London by Lord Roseberry as Chairman of the London County Council in March 1891:

"Sixty years ago, a great Englishman, Cobbet, called it (London) a wen. If it was a wen then, what is it now ? A tumour, an elephantiasis, sucking into its gorged system half the life and the blood and the bone of the rural districts"[2].

In our own times, the instinctive reactions of the Victorian bourgeoisie have often been strikingly paralleled by the authorities in developing countries when, from the nineteen fifties, many countries entered the fastest phases of urbanization, involving unprecedented numbers of people. Governments saw the process in predominantly negative terms. It induced fears and anxieties, horrors and, sometimes, compassion for the millions of city dwellers who were victims of the process and had been robbed of some golden age when all had a place, roots, and an understood relationship to nature. There were infinite possibilities for romanticizing the village, inventing rural images of bliss

---

2 Cited by Donald Foley in *Controlling London's growth: planning the great Wen, 1940-1960*, University of California Press, Berkeley and Los Angeles, 1963, p.(vi).

as remote from reality as Marx's image of the idiocy of rural life.

A case was developed which became part of the conventional wisdom (as often it had already become in developed countries). Appalling city conditions were the result of a maldistribution of a poor population, "imbalances" between urban and rural areas and within urban areas, as measured in both the absolute size of cities and the densities of city populations. These two imbalances were seen as the symptoms of a profound social illness, the source of a wide range of social maladies – the lack of adequate services, congested and dirty streets, poor housing, squatting and slums, malnutrition, crime, disease and disorder. Cities were the most marked signs of "overpopulation" or "population saturation" (water imagery proved an irrepressible companion to these fears). In an important sense, it seemed, poverty and other manifest social ills were *locational* questions – people were in the wrong place; and the migrant, moving from one place to another, now became the striking evidence of a breakdown in the natural order of society. It followed that social ills could be remedied or at least significantly ameliorated by the relocation of people.

The remedies flowed from the diagnosis. Within the city, the control of land uses could be employed to lower densities and reduce movement; highly aggregated zoning would end the concentration of homes round factories and create ordered residential neighbourhoods. For the country at large, governments sought to decentralize from cities, populations and, what attracted migrants, sources of employment, both to smaller centres but also, sometimes, to backward areas. Furthermore, governments frequently pursued rural development, not as an end in itself or as an effort to increase the utilization of all national resources, but as a means supposedly of discouraging outmigration to the cities.

A 1981 United Nations survey of 126 governments in developing countries found that 123 "continued to be far from satisfied with their migration trends and patterns of population distribution, and many considered population distribution issues to be among their most important problems"[3]. Three quarters of the governments concerned claimed to be pursuing policies to slow or reverse migration as part of

---

3 United Nations, *Fifth population enquiry among governments: monitoring government perceptions and policies on demographic trends and levels in relation to development as of 1982*, Population Division, United Nations, New York, 1984, p.19.

INTRODUCTION

a strategy of decentralization.

Political differences did not seem to affect the issue – governments of the political Right and the Left were apparently united in the perception of the grave dangers of urbanization. The Government of the People's Republic of China was one of the more strict in seeking to prevent urbanization. From the late fifties until the late seventies, tight control was exercized over rural–urban migration, and in the sixties there were periodic mass removals of urban inhabitants for relocation in rural areas. Other governments pursued part of the programme. For example, both Tanzania and Indonesia tried at various times to control migration to the cities. The Government of the Philippines in the early sixties tried to charge inmigrants to Manila a fee for entry to public schools (free education was available only to existing urban residents). The measure proved difficult to enforce, a continuous source of corruption, and without observable effects upon inmigration. Many other countries have, from time to time, tried to expel sections of the urban population or squatters (for example, Congo, Niger, Zaire, South Korea, India etc.). In essence, such policies – whatever their declared purposes – had the effect of classifying the rural population as foreigners and excluding or expelling them from the urban country; it was perverse since often the policy was supposedly to help the rural inhabitants.

An academic case: "urban bias"

Separately, more sophisticated economic critiques of urbanization emerged, some of which proved influential in shaping government perceptions of, not just dangers and fears, but the basic process of economic development. There were many threads to the case – for example, it was said that cities appropriated a disproportionate and economically unjustified share of national resources[4]; or, a case familiar

---

4 W. Arthur Lewis connected this to developing country borrowing practices and the cumulative debt of developing countries – cf. *Evaluation of the international economic order*, Discussion Paper 74, Woodrow Wilson School Research Programme in Development Studies, Princeton University, Princeton NJ, 1977, pp.39–40; for a critique, see Johannes F. Linn, "The costs of urbanization in developing countries", *Economic Development and Cultural Change*, 30/3, Chicago, April 1982, pp.625–48.

INTRODUCTION

in Europe, that national capitals were subsidized by the country at large[5].

A broader case emerged in the late 1950s, summarized in the introduction by Professor Bert Hoselitz of the University of Chicago of the term "over-urbanization"[6]. In essence, Hoselitz argued that in nineteenth century developing Europe, urban and industrial employment – with rising average productivity and incomes – expanded, drawing workers off the land as urban opportunities increased, and making possible parallel increases in rural productivity. Workers were, in the popular terminology, "pulled" into the urban areas. Cities thus played the rôle of "engines of economic development". By contrast, in contemporary developing countries, high rates of rural population growth with limited land, increased poverty and drove the rural poor to seek sanctuary in the cities (they were "pushed" out of rural areas). The capital intensity of modern manufacturing, however, limited the increase in employment to well below the labour supply, forcing the migrants into unemployment. The cities became, not engines of growth, but welfare centres for the rural poor where the mass could use their now concentrated political leverage to extract further benefits at the expense of the countryside and the growth of urban productivity.

The case was later refined in a path-breaking model of the urban labour market in developing countries, formulated by Michael Todaro[7].

---

5 For France, see the refutation by Rémy Prud'homme, "Does Paris subsidize the rest of France?" in H. J. Ewers, J. B. Goddard, H. Matzerath (eds), *The future of the metropolis – Berlin, London, Paris, New York: economic aspects*, Walter de Gruyter, Berlin and New York, 1986, pp.285–96. See also Laurent Davezies et al., "La contribution des grandes villes au développement: Abidjan subventionne-t-elle le reste de la Côte d'Ivoire?" *Revue d'Economie Régionale et Urbaine*, no.4, Paris, 1987, and *The metropolis subsidizes the rest of the country: a comparative study of Paris, Casablanca and Abidjan* (mimeo), OEIL (Observatoire de l'Economie et des Institutions Locales), Paris, May 1987.

6 The rôle of urbanization in economic development: some international comparisons, in Roy Turner (ed.), *India's urban future*, University of California Press, Berkeley, 1962, pp.157–81.

7 "A model of labour migration and urban unemployment in less developed countries", *American Economic Review*, 59(1), 1969, pp.138–48. See also J. R. Harris & Michael Todaro, "Migration, unemployment and development: a two-sector model", ibid, 60(1), 1970, pp.126–42; M. P. Todaro, "Urban job expansion, induced migration and rising unemployment", *Journal of Development*

INTRODUCTION

This introduced the modification of expectations to explain why migration could continue even though the possibilities of securing employment were poor. Migration was determined by the differential between average urban and rural wage income. Urban wages were sustained at high levels through the operation of government minimum pay legislation and/or trade union controls. As a result, waged employment was paid significantly more than the opportunity cost of labour, and employers therefore sought to substitute capital for labour and thereby limited the growth of employment. Rural workers, faced with the high urban-rural wage differentials, continued to move to the city even though they had poor chances of securing work, hoping that in time they would secure waged employment. While they waited, they were unemployed or underemployed in petty and miscellaneous activity where the marginal productivity of labour was close to zero, what became known as the "informal sector".

Already in this account the rôle of mistaken policy – sustaining formal sector wages at a high level – was crucial. Later, the case was broadened into a more general one. The emerging neoclassical critique of strategies of industrialization based upon import substitution saw "overurbanization" as one byproduct of a mistaken macroeconomic policy package. Subsidizing interest rates for investment in, and the provision of other incentives and subsidized input prices for, manufacturing, along with the protection of industrial output from competition with imports, the holding down of prices paid for agricultural output (often through State trading monopolies, designed to funnel resources from agriculture to industry), all changed the terms of trade and thus the rates of return between the urban and rural sectors. It overpriced urban and underpriced rural labour. It also, it was said, led to high capital intensity in industry and thus a poor rate of growth of manufacturing employment. In sum the expression of the comparative advantage of the developing economy – abundant supplies of relatively cheap labour – was entirely frustrated[8]. Michael Lipton's

---

Studies, 3(3), 1976, pp.211-25; and M. P. Todaro, "Internal migration in developing countries: a survey", in Richard A. Easterlin (ed.), *Population and economic change in developing countries*, University of Chicago Press for the National Bureau of Economic Research, Chicago, 1980.

8 An early exposition of the case was included in the final volume of a major series of OECD country studies of economic development – I. M. D. Little, T. Skitovsky, Maurice Scott, *Industry and trade in some developing countries*, The Development Centre, OECD/Oxford University Press, London, 1970.

INTRODUCTION

influential *Why the poor stay poor: urban bias in world development*[9] summarized and illustrated many of these points (without the same emphasis upon import substituting strategies), making the systematic bias of the urban upper classes, public and private, the centrepiece of a political economy of development in which the struggle between urban and rural classes dominated society.

The case, intellectually, was a powerful one, answering as it did a diversity of different questions. It became politically powerful when, in response to the continuing crisis of sub-Saharan Africa in the seventies, the World Bank's Structural Adjustment Lending programme was developed from a diagnosis which took over both the critique of industrialization strategies based upon import substitution and the arguments about "over-urbanization"[10]. The restoration of sub-Saharan Africa's capacity to export its primary commodities required an end to the diversion of resources from rural to urban sectors, and this, it was expected, would eliminate most of the wage gap between the two, leading either to an end of net urban–rural migration or possibly reverse migration from the cities to the countryside.

Powerful the case may have been, but it rested on shaky conceptual assumptions and inadequate empirical foundations. For example, if migration was not sensitive to income differences but was the product of either *relative* not absolute deprivation in the village, or of family strategies to diversify income sources and risks[11], it might be entirely unsusceptible to influence by the package of changes included in Structural Adjustment. Furthermore, empirically, the data on urban unemployment is rarely good enough to detect a secular trend to increase, nor, at a moment of time, does it show any correlation between unemployment and migration. Urban real wages have in general not been fixed by governments or trade unions; in sub-Saharan

---

9 Temple Smith, London, 1977. For an opposite case, cf. Ashok Mitra, *Terms of trade and class relations*, Frank Cass, London, 1977, and a rebuttal, T. J. Byres, "Of neo-populist pipe dreams: Daedalus in the third world and the myth of urban bias", *The Journal of Peasant Studies*, 6/2, Jan. 1979, pp.210–44.

10 The original case was laid out in what became known as the "Berg Report" – World Bank, *Accelerated development in sub-Saharan Africa*, World Bank, Washington DC, 1981; cf. also *Towards sustainable development in sub-Saharan Africa: from crisis to sustained growth – a long-term perspective*, World Bank, Washington DC, Nov. 1989.

11 This is explored econometrically in several essays in Oded Stark's *The migration of labour*, Basil Blackwell, Cambridge (Mass.), 1991.

Africa, they have been in fairly continuous decline since 1970[12]. It appears in general that it is not the rural poor who migrate to cities, and the contribution of migration to urban population growth is, in many countries, relatively small. Rural incomes are not uniformly below urban in comparable occupations (although in aggregate they are). Formal sector incomes and conditions are not systematically better than informal ones, nor do the self-employed necessarily earn less than the employed; migrants are not overrepresented in informal sector activities. Peter Gregory has put together many of these elements in a powerful critique of the overall arguments as they affected macroeconomic policy in Mexico[13].

In general, it would seem, then that while the content of urban economic activity has changed radically (particularly as it affects urban productivity), it remains true that a growing and changing composition of urban output selects a particular level and type of migrant; migrants are not expelled from impoverished agriculture. There can be little general sense to the idea that cities are the wrong size in terms of population, that "over-urbanization" can mean anything in normal circumstances (as opposed to when large numbers of refugees or famine victims temporarily flee to the cities).

Aid donors

However, whatever the academic arguments, most aid agencies became committed to an almost exclusive orientation on rural development and were often hostile to projects which were explicitly urban. Of course, aid agencies were often involved in sectoral projects which were implicitly urban – in the fields of transport, water supply, industry, ports, power generation etc.. The arguments for a rural orientation were often that the majority of people lived in the rural areas in, particularly, Low Income developing countries, and a majority of the poor were

---

12 Philip Amos, *African development and urban change* (mimeo), Development and Project Planning Centre, University of Bradford, Oct. 1988, p.14.

13 *The myth of market failure: employment and the labour market in Mexico*, World Bank Research Report, John Hopkins University Press, Baltimore, 1986. See also S. Kannapan, "Urban employment and labour markets in developing nations", *Economic Development and Cultural Change*, **33/4**, 1985, pp.699–730.

INTRODUCTION

there; the cities, it was said, had already received disproportionate government investment due to "urban bias", so aid should be employed to right the balance. The World Bank was almost alone in sustained explicitly urban lending programmes through the past fifteen years or so (starting with its first loans to Calcutta from 1972); the urban projects were heavily dominated by housing and infrastructure provision.

However, in the late 1980s, there was an increasing realization that over the following two or three decades a majority of people in most developing countries would come to live in cities and towns. A majority of the poor would become urban within the medium term. Furthermore and more importantly, it came to be realized that the most dynamic sources of economic development and of national savings were in the cities. The World Bank produced figures to suggest that sixty per cent of the value of output of developing countries and eighty per cent of the increment in output was generated in urban areas. Urban productivity was thus crucial to national development – including the development of rural areas – and to improving the conditions of the poor.

The reconsideration was signalled by a conference of aid agencies called by OECD in 1986 and another held two years later in Canada. Congress requested a new policy directive from USAID on medium term urban assistance in 1989, and a major conference of aid donors was called at Lille by the French Government in November of the same year with the firmly committed title: "Cities, the mainspring of economic development in developing countries"[14]. Simultaneously, the British Overseas Development Administration revised its orientation away from an exclusively rural one, and other bilateral aid donors began to rethink the emphasis of their aid programmes.

At the same time, the whole stress of government programmes and of aid in developing countries was beginning to change radically. In the earlier phases, without too much simplification, underdevelopment had been identified as basically a shortage of capital, so the rôle of government was to seek domestic and foreign resources to target them

---

14 Lille International Meeting: *Cities: the mainspring of economic development in developing countries*, Proceedings (Vol. I) and Papers (Vol. II), Ministries of Foreign Affairs; Co-operation and Development; Public Works, Housing, Transport and Maritime Affairs, with the United Towns Organisation and the City of Lille, Paris, 1990.

on the key bottlenecks restricting growth; aid donors saw their rôle as being to help to expand the supply of capital, to choose those capital projects with maximum effect in relieving constraints. However, in the 1980s, the diagnosis of development has come to focus on skills, policy and institutions. Government now supposedly should seek to facilitate action by its citizens, private firms or non-governmental organizations, to provide for themselves such services and at such standards as people themselves might choose. The capital project now became replaced by the programme of technical assistance and "enabling".

This concept of an "enabling" approach was first enunciated in the United Nations Centre for Human Settlements, whose *Global strategy for shelter to the year 2000* was adopted by the Commission for Human Settlements in 1988, and subsequently by the UN General Assembly. Stressing the need for governments to make fundamental changes in their approaches to shelter, the Strategy stated that they should concentrate more on the creation of incentives and facilitating measures so as to enable housing and other urban services to be provided by householders themselves, community organizations, NGOs, the private sector and so on, and less on actual implementation. In this way, the full potential of all the actors in shelter production and improvement would be mobilized.

In 1991, the World Bank crystallized and defined the new orthodoxy on the urban sector in *Urban policy and economic development: an agenda for the 1990s*[15]. This combined both the emphasis on the economically productive rôle of the cities and the style of assistance relating to governments as facilitators rather than providers. Shortly afterwards, the United Nations Development Programme followed this initiative with a strategy paper, *Cities, people and poverty: urban development cooperation for the 1990s*. This was even more explicit in emphasizing the new style of aid assistance and in responding to governments in terms of their priorities rather than what the aid donor preferred. The UNDP sees its document as complementary to the Bank's, stressing the social or human dimension of economic development rather than simply the economics.

The Bank document emphasized that the key issue in national and local management of cities was enhancing productivity. Within that, two further priorities were laid down – ameliorating poverty and protecting and improving the environment. It outlined some suggested

---

15 Summaries of these two documents are included in the Appendices.

INTRODUCTION

lines of enquiry on the factors restricting productivity, but emphasized that a significant expansion in research was required to identify clearly the key factors restricting the growth of productivity, the relief of poverty and the improvement of the urban environment. The emphasis was now on policy, politics and participation, not the bricks and mortar of the old projects, and on substantial expansion.

However, while there were a wealth of illustrative examples in the Bank's document, it was not clear what the new policy orientation would mean in practice: what were governments, national and local, and aid donors to do about it ? To seek to go some way to answering these questions, the Development Planning Unit called a workshop in November 1991 in London. Supported by the Overseas Development Administration (the Permanent Secretary of the Ministry opened the proceedings), the workshop was originally intended for a small group of people drawn from bilateral and multilateral aid agencies and from the senior echelons of the governments of selected developing countries. In fact, the pressure to attend the workshop was considerable and the final number of participants was more than 55 (the participants list is included here as an appendix).

The programme (also included as an appendix) was designed to hear presentations from the main officials concerned in the World Bank and UNDP on their interpretation of the documents and how far they had moved in seeking to make them operational. The following session was aimed to provide an opportunity for the representatives from developing countries to react to the new policy statements and assess how far they might be useful. The programme also included a session to consider the joint programme on urban management between the UNDP, the Bank and the United Nations agency principally concerned with the urban sector, the UN Centre for Human Settlements (Habitat). Finally, a central session concerned how far the experience of those governments which had attempted national urban policy packages had been successful and whether they might throw light on how far the new policy documents would be effective; this considered two papers: "National urban development policies and strategies: a review of country experience" (by Kenneth Watts), and "Productivity and poverty in the cities of the developing countries" (by Nigel Harris).

Originally, the workshop was intended to be informal, without formal papers (apart from the two already published policy documents, and the two papers mentioned in the previous paragraph), in order that the participants could react freely to the issues concerned. Notes were taken and a video film made of the proceedings (it is now being edited and will shortly be on sale), but it was not intended to produce a volume of proceedings. However, in the event, the discussions proved to be of great interest and led to a change of mind during the workshop, suggesting that a much wider audience would find the occasion instructive. The interest was from many different angles – from the question of how policies are formulated and implemented to the operational significance of the new appraisal of urbanization and the new style of aid programmes. The discussion was strikingly free and open, given that more normally officials from government and international organizations are likely to treat each other with diplomatic distance.

The urban agenda in the wider international perspective

The discussions that took place in the Workshop highlighted the need for important changes to take place, in the ways that cities are regarded, how they work, the contribution they make to the economy of nations, and how they are managed. All three of the major international donors – the World Bank, the UNDP and UNCHS – signalled a change in their ways of working, away from the traditional project approach to one that emphasizes process, that seizes opportunities as they arise, that stresses continuity, and, recognising the multi-sectoral nature of urban activities, also stresses the need to look at city issues in a holistic way. This message was conveyed to the other donor representatives at the workshop, in the expectation that they would follow suit.

In a certain sense this may have been a rhetorical exercise for, as Tim Lankester said in his opening address, the workshop was attended by people who were already of the same mind on many of these issues. Yet the ideas expressed in the workshop have wider resonances, and can be discerned in the approaches by the international community to problems associated with the *general development status* of nations, and the ways in which the poorer nations can be helped to grow faster. For example, two years ago the United Nations General Assembly passed a resolution that expressed concern that many internationally funded programmes had not made more of an impact. (To quote Lankester again: "the basic approach doesn't seem to be in question, . . . [so] why does so little appear to have been done on the ground?") Indeed, at the end of 1991, the UNGA once more expressed disappointment at the lack of progress that had been made in moving towards a more

INTRODUCTION

coordinated approach to assistance in all development sectors. Why is this so?

Certainly, these resolutions touch upon many of the issues that are highlighted in this workshop as urban issues: the need for "maximum participation of populations, local communities and organizations, including NGOs in the development process"; to take measures to eradicate poverty; to "emphasize the human dimension of development through training and education etc". In responding to such needs, the UN system is urged to "shift from a project approach to a programme approach . . . and develop more programme-orientated mechanisms for the provision of technical cooperation, with a view to allowing more flexible and effective support of national programmes."

This last point, underlining the primacy of national plans and priorities "which constitute the only viable frame of reference for the national programming of operational activities for development of the United Nations system", is an important one; and it has to be borne in mind when considering the particular approaches of the organizations represented at the workshop. The World Bank is a highly centralized agency, whose policies may well ultimately filter through to its lending programmes, and whose conditionalities – the terms under which it lends its funds – carry weight. The UN system, on the other hand, recognizes the primacy of government plans and priorities; and although it may stress the importance of certain global themes, it cannot impose them on governments. This primacy of national governments in decision-making is reflected in the comparatively decentralized nature of the UN system, whose country representatives have powers of negotiation, within the framework of UNDP general policy, that exceed those of the Bank's country representatives.

The question as to why so little has been done on the ground resolves itself into two issues: the extent to which the UN system is able to change its own agenda, and the extent to which it is able to adopt an advocacy rôle with governments, and promote changes in their agendas. As will be seen from Mike Cohen's, Shabbir Cheema's and Mark Hildebrand's interventions at the workshop, important steps are being taken in the World Bank, the UNDP and UNCHS on the first account. The second is an issue that is the subject of much debate. Certainly some UN agencies, particularly UNICEF, have a strongly avocational style; but although General Assembly resolutions, and those adopted by the UNDP Governing Council, carry considerable weight in determining general policy stances by the system, there are limits to the degree of persuasion the system as a whole may adopt.

One point is, however, certain: that the success achieved in gaining acceptance for the ideas expressed in this workshop will depend ultimately on the quality of the papers presented by the organizations concerned to the world community; and although both the Bank and the UNDP urban papers are presented in some sense as internal documents, with the avowed aim of changing ideas within the respective organizations, they contain important ideas that are of global interest. Thus, the objective of this workshop will have been achieved in at least one particular, if it has given wider currency to these papers.

Most governments in developing countries – and not a few in the developed countries – have not done well in coping with the processes of rapid economic change as they affect cities. The record of the past forty years in this respect is a melancholy one, relieved only by the enormous capacities of people to provide for themselves, to make their own cities, despite the obstacles so often put in their way by official agencies. The proof that the new policy statements can offer a new deal will be settled not in London, but in the capacities of the urban inhabitants of developing countries, and the possibilities of national and local governments in developing countries succeeding in changing their style sufficiently radically to make it possible to cope with the effects of the rapid urbanization which is already under way. Given the lessons drawn from the past period of urban and rural aid, the new orientation and the new style, the workshop was perhaps more optimistic on this score than has been possible for a long time.

NIGEL HARRIS

Opening Address
TIM LANKESTER
Permanent Secretary,
Overseas Development Administration

Ladies and gentlemen,

It gives me great pleasure to welcome you to London and to open this international workshop. I would like to commend the Development Planning Unit of University College London for their initiative in bringing together such a prestigious group of experts in the field of urban development, and to thank them for the practical arrangements which they have made in order to bring the workshop to fruition this morning.

This is an opportune time to be convening such a meeting. The United Nations Global Strategy for Shelter to the Year 2000 was adopted by the General Assembly at the end of 1988. This strategy, based upon its concept of the enabling environment for shelter provision, is increasingly being accepted in principle and a few countries have now had initial experience in drawing up their own national shelter strategies.

This year, we have seen the publication of two important policy papers: one by the World Bank on the Urban Policy Agenda for the 1990s, and one by the UNDP: Cities, People and Poverty. These papers greatly advance our thinking for dealing with the challenge of urbanization in the years ahead.

I am delighted that the World Bank and the UNDP have agreed to lead off these discussions with the introduction of their papers, and I welcome particularly Mike Cohen and his team from the Urban Development Department of the World Bank, and Shabbir Cheema from UNDP.

I am also very pleased to see so many representatives of our partner donor agencies here this morning. I am pleased that so many of you were able to accept DPU's invitation to take part, and that other bilateral agencies have joined the ODA in sponsoring the attendance of a significant number of important people from developing countries concerned with urban policy. The presence of representatives from the developing world will also greatly enhance the practical relevance of the discussions over the next two days.

I know I do not need to recapitulate the magnitude or the severity of the urbanization situation in developing countries. But I hope that the problems (which urbanization poses) will not be allowed exclusively to dominate the discussions. For it seems to me that the urbanization process not only poses problems; it also offers great opportunities. Most obviously, urban development can be a very positive element indeed in a country's overall economic and social development. Slightly less obviously, urbanization offers opportunities for tackling some of the problems that cause countries and their peoples to be very poor. Opportunities – notwithstanding the colossal difficulties encountered in rapid urban growth – may be easier to take up in urban rather than in rural areas, whether because of economies of scale or because urban society is more fluid, less fixed in its ways, or more modern.

Let me give one or two examples. Governments the world over – not just the donor agencies – are now emphasizing the importance of better administration, better governance if there is to be sustained economic and social development. Nowhere is this more important than in cities. The people of large cities are arguably the worst affected by bad government. They are usually the most politically conscious and therefore well capable of causing political difficulties at a national level if city government fails. The imperative for improvements in city government is very great, and in many cases not infeasible given the political will. The reform of urban government, particularly in large cities, would therefore seem an excellent priority for putting into practice the principles of accountable, transparent and efficient administration.

Secondly, the concentration of people in urban areas should make programmes of poverty reduction and health and education provision more cost effective.

The breakdown of traditional social and political systems, which the urbanization process inevitably involves, opens up new opportunities for exciting and innovative programmes of community development.

There are in the urban areas, I would suggest, excellent opportunities for pursuing our concerns with enhancing the rôle of women. It should be easier, in urban areas, to mobilize women's groups and organize literacy classes. It should be easier to spread health education messages. These should have multiple benefits in important fields such as improving child health and the reduction of AIDS.

The UNDP paper and the World Bank policy papers exhibit a substantial agreement as to the approach to be adopted to dealing with the problems of urbanization. There are differences of emphasis, naturally, but the basic approach – namely the need to get the enabling environment right, and strengthening urban management, so as to loosen the constraints on urban productivity – does not seem to be in question. The same approach is at the heart of the UN's Global Shelter Strategy. It also runs through much of the academic literature on urbanization being produced at the present time.

In the ODA we held a seminar to mark Habitat Day on the 7th October. There again was demonstrated a considerable consensus running through the presentations by consultants, academics and aid practitioners alike as to the endorsement of this principle. There can be few current development issues which appear to command such intellectual consensus.

And yet I have a feeling that, in spite of this consensus, policy and practice in most of the developing world are still lagging sadly behind. Perhaps it is still early days, but if there is so much agreement on what needs to be done, why, I ask myself, does so little actually appear to be happening on the ground? I hope, therefore, that within the next couple of days you will spend some time addressing what may be the obstacles to putting the new urban agenda into practice and how these may be overcome.

I hope you will also bear in mind that this is a gathering of the converted. You, I am sure, do not need to persuade each other, and you do not need to persuade me, of the importance of the urban problem in developing countries and the priority which needs to be given to it. However, I suggest that this is still not the universal perception amongst the development community.

Many of our development institutions are still, understandably, working with the legacy of the rural development emphasis of the seventies, and there are still valid arguments which can be advanced to support this. There is still a lot of poverty in rural areas, more indeed than in urban areas, environmental degradation is occurring in rural areas, and suspicions of urban bias in public expenditure allocations may not always be misplaced.

It is necessary, therefore, for us to consider not only the needs of the urban areas themselves, but also the rôle of urban areas in relation to the development of the whole of national economies – that is to say the whole issue of urban-rural linkages and the urban linkage with macro-economic aggregates. The DAC[16] meeting on urbanization this time next year will provide an opportunity for spreading the message for the need for a balanced assessment of the importance of urban areas in national development.

Finally, since much of what you will be discussing will impinge upon policy, it would be helpful to bear in mind the need for a coordinated approach. We have a lot of experience now on policy dialogue with developing countries in the context of structural adjustment. What we have learnt from that experience is that this dialogue can only be effective when there is a

---

16 Development Assistance Committee of OECD.

consistency of approach between those involved in the discussions. It is certainly not helpful to the developing countries to have different aid donors pursuing their own priorities and speaking with different voices.

There is room in the challenge of urbanization for us all, but it is important that we all work together. We do need to ensure that adequate mechanisms for co-ordination of donor and recipient policies and programmes are in place, so that assistance can be co-operative and not competitive. We have also learnt that policy reform is only really effective where the national government is committed to it and takes the leading rôle in design and implementation.

I wish you all a very productive two days' discussions and I look forward to reading the outcome of your deliberations in due course.

PART I
The discussion

CHAPTER ONE
The new agendas

Urban policy and economic development – the agenda
Michael Cohen *Chief, Urban Development Division, World Bank*

Introduction

I want to be frank in describing where I think we are in the process.

The main purpose of the Bank's policy paper is to make the argument that urban issues are macrodevelopment issues, that is to say, that the success of many of the key objectives of development strategy are tied up in our approach and follow-through on urban issues. We look at the question of what are macro-objectives for countries and for the developing community, whether we want to talk about sound macroeconomic management, poverty alleviation, or improved management of the environment, improving the intellectual foundations of development assistance and development performance in countries. Many of these objectives can be achieved only if there is a much more thoughtful and policy-orientated approach in the urban areas. For many people who have worked on urban issues for a long time, I think there is a feeling that there were messages contained in that experience but which somehow did not really reach people making general development policies, whether in government at a national level or in the general community.

When we started out with this policy paper, we realized that what we were talking about is not a sectoral policy. We are trying to figure out what is the linkage between what goes on in cities and the broader development objectives to which we all aspire.

In seeking that objective, the interesting question that arises is what is the language of discourse between those of us who have worked on the urban sector and those people who work on macro-questions.

From 1986 to 1989 I worked as a country operations division chief in the Bank. I was responsible for Pakistan and Turkey. We had a very large lending programme for both of those countries, very active at the macro-level. We were working with the IMF and with the community at large and thinking about a broad set of issues. But as I watched my macroeconomic colleagues and particularly as I watched the IMF in discussion about macro-policy, there was always a great discussion about growth, about the need to get countries growing again, to make sure that the fiscal deficit was under control and to monitor a whole range of macro-variables. But I found that very rarely was there a concern about the composition of growth. What was the rôle of infrastructure? Where did growth occur? Where were the distortions in the economy occurring? Where are the possible sources of improvement in productivity? They are all sets of questions that the macro-people just did not raise and I found that somehow strange. It was not just that it applied to urban questions but they really were not talking about the rôle of agriculture or even the rôle of energy. People could say that these were important, but they never quite came to the conclusion that we absolutely need this amount of energy in order to support industry, in order to support the industrial contribution to the growth of the gross domestic product.

This absence of a linkage between what was going on in sectors and the macro-performance seemed striking. When I was given the opportunity to come back to work on my own professional interest, on urban questions, I brought a different perspective after having worked on macro-issues for three and a half years. I realized that this was not simply a question of professional myopia on both sides, that is, a very limited perspective, but rather there were serious conceptual and operational problems on how one would link the sectoral questions with macro-strategy.

The premise in starting on the urban strategy work was that the stakes were large. We knew that in writing the policy paper, we had to take on not just our sectoral colleagues and convince them that they ought to do things differently, but that we were taking on in effect the whole institution. What that meant was that we had to be able to convince, for example, our chief economists, our regional vice-presidents. This was not science fiction as an approach. It could change the way the institution operated, the way it thought about development.

The agenda items

Let me give you a progress report on this process. What I would like to do is to organize my remarks around the elements of the agenda and ask the question: "What were we doing before 1991 in this area and what would we do differently now?" and then to pose the question "How are we organizing ourselves for the future on this particular agenda item?"

The first agenda item was the question of urban productivity. The argument in the policy paper about productivity basically identified four constraints that we perceived to be restricting the growth of productivity that needed to be addressed. The first was the question of infrastructure deficiencies. One might say this is an old question, a traditional issue, about the operations and maintenance of infrastructure. Governments and the community have worried about these things for a long time: what's new?

A couple of things are new. The first thing is that we propose to look at urban infrastructure not from the supply side. We propose to ask the question, what are the constraints on those people, firms and households in urban areas which come from infrastructural deficiencies? How do these infrastructural deficiencies increase the cost of doing business or, as Mr Lancaster said, affect the efficiency of investment, public and private? The paper uses the example of Lagos, Nigeria where research demonstrated the impact of infrastructure deficiencies on the behaviour of small firms. Typically they spent 35 per cent of fixed investment on providing infrastructure for themselves to make up for the absence of public infrastructure.

It was not simply a question of the absolute deficiencies that occurred in power, waste management, etc., but also the question of the composition of infrastructure. We noted that, for example, São Paulo had twice as many cars as telephones. One might say that is an interesting touristic finding. Now what would you do with that?

The proposal would be to look at other cities and ask: what is the composition of infrastructure and how would you identify the critical infrastructure constraints that affect behaviour and the productivity in a city? That is a city-wide question. Here is the difference between the past and the future: it is not going into a neighbourhood and if there is a serious water-supply or drainage problem, proposing to solve it through a slum upgrading programme. The slum upgrading programme has a certain rationale which makes sense at a household level but cannot be related to the efficiency of the city as a whole, the efficiency of investment both public and private. We propose to ask a broader question at the level of the city. What are the more severe constraints? It may turn out that these are not infrastructure which has traditionally been handled by urban types. It may be telecommunications, public transportation, drainage. We need to take a city-wide look at infrastructure.

On the infrastructure side, there has been experience in developing countries of the differential performance of public and private sectors in infrastructure provision. It is appropriate to ask: "what is the most efficient way in which one can deliver, manage and own infrastructure systems?" We started in the policy paper but now, much more aggressively, to ask the question for each type of infrastructure: "Should the Bank be actively behind private sector provision in infrastructure of a particular type?" For example, I wonder about garbage collection. We financed 71 garbage collection systems around the world. Almost every single one of them has been in the public sector. That meant we bought garbage trucks for municipalities to go and collect garbage. Typically it accounted for 50 per cent of municipal budgets. Is this sensible? Maybe we ought to be trying to set up a fund which can support private sector collection of garbage and the purchase of trucks, etc?

The second constraint on productivity which we identified was the regulatory framework. There are people in this room who have visited various cities and looked at the building codes. Sometimes we have gone in together. We have said zoning makes no sense, the building code is too expensive and that is part of the regulatory framework. But that is the past. There is another set of regulations; for example in the Nigeria case it turned out that when private sector enterprises generated electricity, if they had an excess they were unable to sell it back to the public grid because there was a rule saying that the public sector would not accept private sector generated electricity. It is an inefficient regulation. It doesn't make sense. One need not go into the description of regulations in Peru or other kinds of examples, but we think that it is necessary, again at the city level, to look at the regulatory framework: what are the costs and benefits of all these regulations? Here we are proposing to carry out regulatory audits; that is, a cost-benefit balance sheet of the system of regulations in particular cities. We have started this in Mexico, and a number of our colleagues have had discussions with other countries, as a way of cleaning out the regulatory web which constrains economic activity. Is it really necessary that the distance between two buildings should be equal to their height? I have seen that in ten different countries and one wonders what is the magic of those kinds of regulations.

This is not an onslaught on all regulations. There are certainly issues of health, fire hazards and certain kinds of waste for which clearly there has to be a regulatory framework. This is not an indiscriminate attack on regulation, but the point is that we need to assess the costs and benefits of these systems.

The third constraint which we identified in the paper is local government. We are not really proposing to do very much that is different. There has been substantial support by the Bank for strengthening local government on the operational and financial side. We have been doing this for ten years, but there is one important policy lever which marks a significant departure for the Bank compared to the past. We know the attitude of central government to local government determines the performance of local government in many of its functions. Yet when we look at our own projects, there were very few cases where the Bank took a serious position on central–local governmental relations, on the issue of central or local financial relations and autonomy. So we have made, as a precondition of our own support for municipal development – conditionality – that we have a serious dialogue on central and local relations.

What has been the response in the Bank to this? We are starting studies in 22 countries in this fiscal year on central and local financial relations. What are the terms of decentralization? What happens if there is a local government deficit? What would be the response? It is clear that this is a very political area, very sensitive. I was told very forcefully by ministers of finance in both Pakistan and Turkey to stay out of it. We told them that we would not pursue urban development unless we could address these questions.

The fourth constraint we identified is the weakness of the financial system. We know that most of the assets, public and private, in the city are of long duration. They are not going to be financed by disposable cash. We have to acknowledge that our whole approach to the financial sector, through the banking systems regulations and the availability of credit, must be linked with our financial sector colleagues if we are to make a serious approach to urban development.

We tried out an earlier draft of the urban policy paper at some meetings in Delhi about eighteen months ago. There was an interesting comment by someone about an hypothesis: he said that between 1950 and 1980, Latin America had gone from 30 per cent urban to 60 per cent urban, and so there were tremendous financial resources devoted to the urbanization process, both public and private. The hypothesis was that the method of financing urbanization had been the underlying cause of the debt crisis in Latin America, of the financial weakening. When an external shock hit Latin America in the 1980s, there had not been sufficient resources for urbanization at the local level. The system of transfers, the rôle of financial institutions in Brazil and Mexico, had not been strong enough to withstand the shocks, because they had a very distorted approach to the financing of urbanization. It is hard to confirm this hypothesis, but it is interesting because it raises all kind of questions when we look at other regions which are less urbanized, where urbanization is going to be rapid. We have to think about the financing of organization and of infrastructure. The key point on productivity is that there are four constraints and we propose to do some things differently in each one of these areas.

Let me turn to the area of *urban poverty*. This is something that we have identified ourselves with professionally, institutionally, some even emotionally, believing that this is the business we have to do: to address the question of the urban poor. We have been active in supporting slum up-grading programmes, sites and service, etc. Yet I think if we are realistic and self-critical, one cannot help but be struck that by 1990 urban poverty has not really been alleviated very much. The demographic pressures continue. The responses of government seem not to have changed in many regards and even though the donor community can point to a handful of projects which are effective, I think we have to be modest about what has happened.

In the policy paper we distinguish between two kinds of urban poverty: first, the poverty that is somewhat classical and structural, driven by high demographic growth, low productivity of households, inadequate investment, health and education. This is the kind of urban poverty that we somewhat understand. I think there is greater appreciation of the impact on women and children in the 1980s, but it is not too different from what was described a generation ago.

Secondly, addition there is the urban poverty that has been borne of economic change, of the debt crisis, of the need for adjustment, of the recession and even of growth itself. At the

Bank's Annual Meeting in Bangkok, I was struck by an interesting comment by the Prime Minister of Thailand. As everyone was praising Thailand for its economic growth experience, the Prime Minister's main message was that, even though Thailand had experienced real growth, the most important political fact on his mind was the disparity between those who profited from growth and all those who have been left behind. The fact that he articulated that to the Board of Governors was quite interesting.

The point here is that even in the growing economies, income distribution questions are still serious. Urban poverty, both the structural-classical type and that which results from adjustment and economic change, as a statistical phenomenon is much more serious. In the paper we argue that a quarter of the world's urban population, that is about 330 million out of about 1.3 billion people, are in absolute urban poverty. All the numbers of projected increase in urban population will certainly accentuate that. When you think about demographic projections, it is not as if the increased urban population is going to be rich. It will tend to be low income people with larger families on the periphery of cities.

What do we propose to do here? I would refer back to the basic strategy that the Bank elaborated in the *World development report*[17], where we talk about first, increasing the demand for labour of the poor and thinking about the policy impacts, again at the macro-level; secondly, investing much more actively in health and education, in the productivity of the poor – that is the strategy; thirdly, thinking about safety-nets and compensatory measures to deal with the so-called problems of transition. This has been the Bank's view at the macro-level. What does this mean in urban terms, in city terms?

In terms of increasing the demand for labour by the poor, there have been a series of projects which the Bank has financed in West Africa, which are interesting. They involve both the privatization of municipal services and an insistence on labour

---

17 *World development report 1990: poverty.* Washington DC: World Bank.

intensive methods. In countries such as Niger, Senegal and Mali, urban services are privatized and labour intensive methods are used to increase the work of the poor. We are beginning to think more actively about some of the trade policy implications, and some of the industrial policies – to be more clear about the need to increase the demand for labour.

At the same time we believe we need to reverse an important trend which has occurred in urban lending, which we have seen at the Bank and in other programmes. This is the disappearance of the social service component of urban lending in the 1980s. For example in the 1970s, we observed that about 10 per cent of the project costs of almost any one of our operations included markets, health clinics, schools, nutrition and family planning programs. Last year only one-tenth of 1 per cent of project costs went into social services in urban lending. It has become concentrated in a narrow sense, either in housing or residential infrastructure. My urban project colleagues say: it is as if you believe that if you house and water people, they will not be poor. Pardon the crude expression here but it obviously does not make any sense. There has to be a much more integrated view of the needs of the poor in the neighbourhoods of the city as a whole.

This brings up a new dimension which is another category we have not used in the Bank in a serious way: social policy. The question we are now posing is: what should urban social policy be? Is it possible to think about improving the productivity or addressing the needs of the poor by a clinic here, an upgrading programme there? Do we not have to be much more multi-sectoral? We are undertaking research into the impact of adjustment on urban households.

We have started to look at the question of the whole safety-net approach which has also been used to deal with the transitions of urban poverty, and here we have some disturbing news to report. There are something like thirty social safety-net programmes financed by the Bank and other donors. Frequently these are joint activities, many in Africa, many intended to deal with, again, the transitional problems of adjustment. The content of these safety-net programmes involves typically a little bit of transport, a little health, a little education, occasionally some food. If you looked at each of those components and asked whether they made sense in the policy context of education, of food, or of transport, in the country, much less in the city, I do not think you would be deceived. You would realize that they do not in fact relate to the overall policy framework. Even worse, they are not sustainable in their impact beyond a very short time. We have just produced an important paper where we look at these compensatory measures. We think, from an urban point of view, that these are not adequate responses to the urban impact of adjustment and macroeconomic change. It does not mean we have the answers, but we are now starting discussions in the Bank to look at these safety-net programmes in a much more serious way.

To come back to the question of what is different between the past and the future. In the past we had neighbourhood-level projects; perhaps the best were those broader city-wide programmes such as the Kampong Improvement Program in Indonesia or bustee improvement in Calcutta. A number of you were associated with these and maybe they reached a significant number of people. But it is clear that they are not reaching the numbers that one needs to think about. I do not think that the policy context is adequate to that approach. We need to put a lot more emphasis on urban poverty.

Let me turn to the *urban environment*. Our performance is miserable. We started to look at the urban environment in preparation for the policy paper. We collected data on our performance and then we went back to the 1971 projects where the Bank had financed garbage collection. We observed that there was not a single case where the garbage trucks had led to a broader discussion of urban environmental policy. We financed drainage, water supply, garbage collection, but we had not really raised the question: what are the primary environmental issues facing a particular urban area, and where are the data to make accurate observations about this? What would be the policy standards one would wish to aspire to; for example, what would be a clean air standard, an air-pollution standard? Should there be some normative view on waste management; how much should be collected, how should it be handled, how do we relate landfill and disposal to the question of the collection and the broader use of land in the area? Even if we had a normative view, have we dealt with the institutional framework of environmental management? Frankly, I do not think we have. I cannot find a single project where this has been done effectively. We ended up taking this finding through the management who were full of incredulity.

The urban environment is something that really requires a lot of thinking. There is an irony here because, after all, in the past two years the green agenda has captured the political and public imagination in many countries. Yet our observation is that the green agenda seems to be about broad global issues: warming, deforestation. In some sense we do not have responsibility for those things. There is a global environment fund, there are broader concerns, but what can people do about cities? We would argue that in parallel to the green agenda there is the brown agenda: dirty air, dirty water which impacts right now, not in the next generation. It affects the productivity that we started with in terms of the contribution of the city to overall productivity. It affects the poverty that we were interested in addressing, although many of the causal links are unclear: do the poor create environmental degradation or are they the victims of it? There are clearly all kinds of causal connections, which we will not debate.

There is an agenda of environmental concern which we think is being neglected. If one looks at the agenda for the UNCED conference in Rio, the first item was environment, but it was not about people; it was all about natural resources. Nor did we see institutions and responsibility. Part of the agenda should be an issue about local responsibility and about institutional strengthening.

I have said a little on what we did in the past. We are not proud of that, but what are we doing in the future? In our lending program, we are receiving lots of requests to work on the urban environment, but the question is who in the Bank is receiving them? An example: in the case of Brazil, one of my colleagues discovered that the people working on municipal infrastructure had been asked by the city authorities to work on the environment. The people working on industrial projects had been asked, but they were not even talking to each other. So we have now pulled them together and said we want to work in a concerted effort to think about environmental areas; for example, the São Paulo area, the water basin and the impact of industrial waste on water supply, all the way down stream to Cubatão. We are thinking about a co-ordinated environmental response which looks broadly at river basins and water sheds and is cross jurisdictional. This is complicated, costly and data intensive, because in many cases we do not know the quality of environmental standards in the beginning. We do not have normative standards, nor do we have the institutional framework. What is happening is we are getting very large numbers of requests: there are six urban environmental projects in the pipeline for China for the next three years. We are getting a strong interest from that Government, which has something like 70 cities with over a million people. We are learning that this is something we really have to respond to.

We are developing an urban environment policy paper which will come out next year. This seeks to look at operational experience and tries to figure out in specific terms what kinds of things we ought to be doing. It is clear that one of the major areas is investment simply in data. With all the efforts, for example, in the water decade, we are surprised that there is very inadequate data on water quality round the world.

The paper argues that cities are becoming more important for macroeconomic development, for the achievement of our most important development objectives, in terms of growth, poverty alleviation and environmental management. We have the impression that urban understanding has actually diminished during the 1980s. The urban studies industry, as it might have been called in the 1970s, boomed then, and it reflected urban crisis in the north and great interest in the squatter settlements of Latin America, Africa and Asia. There were a lot of studies going on. In the 1980s, a lot of urban research stopped, despite the tremendous changes which occurred. High inflation in Brazil is a good example. Brazil is a country where there are 1,000 dissertations. If you look at them, there is not one I would want to put money behind because there has been a 1,000 per cent inflation. The meaning of minimum wages has changed. The relationship between men and women's earning power, between sectors of the economy has changed. The whole adjustment process and economic crisis has changed everything, so the basic quantitive understanding is out of date. From the point of view of the impact on households, the rôle of labour markets, the performance of infrastructure, what has happened in the neighbourhoods, the whole problem of the mega-city, there is a very rich agenda for urban research, which itself becomes a policy issue. How can we assume that the developing countries can make informed policy decisions without adequate urban understanding? In some of my travels I talk to Governments and say "How do you know that you know? What do you think you know about some of these questions?" Most people are disturbed because I do not think there has been adequate investment made in the urban research and understanding business.

We have been working closely with the Ford Foundation which is now undertaking an assessment of urban research in the developing world. They are hoping to convene a global conference on urban research in December 1992. The question we have raised in the policy paper is whether there has to be something analogous to what has been done in international agricultural research, that is a Research and Development programme to prepare something analogous to the green revolution.

These are the four issues we think are important and we are proposing to do things somewhat differently. In practical terms, let me give you some numbers to show the magnitude of what is going on.

Between 1972 and 1991 we financed 188 urban operations. We have 150 more in the pipeline for the next five years – this reflects a decision not by the Board or by the President. It reflects country requests. In fact some of the senior management asked us as we brought the policy paper through the institution: "Where do these numbers come from?" They came from developing country governments. This is not something that was supply driven. There is a tremendous explosion of demands for assistance.

We have been financing roughly one and a half billion dollars a year in urban lending. We are anticipating moving up to about 3 billion a year. Last year we did 16 urban operations. I believe next year or the year after we will have 34 operations coming up. There is a tremendous increase in the numbers, in the money involved and the content of what we do.

One of the messages of the policy paper is that policy and institutional development are the keys to addressing this agenda. Since this policy paper was approved by the Board in January 1991, we have already programmed a doubling of what we call programme sector work, analytical studies which lead to project work. There is a doubling from 1991 to 1992, and in 1993 there is a substantial increase. By the end of 1993, we will have done four to five times as much analytical work on urban issues as we have done in fiscal 1991. The institution is responding in budgetary terms to the kinds of task and work that need to be done.

What are the implications for the urban aid system? What are the implications for developing countries to try to shift the agenda, to do things differently? I would like to bring in the notion of collaboration between UNDP and Habitat (UNCHS). Raising this policy agenda is not something that can be done simply through the transfer of capital resources, which is the Bank's comparative advantage. We must have a much more collaborative model of development assistance which emphasizes institutional development and policy dialogue. We cannot do this work through the feasibility studies of the 1970s and 1980s. There is not necessarily a linear process by which one identifies needs, does social surveys and preliminary engineering, does the cost tables and that is it. We have all been through that process and we don't think that is the way to go.

We must first of all work with developing countries to listen to what they believe their priorities are. Hence we raise the question of the urban management consultation, a device supported by the urban management programme as a way of eliciting a sense of priorities and entering into a dialogue about the meaning of policy reform. Institutional development is something that the World Bank and some of the institutions which transfer big capital resources may not in fact be good at. We are not particularly pleased with our own record in the urban sector on this. The bilaterals have an important rôle to play in training and institutional strengthening. Institutional assessment is something that needs much more attention. We are really looking at a model of urban assistance in which the institutions use their comparative advantage much more explicitly. We wonder whether a bilateral that is putting for example 40 million dollars a year into the urban sector should be buying pipe with that money. I am not sure that it makes sense. On the other hand, that 40 million dollars can really be used effectively with smaller inputs, not into a big project cycle, and figuring what would be the appropriate moment in the policy reform and institutional development processes in which to act is the key.

Let me give you one final example of what this means in practical terms in Mexico. We were invited to present our policy paper by the Minister of Urban Development and Environment in Mexico. I spent a day talking about the context. A couple of weeks later, the Mexicans called the Bank and said:

"We are very worried, the free-trade agreement is coming, we are expecting that the towns of northern Mexico will receive even more of an onslaught from American private investment. There are 1,200 American companies already there and if you look at these towns, the whole question of public and private investment is not clear. Urban poverty is increasing, the environmental conditions are out of control. We need to think about some other response. We don't want to talk about a Bank operation – we just want to talk about the situation."

We said we would send some people who would think about it, but the condition was that nobody would have any money in their pocket. What we wanted to do was to think about these things together – what would be an urban policy response, which is not project led? We sent a mission, talked about these issues, and there was a case study done on one city[18]. There will be discussions with the government about the content of that, but the interesting thing that has happened, with the Mexicans and with our own operational division, is that somehow the pressure to lend is off, to come up with a dollar amount in response. It is a much more open policy discussion about what should the Mexicans think about here, what would be the response, not in one town or a neighbourhood of one town? How can they think about an urban policy that is consistent with the macro-changes that have occurred in Mexican policy in the past 10 years? The stakes have gone way up. The interlocutors are not the Ministry of Urban Development or the Mayors, but the Ministry of Finance, the Ministry of Planning. These are in fact macro-questions. The whole way of rethinking this is a small step on the way to changing the way of doing business. Then we will have a much more serious impact.

The challenge of urbanization
Shabbir Cheema *Principal Technical Adviser*
Bureau for Programme Policy and Evaluation
United Nations Development Programme

The first important point in urbanization is that the size of the urban population and the numbers involved are so huge that no public policy can ignore this process. Urbanization is one of the single most important phenomena in developing countries, transforming them with major social, economic and political implications. It is not easy to control a large number of well-organized areas. There are a lot of political implications and any national policy has to take that into consideration.

The second major point is that when we discuss our strategy

---

18 *Juarez: report of an urban management mission* (mimeo). Washington DC: World Bank, August 1991.

for the 1990s, we must see that action takes place within the framework of human development, which UNDP has defined as: the enlarging of human choices including access to income, employment opportunities, education, health, and a safe physical environment. We must see urbanization within the broader human development framework. Our thinking about development has changed; and when we look at the urban phenomenon, we look at human conditions in the cities in developing countries, and how to increase peoples' choices and improve their living environment.

Another introductory remark is that UNDP as the central co-ordinating agency of the United Nations system, like all organizations which must compete and continuously show relevance in what they are doing, has in many ways undergone significant changes in the past two or three years. Within this climate of change, about two years ago we started a process toward an urban policy paper; I consulted "wise men" from developing countries, in order to produce UNDP's first Urban Sector Strategy Paper.

We felt that to be effective as a central funding and co-ordinating organization of the UN system, we must be able to forge collaborative efforts, inter-institutional co-operation, and be able to give substantial input to that process. Co-ordination accompanied by substantial inputs is critical. A lot of the bilaterals are learning that to be effective they must examine critically what they are supporting. That has led to a situation in 1991 where the bilaterals, multilaterals and governments in developing countries are sitting together and discussing issues from their own perspective. The end product is that we are, for the first time in the urban sector, beginning to recognize the different perspectives of the developing countries, of the bilateral donors and of the multilateral donors. Although it was mentioned earlier that we do not need to convince each other (we are already converted), the reality remains that there were not as many forums for discussion and communication on substantial issues among these three groups as we have today. This meeting is a very useful initiative.

In February 1990, UNDP's governing council changed the mode

of operation of UNDP. The council suggested that UNDP should become more thematic and that there are a few global themes that are critical. With that sharper focus, UNDP could perhaps more effectively utilize its limited resources for technical co-operation. The six global themes are: poverty alleviation and grassroots participation, women in development, natural resources and the environment, technical co-operation among developing countries, management development and the transfer and adaptation of technology. The idea was that once this was done the comparative advantages of UNDP as an organization could be enhanced. This was approved by UNDP's Governing Council, consisting of representatives from our recipient and donor countries. When the change happened within UNDP, we realized that cities are the areas where many of these issues and innovations take place: some of the most successful informal sector activities; some of the most innovative income generating activities for women; and a lot of private sector initiatives providing urban services. Urban areas provide a setting in which the specific themes could be examined because in some ways urban areas are integrating mechanisms. That was the beginning of seeing that it was essential to look at UNDP assistance from a holistic perspective and to have a thematic assessment of UNDP's past work.

We undertook an assessment of UNDP's urban programmes. Since 1971, UNDP has provided close to 2.5 billion dollars in urban-related projects and close to half a billion in directly targeted urban assistance. We did a case study in a few countries, and analyzed the data that we had at Headquarters. Then we undertook case studies of fifty specific projects. We were able to reach some conclusions about the strengths and weaknesses of UNDP assistance in the past[19]. The response that I got from some of the senior managers at UNDP was that we were evaluating UNDP's past performance with criteria that did not exist at that time. In some ways, this was a valid comment.

---

19 *Assistance in the urban sector – a thematic assessment*. New York: Bureau for Programme, Policy and Evaluation, UNDP (January 1991).

But at the same time, I told them that because we did not want to make the same mistakes we had made before, it was necessary to make the assessment that we had made, to identify the constraints which impeded the implementation of programmes, in order to improve the effectiveness of our assistance.

I wish to discuss the challenges which constitute UNDP's Urban Development Co-operation Strategy. First, I will explain what our perception of those challenges is, mentioning some of the things UNDP has done and is likely to do in the future, and pointing out our collaboration with other agencies. We have said that the strategy paper, *Cities, people and poverty*, is a UNDP policy statement. What we are actually presenting is a different way of doing business.

What is critical, based on our *Human development report*, 1991[20], is that economic viability and productivity need to be accompanied by social justice, sustainability and participation. These are the goals that we need to pursue. Removing constraints on urban productivity is a necessary but not a sufficient condition to improve the situation of the poor in the cities of developing countries. It is not an either/or situation. But in many cases the trickle-down effect just has not taken place.

Urban development must be more holistic in perspective. We cannot have a project approach and expect a radical transformation. To expect a significant transformation, our own concept should be significant enough to incorporate various dimensions. When we drew up our agenda for the 1990s, the challenge of *urban poverty* was central. This is the first challenge of UNDP strategy. There is a lot of debate about the determinants of urban poverty: what leads to urban poverty in developing countries? What are the appropriate policy and programme responses to dealing with urban poverty? There seems to be general agreement that we must organize the urban poor at the community level to increase their capacity to make demands on

---

20 UNDP *Human development report, 1991*. New York: Oxford University Press (1991).

the urban system, to safeguard their interests. That is the way the system, any system, works; the organizational capacity of the poor must be strengthened to put pressure from below, so that their interests are safeguarded.

Increasing the productivity of the poor is critical. This can be done by strengthening small enterprises in the informal sector. There is a need to support these enterprises through mechanisms such as community financing. There is now a clear recognition that government does not need to formalize the informal sector. I think that because in many developing countries 60–70 per cent of employment is generated in the informal sector, it is difficult for anyone to ignore them. They are the major part of the urban development process.

The magnitude, in terms of numbers, of the urban poor in developing countries and their contribution to economic development (despite the hostility of the government in many countries) is very significant. Yet when we make the assessment of UNDP assistance, covering close to 250 urban and human settlement programmes, we found that only about 10–15 per cent were directly related to poverty alleviation. Indeed only 3–5 per cent were creating income-generating activities for the poor. If we consider urban poverty to be such a critical issue, why was it that in the international assistance programmes the issue did not come forward? We found that 25–30 per cent of our assistance went into the preparation of master and structural plans, which are now implemented in most countries. We supported those from 1971 to 1989. When I presented these figures to our senior management, I reminded them that in 1989 UNDP had laid down these six themes. We need to look at what UNDP did in the past, but we do not want to make a sweeping statement that suddenly we have discovered that poverty is important.

We can already see the results of our new strategy. Three weeks ago, we received a request from the government of Indonesia to assist in preparing a five year programme on urban poverty with an eight or ten page terms of reference.

When we at UNDP talked about a global agenda, our approach was the following: there are some global themes that we find critical. How are the global themes delineated? I think through the collective wisdom of people like those in this room, we discuss and analyze at a global level. But when we take those themes to the countries, and they become central issues for the dialogue with our government counterparts, we do not feel it is our rôle to force any government in terms of conditionality that this must be done. But we want to use these themes as substantive, the focal point for initiating country-based dialogue. We want UNDP to be playing a mediation rôle between the bilateral and other international donors and recipients to increase the capacity of the developing countries to speak from a position of strength and intellectual capacity. When we take these issues to our counterparts in developing countries (and some of them are sitting here) we want them to see how these themes fit in the country's specific situation. Since we started this process, we have seen in Indonesia and Mozambique major programmes on urban poverty being initiated. In Thailand, one fifth of the total UNDP programme is going to the reduction of inter-regional disparities by delineating a programme on urban poverty in regional cities. This relates to the statement the Prime Minister of Thailand made at the World Bank meeting on why he considered poverty such a big problem. The initiatives emerge from a country-based dialogue between the UNDP staff and our Habitat on the one hand and the government counterpart on the other. It is a collaboration. It is not conditionality. This is the essence of technical co-operation, technical assistance. We consider at UNDP that this is one of our comparative advantages.

Let me come to the second challenge on the urban development agenda: *enabling and participative strategies for the provision of infrastructure and services*. Governments in developing countries do not have adequate resources and capacity to provide services, infrastructure and housing to the increasing number of urban poor. In the 1960s governments did try to provide housing through the creation of development authorities. Since then, we have seen significant changes in public policies, and in the attitude of the government. There have been various stages in the evolution of the provision of services culminating in the late 1980s and 1990s in a recognition of the rôle of informal settlements as a critical component of the urban development process; that is, where we have been playing an active rôle through the "Global Shelter Programme to the year 2000". A lot of our work in UNDP and Habitat has been in the preparation of national shelter strategies. There are three or four critical issues we need to be dealing with: access of the urban poor to land, to credit and to adequate working conditions, and the issue of appropriate building codes and standards, and regulatory frameworks. This is an argument for community participation, enabling communities to respond to their own issues.

Governments are very receptive to the enabling and participative approach to infrastructure, especially if international donors are able to present an integrated package which is identified through dialogue. In each of the programmes in Thailand, Mozambique and soon in Bangladesh, we expect that this will be the critical component in specific areas rather than studies at a more macro-level (which take three years to undertake and end up in the desk of the Secretary who doesn't want to share it with anybody). Technical assistance should be a process. The people involved in technical assistance should be part of a process, learning with the counterpart rather than coming in with a couple of solutions which they give to the government. The situation in developing countries has changed radically. In view of the increasing capacity of developing countries, international technical assistance agencies really have to be at the cutting edge of the field to be taken seriously. International experts have to know the context of the developing country.

Let me come to the third challenge: *improving the urban environment*. This is critical. We do not look at the urban environment from a global perspective. Improving the living condition of the poor at the local level is the real issue. In fact we have the Global Environmental Facility that we are managing in co-operation with the World Bank, but the response at a meeting in New York a few weeks ago attended by recipient countries, was: "Can you use this money to support some urban environmental programmes?" The issues of solid waste management, urban transport, and alternative transportation systems in developing countries stimulate a lot of requests. In the past we did not have many integrated urban environmental improvement programmes. We may have a water scheme in an urban area and a slum improvement programme in a settlement, we might have educational facilities, and curriculum development programmes in a particular city, but there were not many integrated urban development programmes. That is an issue on which there is focused a lot of interest. We have ensured that urban environmental issues are incorporated in the Agenda 21 of UNCED. One of the initiatives we hope to launch in the early part of next year is a Local Initiative Facility for Urban Environment (LIFE), for which resources can be mobilized to support community-based initiatives in developing countries. We already have a major programme in Asia which we call Asia Pacific 2000 which supports NGOs to improve the urban environment. Under that programme which covers 8 countries, we provide through national steering committees small grants of $50,000 to $200,000 for innovative local initiatives aimed at improving the urban environment. I have been told by many people that these small-scale initiatives are not sustainable; my response is that many national policies are not sustainable. There is a certain opposition to local level initiatives, just because it does not fit into our limited definition of sustainability. UNDP's position in supporting community-based initiatives gives it a comparative advantage at national, regional or global levels.

The fourth challenge is *strengthening the capacity of local government administration*. Much has been said and written about this, but the fact remains that international assistance to strengthen local government has been inadequate, and often monopolized by central government Ministries and Departments. In the mid 1980s, Sivaramakrishnan wrote an excellent book on urban management[21] in which he pointed to a crisis. Infrastructure had been built with foreign assistance without strengthening the capacity of local governments to maintain it.

---

21 K. C. Sivaramakrishnan & Leslie Green (1986). *Metropolitan management: the Asian experience*. New York: World Bank/Oxford University Press.

It took ten years for the international community to get the message and incorporate it into programmes.

We do not want to look at local government purely from the economic perspective. We also want to see that urban local government is the focal point for strengthening participation and democratic processes, and local relationships between municipalities and the community. The decentralization of power and resources, municipal finance, and improving the management capacity are issues we are stressing in our next programme cycle. We will be supporting many projects that will be possible only in this new age of democracy. Many countries, where we could not work directly with municipalities in the past, we can work with today.

Yesterday in a meeting on the Municipal Development Programme for sub-Saharan Africa, somebody raised an interesting issue. We were discussing the programme that UNDP is supporting[22]. Somebody asked: "How did you determine the demand for these 15 projects that you are undertaking?" The manager gave a frank answer: "Some of it is through requests from countries, but generated by a group of our people, sitting here; we thought that was a very important issue". We have to see what the issues are and try to support them, but not through a limited definition of what a demand-driven programme is. Promotion, advocacy, and demand-driven are all related concepts, and we should have a dialogue among the partners, where we recognize that our developing country counterparts may not have the technical knowledge required on an issue. They do have a much better understanding of the local situation and cultural dynamics. In the 1990s, issues are primarily institutional and managerial, not technical. Thus it becomes important for us to recognize that our collaborators from developing countries have considerably better understanding of the institutional and cultural contexts.

The final agenda item is the challenge of expanding *the rôle of the private sector*. Here again there is a recognition that we need

---

22 The UNDP–World Bank–UNCHS Urban Management Programme.

to draw on the full complement of human energy in the cities. The government cannot do everything alone; a lot of capacity is available in urban programmes, that we intend to support. There is resistance in some countries. We can do it easier and faster in other countries. Dialogue is of the essence. The dialogue at the global and regional level should not be confused with dialogue at the national level. The national level is where the real action is. We must think globally and act locally.

I would just like to sum up by saying that we have decided to take a more active rôle in UNDP, in advocating ideas and themes on the global level on which we feel there is a global consensus. Let me present to you an optimistic perspective of the way we look at it. If we wait for the big organizations to change before we promote these ideas, no significant change will take place. If in our individual capacity as the chiefs of various units, serving as focal points in various organizations, we can make a 10 per cent change in the way we do business, I think we have done something useful. That is the spirit with which we are trying to present this UNDP policy paper. Its strength will depend on the co-operation of our colleagues, particularly my colleagues from Habitat, whom I must acknowledge, have helped us a lot in UNDP in developing these ideas and giving us feedback from the field.

The discussion
CHAIRMEN: Patrick Wakely & Paul Ackroyd
PARTICIPANTS: Jorge Hardoy, Arif Hasan,
David Leibson, Patrick McAuslan, P. S. A. Sundaram

The discussion took up and elaborated qualifications to the points made by the opening speakers. In particular, the realistic possibilities of popular participation received much attention. One participant stressed that the situation in many of Asia's cities had changed in the late eighties and nineties. Although government efficiency had improved, the capacity to implement public policy, rules and regulations seemed to have declined to the point where government action had become increasingly irrelevant for the mass of city dwellers. Informal sector activities had increased in scope, efficiency and confidence relative to government. But the formal sector – including the state and professionals – was increasingly restricted to upper income groups, and the rich were isolated in ghettoes. Much of the formal legislation and regulation governing cities was increasingly irrelevant and out-of-date. Ignored by the formal institutions of society, a second generation of slum dwellers was growing up who were quite different to their parents: more alienated and prone to violence. Local community action had become more regularized without yet becoming politicized, so that it still did not provide acceptable outlets for the frustrations of the young.

Despite continuing expressions of interest in greater popular participation, governments seemed quite remote from the reality. So far as the mass of the urban population were concerned, there were four main obstacles to greater involvement in, for example, infrastructure provision: psychological (the assumption that governments would always provide services); economic (the high costs of facilities); sociological (people were alienated from the public processes involved); and technical (people lacked the capacities to modify or set standards, etc.; the NGOs would have an important rôle here). However, outside the formal system, these barriers had in practice been overcome, but it was not clear that they could be superseded within the public domain. For these reasons, it was not obvious what rôle local communities would be able to play if powers were decentralized to a local level.

The discussion underlined the opening speaker's emphasis on the importance of urban government and the political agenda. How could governments be persuaded to adopt the types of new approaches outlined in the two policy documents – or rather, since governments often formally agreed with those approaches, how could they be induced to act on them ? This gap between declaration and implementation could be seen in the failure to involve the "other half" of the city, its women, and involve them not just in the elementary tasks of building the city, but in the formulation of city policy.

The two policy documents hardly covered the great diversity of political conditions in Third World cities. They seemed to imply that the opportunities for progress were equally the same everywhere, for example in democracies and dictatorships. Yet many people vanished for trying to follow some of the things recommended in the documents. In Latin America, a fourth generation of squatters now existed – and even where the right to participate was constitutionally guaranteed, they were often still not represented in the dominant political process. As a result, the poor and the NGOs that represented them often worked under great constraints; the context had to be changed radically before there could be hope that they could work effectively – and then the agendas would become capable of implementation.

The World Bank, another workshop participant noted, dealt with governments and official agencies, when the people it now sought to influence were outside official bodies. Yet there still remained an important rôle for the state – it was not enough just to talk of removing restrictions. Of course, "the state" was not one single agency – it varied considerably between its different components, particularly between the central, provincial and local powers. Nor was the attitude of public authorities to the wider society uniform. How many political leaders felt threatened by the activity of NGOs and community groups ? This was a key question if, as the two policy documents suggested, increasing activities were to be transferred from the public sector to other agencies.

However, the state would still have to provide services in many areas. The private sector, for example, had not been effective in meeting the needs of the poor. Some people could not "compete in the market"; the most striking cases included the disabled and handicapped. The state was needed to ensure there were safeguards against exploitation, for example, maintaining standards in safety or food quality. Simple decontrol could quite often lead to increased risks and hazards in society. In housing in India, 90 per cent of the private stock could not be afforded by

75 per cent of the urban population; only the public sector could ensure some measure of shelter for many people. Again, posing issues in terms of a "bottom up" or "top down" approach, *either* the community *or* the state, was not correct – we would still need both and increased sensitivity in handling their interaction.

The problems of Third World cities had to compete for attention and funds with a host of other issues, particularly in a period when major changes were taking place in the world. The generalized shift to market economies and to democratic government had direct effects on the urban sector. But also the dramatic changes in Eastern Europe and the Soviet Union increasingly claimed the attention of aid donors and governments. The radical structural adjustment of the economies of the developed countries – not just the developing – also dominated political perceptions. So, important as the content of the two documents was, it was the capacity to attract resources in a context of strongly competing political interests that would determine how effective they would be.

Summing up
Michael Cohen & Shabbir Cheema

Michael Cohen

The comments have not disappointed me in their content. There have been some important observations: given the political realities, the imprecision with which one talks about "the private sector" and the rôle of the state, looking at it from the developed countries' point of view are very important qualifications.

The vision that is implied in the urban agenda, what we think we are doing here, is to say we acknowledge picking up on the trends, that the rôle of the state has changed, that perhaps the discrepancy between expectations and delivery is much larger than we understood at the outset and that we will not expect that the state will do certain things.

We did not pay enough attention to the political and social power of communities, particularly on the political side. Some of my political scientist friends say: you blew it; you really did not acknowledge what was going on at the political level. My reply is that maybe we were not explicit but what we were trying to apply was an increasingly decentralized view in the way in which cities are managed, that the rôle of central government is no longer tenable in the long term, that one presumes that there does have to be a local context in the way that these things are worked out and that our efforts in the past to support the local context have not been particularly successful.

We have 84 municipal development projects under implementation around the world. The fact that we do not address the centre-local relations means that we cannot expect that action at the municipal level will be able to create the political context within which communities can be supported, facilitated and enabled, in which there can be an adequate division of labour between public and private at the local level. That is a rather important mistake in terms of this connection with the locality. These important issues of productivity, poverty, etc. are going to be thought out within a local context and we are trying to reinforce this through intervention, through support on the policy institutional side, the reinforcement of the local context; that is the first part.

What do we expect to occur in the local context? We would expect that governments at the local level would have to acknowledge that municipalities cannot provide all the housing. They never have. They cannot be expected to continue. But if reinforced from a central level, they will perhaps have the confidence and also some efficacy with regard to enabling communities to take on responsibility. At the same time, we are really concerned about efficiency. One can't help but be worried about the efficiency of investment, the way in which things are done, the costs. For me, the interesting part of the analysis of infrastructure inefficiencies in Nigeria was that the firms and enterprises that were most affected by deficiencies were the small firms; it was not the big firms[23]. The big firms could find their own generators, build their own wells and take care of their services. The smaller firms felt the impact of inefficiency, so there was an equity implication as a result of inefficiency. If we can somehow support local contacts, we may be able to have results in terms of both efficiency and equity, in service delivery, and as a part of this empowerment, supporting political space.

We received a report on Hungary called *Privatization through decentralization*[24]. I had a discussion with the people who put it together and asked what were we trying to do here. The local people were saying clearly that the central rôle of the state was not acceptable any more. They wanted decentralization, differentiation of these activities. This goes back to distinguishing different rôles and responsibilities. There is going to be a broad range of outcomes which we cannot foresee ahead of time.

The barriers to participation are important. They are barriers for communities and international agencies which have the nerve to think they can relate to communities. To put it the other way round: psychological, social, economic and technical barriers obstruct us. I am not convinced that the notion of international officials jetting in to deal with these problems is meaningful; to believe that they are relating to communities. For that reason, the level of abstraction in our urban policy paper was intended to communicate that we do not think we ought to be down there looking at building codes and costs. I do not think we can do that. It is a lot of fun and you learn a lot of things, although I doubt if we can ever reach the scale and do this in a socially sensitive way. Our rôle is through communication with central governments to encourage a decentralized operation to support processes that have already gone on, to create political space, to get on with some of the economic and social activities that need to occur. One of the differences here in the Bank is that there are

---

23 Kyu Sik Lee & Alex Anas (1990). *Impacts of infrastructure deficiencies on Nigerian manufacturing: private alternatives and policy options*. Washington DC: World Bank Research Publication.
24 Robert Buckley et al. (1991). *Privatization through decentralization*. Washington DC: World Bank Draft Report.

some people who are romantic; they say we have got to be involved in neighbourhoods. I wish I could say yes, but I do not have a lot of confidence in that. We are too big. I think we could inflict a lot of damage. We have got to have a set of intermediaries. In effect what we are trying to talk about is reinforcing a local institutional framework.

Coming back to democracy and dictatorship, and distinguishing political realities, what we are talking about here is almost the political economy of urban assistance, of what is going to happen at the city level itself. These are going to be determined by political conditions. I want to turn that around and make that economic for a second. If you say that we want to have a user-driven or demand-driven approach to these things, when we talk to some countries, they say: "We do not want to hear about this stuff – decentralization". Fifty years ago they did not want to hear about slum upgrading; the bulldozer was the instrument of preference. We did not work in the tyrannical 1970s on shelter; governments were not interested in what we were talking about and we did not do it. At this point unless we are talking about some sort of decentralization process, the institutional choices, we also do not want to come in to do business just to push a project. Understanding that and being under self control, without trying to projectize everything and get it out, that is the really important distinction. There have been a number of governments in the past six months who have said to us in the Bank: "We do not buy into the decentralization idea" and that is fine. The Bank does not have to be a full service Bank – to use an American term – and come in here and work on urban and other things.

Again, what we think we are doing is broadening the possibilities. If the institutional framework can broaden the space, then perhaps there can be other kinds of interaction.

Shabbir Cheema

The question of so-called conflict between the central and local government is critical. It is the essence of decentralization. A couple of years ago when we did some work on decentralization, including a review of material from about two hundred case studies in developing countries, we recognized that it is a question of power, and that the central government does not want to lose their control. We concluded that it is really a question of the reorientation of the actors involved. Decentralization does not mean abolishing the centre. It means giving different kinds of rôles to the centre, and in that sense re-orientating the key actors. In discussions with Ministers of local government in the developing countries, a typical response I get is, "You know, Mr Cheema, my Ministry is not that important". I ask, "Why?" "Because I do not control the budget – the Ministry of Public Works is very important". Within the local political culture, he feels left out, which leads to a situation where the person does not recognize the significance of his own rôle. Thus it is both a question of power as well as re-orientating various political actors involved in that process.

When we are dealing with this kind of issue, nobody in the international agencies is in a position to say that this is the task that needs to be done. What is important is to create a framework, let the key actors discuss the situation and let the solution emerge through that process. That solution will be more lasting than one imposed from outside and which has been characterized by dissension. If you review the literature on administrative reform in developing countries during the past 40 years, one thing becomes very clear: the greater the scope of administrative reform, the greater the possibility of its failure. If a Prime Minister or President signs a decentralization bill, everything has to be restructured. The bill appears in 24 hours and the whole proposal will disappear in 24 hours too.

The issue was raised concerning how we need to address the problems of the other half of the urban population. That is precisely the issue we are trying to convey: that the urban development processes are really the other half of the urban population. There are so many constraints in dealing with them, the constraints from international agencies, from the national and central governments, and in some cases from the municipalities. In that sense, it is very important that we re-appraise the rôle of the international community dealing with technical assistance co-operation. It is our responsibility to make sure that we provide a framework, and we help facilitate that framework in which community initiatives can take place. If our dialogue is at the policy level, at the national level, without incorporating community concerns, there will be conflicts among different actors. The national setting is not an homogeneous one, and everybody within the national context is only talking about centralization and decentralization. There is a discussion, an informed debate, going on. The international community can help that processes by providing evidence and information, from the experiences of other countries, and indeed strengthening the rôle of local innovators, the people who agree with our point of view but are not heard within their own countries. In that sense international technical co-operation has a critical rôle to play in strengthening community based initiatives in developing countries.

Let me make another comment concerning democratic, open government. In UNDP's *Human development report*[25], we ranked countries according to their support of freedom, and there was a lot of criticism. So we went back to the governments and said that next year we will delineate a different index for human freedom. What we are doing now is putting together a team consisting of prominent persons from the developing countries. I do not have the data with me but I will not be surprised if the score remains more or less the same. We took the risk and we did the right thing. There was a lot of criticism. People from developing countries said, "How can you talk about democracy in the national political context but not in the international economic system?" Many people did not have an answer to that question and it was left unanswered. So it is easy to raise the questions, but the answers are very complex.

Finally, how are we going to incorporate these concerns into our own activities? To me it is clear that the people are looking for answers. In all settings there are people who will support

---

25 UNDP-Oxford University Press, New York, 1991.

innovative initiatives, whether it is in international organizations, national government Ministries or Departments. Even in our meeting in Paris[26], the issue was raised – how do we go from these ideas into action? We need a collective orientation, the capacity to be able to work as a team from the international organizations. We need a genuine dialogue with developing countries, not solutions imposed from our side, but a genuine dialogue, sensitive to the cultural and local context. Out of these two will emerge the actions that make these themes operational.

I visited the Asian Development Bank a few years ago and people asked me: "Can you give us guidelines on how to incorporate community participation in our project documents?" I said that in the literature I would have used, there are no guidelines. Our problem many times is that we want guidelines, to incorporate these concerns in our agency specific situation. It cannot be done without a genuine dialogue with our counterparts.

---

26 The Annual Review Meeting of the Urban Management Programme, from which many workshop participants had just come.

CHAPTER TWO
Country experience

Discussion

CHAIRMAN: Nigel Harris
PARTICIPANTS: Michel Fouad, K. C. Sivaramakrishnan, Hendropranoto Suselo, Pervez Tahir, Emiel Wegelin, Gu Wenxuan, William Housego Woolgar

After lunch, participants heard a number of contributions and comments from senior officers of governments considering or attempting to implement national urban policies.

On **Indonesia**, a contributor stressed the need to link the enhancement of urban productivity and the alleviation of poverty to the full development of people. Some urban poverty alleviation programmes may in practice have negative effects on overall human development.

A similar gap between aspiration and achievement was reflected in the hiatus between general policy formulations – as embodied in the two policy documents – and broader policy frameworks of the country concerned. In Indonesia, five yearly reports to the National Assembly constituted part of a 25-year programme of government action. The present long term programme, covering the period 1969 to 1994, stressed in the main economic development, combined with equity and stability, the key political ends of the government. In the next long term programme, the emphasis was upon human development. Thus, the ends of the two documents by the World Bank and the UNDP, to be effective, would have to be formulated within this overall policy framework.

In practice, the current 25-year programme had, in the urban areas, mainly been concerned with infrastructure development, a set of projects with little relationship to any overall strategy of urban development. This was a common and recurrent problem, deriving from institutional deficiencies. In Indonesia, the provision of urban infrastructure and services was project oriented, and this was rooted in the current professional and managerial style. National State policies were fragmented in sectoral objectives, as outlined in the chapters and paragraphs of the five year national development plans. The plans were fed through a structure of sectoral Ministries and specialized general directorates and directorates. Thus, the overall development of urban services could not be part of an intersectoral strategy. This institutional issue was a major problem in the translation from policy to implementation. Unless it could be overcome, the implicit method of the two policy documents could not be pursued. The government did try to overcome the problem through cross sectoral approaches embodied in areal – urban and regional – plans, acting as a counterweight to sectoral narrowness. But these questions were closely interwoven with the political struggles between different sections of the bureaucracy itself, so they were not easily resolved.

The recurrent gap between strategy and implementation was also a gap between two sets of people – those designing policy and those implementing programmes and projects. In Indonesia, the National Planning Board thought about overall strategy, but Ministries executed programmes. It was very difficult to persuade a Ministry to promote certain development strategies unless the National Planning Board made clear that there were specific gains to the Ministry at stake. When national planning agencies did not promote a strategy, line agencies continued to implement projects and programmes. The strategists, like Michael Cohen, were not doing projects; they were the responsibility of the Project Department. The two concerns, strategy and projects, needed to be brought together into a continuing relationship. Perhaps the policy people, from time to time, should change jobs and become project people and vice versa, so that integration could be improved.

The World Bank document stressed the need for more urban research because there had been a considerable decline in the past decade. External economic pressures – a decline in income and the consequent need to cut expenditure – are key factors in this decline. The area of loan projects most easily cut was technical assistance spending, and that usually included research.

An important element in considering research was the need for it to be used rather than just completed. Often few people knew that research had been done. For example, there appeared to be a World Bank study of urban infrastructure in Indonesia, but the document was not available so far, or at least, not disseminated to where it could be most useful, in Indonesia. It was also important to stimulate research in developing countries, not just within the World Bank.

In 1984, the Indonesian government, with help from UNDP, conducted research to define an urban development strategy. Two scenarios were presented – high intensity industrialization with a low level of decentralization, and an agricultural orientation with much more decentralization. The government chose the second – and what happened was the first ! But even with this outcome, what happened needed to be closely monitored, and that was the vindication for research. Of course, much research was irrelevant to the needs of decision takers, but relevant research was much needed, and the help of outsiders was very important in stimulating this.

Research was also seen as playing a key rôle by another speaker, this time in highlighting successes and important innovations, factors linking what individuals could do and the broad macroeconomic performance. Among the urban poor, the situation in many developing countries was not all gloom. There were important cases of success in breaking out of poverty, but a wider audience needed to know about them, why they had been successful and how far the successes could be replicated. This was especially true of the performance of small businesses where often the average size of employment was five workers or fewer. It was here that prosperity was generated. But small businesses needed security of tenure and the provision of basic services – water, power etc.. Aid was not a particularly useful way to help small businesses because it came in relatively large sums which were far beyond the capacity of small firms to absorb efficiently. A question for aid donors was how to reach small business with assistance and what intermediate national and urban institutions were needed to mediate this help.

The experience in **Egypt** was, one speaker argued, quite different to that in other countries since only six per cent of the land area of the country was habitable. The main drive of the national development plans had been to sustain a high rate of economic growth and improve the standard of living of the population, especially the poor, through creating employment. Cairo (now with more than 10 million inhabitants) was to be deconcentrated. After the peace treaty (with Israel) and the introduction of an Open Door economic policy, the approaches were adopted of the reconstruction of the three main cities of the country, the reconstruction of the Suez Canal region and the development of more distant regions. In 1980, the government began the preparation of a national urban policy (NUPS) which was completed by 1983/84[27].

Although the policy was never approved by the relevant Ministry nor the national cabinet, most of its recommendations have been followed. The NUPS projected a Greater Cairo population of 16.5 million by the year 2000, but the later structure plan revised this estimate downwards in the light of a continuing decline in inmigration. The NUPS argued against the orientation on the development of more remote (and usually desert) regions because of high cost. Greater priority should be attached, it said,

---

[27] *National urban policy study: Egypt*, prepared for the Advisory Committee for Reconstruction, Ministry of Redevelopment, by PADCO Inc., with Engineering Consultants and Sharif El-Hakin and Associates, Cairo, 1982, 3 volumes.

to job creation. Much of the strategy was carried out, but there was now a need to review what had happened in the past decade, a new economic and demographic situation. It was important to review the performance of the ten satellite towns established in desert areas and decide where policy needed now to direct attention.

By the end of 1990, the urban population of **China** lived in 467 cities and over 120,000 smaller townships. Continued development would suggest the number of cities would reach 600 by the end of the century, and smaller towns, over 150,000. Problems would become impossible if the increasing urban population moved to the cities. Much more research was needed to develop the basis for policies of regional development.

Macroeconomic and social policy were key elements in the current approaches of the Government of **Pakistan**. But the Government suffered from the well known problems of being remote from the detail of local issues. Cities were undoubtedly productive and governments needed to take advantage of this (although how far urban productivity was the result of a greater share of investment was not clear). But administrative decentralization, so much favoured in the two policy documents, hardly made sense since local government scarcely existed in the country.

The Government of **India** set in operation a major enquiry into urban development, the National Commission on Urbanization[28]. In 1988, this delivered of itself some 14 volumes. The volumes were available in the Ministry of Urban Development by September, and as is the way with civil servants, they were handed down the hierarchy without much attention being paid. However, much of the material was well worth reading, covering every possible dimension of the topic. Yet despite all the effort, the government was no nearer a real comprehension of the issues and a capacity to formulate an appropriate policy response. This was partly because the general approach (urban

---

28 See *Report of the National Commission on Urbanisation*, Government of India, New Delhi, Aug. 1988.

strategy) did not connect with immediate issues of concern to government, and hence to the real opportunities to act.

The same could be said of the two policy documents considered in the workshop. There are so many policy agendas claiming the attention of government and, as an earlier speaker had noted, governments were irrelevant or becoming irrelevant to the mass of the population (although government retained and would retain for a long time great capacity to wreak damage on the population). For action, what was really needed was an appraisal of opportunities that presented themselves. For example, in India there was much talk of liberalization and export promotion. Here was the scope for action. There could be no real increase in the export of shirts and trousers from Bombay to the United States without increased infrastructural provision, without more containers to load them into, roads and trucks to carry them, etc. Thus, there were a set of opportunities to make some steps towards implementing an urban strategy. In reality, strategies become practice only through opportunism.

This was where the question of subsidies arose. A bus in Bombay paid taxes of about 53 pence per kilometer, whereas a private car paid only 2 pence. Something was very wrong here, affecting particularly the relative cost of movement for the poor and the rich. Secondly, the vehicle stock was increasing exponentially. At the Paris meeting[29], the speaker had noted that India produced 1.7 million motorized vehicles (including two-wheelers) per year, but there was no comparable increase in road space to accommodate them. What policy was there on this? What were subsidies doing to the balance between bus and car traffic? The issue was simultaneously a set of macroeconomic questions, issues of national policy, and a city level problem. One could adopt a UNDP approach, showing how much the poor pay for their transport in terms of cash and journey time (the average cost of transport in medium sized towns was three times higher than in metropolitan cities), or a Bank approach in which the issue was national economic policy and relative taxing levels.

---

29 The Urban Management Programme Review Meeting, Nov. 1991.

DISCUSSION

Either offered an entry point to the same issue.

In sum, implementation required exploiting whatever opportunities presented themselves. The ability of developed countries and donor agencies to put across their message might be greater than the capacity of developing countries to absorb it. Opportunism provided a chance of acting whether or not the full strategy was in place or not.

It was remarkable, another speaker observed, that two major agencies, the World Bank and the UNDP, had come to agree on the agenda of issues and policy responses in the urban field. The next task was to turn the tanker round, to implement what had been proposed, and here there were much greater difficulties. Two sets of changes were needed – one in recipient countries, one in donor agencies. The donor agencies were a special problem. The project cycle imposed major constraints on any rapid changes, so a longer planning period was needed for the new policy approaches. That suggested more long term institutional strengthening programmes of technical assistance rather than the conventional feasibility and project approach.

For recipient countries, incentives to change were important, even if change was more related to the independent occurrence of opportunities than adoption of an overall strategy. This could be illustrated in an Indonesian case. The Integrated Urban Infrastructure Development programme there was part of the overall drive to decentralize and integrate sectoral actions in the hands of local rather than central government officers. Rôles and responsibilities had to be redefined. When that had been done, it was possible that half the central government staff involved would become surplus to requirements, and available for transfer to a different government level, whether provincial or local. The problem was how to treat central government staff when implementation of the new policy was underway in order to ensure that the policy was indeed implemented. Incentives to change were thus vital. Furthermore, much more attention needed to be paid to the central government if local government was to become effective.

Response
Michael Cohen

It might be helpful to describe the changes inside the Bank – the kinds of things required inside versus things going on in developing countries.

Let me describe the process that we have been going through. Some of the people that have been involved are here: my colleague, Larry Hannah, who worked in Operations, has joined this effort, as well as managers from the Management Programme. One of the issues which came up was the need to bridge the gap between the policy view and implementation and project experience. One of the messages of the policy paper is that you cannot do institutional and policy reform without a lot of work up front.

We went through an exercise between the end of January 1991 and mid-May. We held about 56 meetings with our operational colleagues from the 19 operating divisions in the Bank and we asked the question: "What is in your pipeline over the next couple of years? If you are going to do a project in 1994, what kind of analytical study should be done in 1992 to be able to make sense of observations in 1994?" In most cases that led to people saying they were in a project cycle and there were all kinds of incentives to generate projects and move them through a particular timeframe. But a lot of people said they did not have contextual information or a good sense of the housing system, or whatever it was, and they needed to do more analytical work. We have now observed, a couple of months later, that the number of pieces of sector work, or what we call analytical work up front, has doubled between 1991 and 1992 in terms of our own planning. It is again going to increase very substantially next year. From 1991 through to 1994 there is almost a four-fold increase in the amount of analytical work that the urban staff is doing with regard to this pipeline. That involves a change in the resource flow. Whereas we used to put a lot of resources into project development, now they go into sector studies.

I was pleased to hear a reference made to the *National Urban*

Policy Study[30] in Egypt, which we did not finance (AID was supporting it). That was important, but the fact is that there are a great many countries where there really are not good policy oriented pieces of work which can serve as a reference point to be revised at a later date. There has been a process of discussion and the studies have started, but what is the nature of the study? Is it going to be like the studies of the 1970s where some external consultants breeze in and in x number of staff weeks they produce something. We believe that we really have to do the business differently. There are two recent cases: the Mexico case I mentioned earlier (reference Footnote 26). In the Ivory Coast, we are trying to take the lead from the government – and here is the point about being selective and opportunistic – to respond to questions. In the Ivory Coast, we say we have been doing housing and a lot of other things but we would like to talk about urban poverty and about urban environment. We do not know whether this will lead to projects or not, but we would like to do it. The result has been to set up working groups; there is going to be no Bank paper prepared, but people will show up in response to their own progress and we will see how it moves. In the Mexican case we are not trying to prepare a huge amount of paper but rather enter into discussion. We are hopeful that this begins to approach the strategic framework; it is a human resource development strategy as well, and it is being explicit that we are not going to do the work, to prepare paper. We are hopeful that this helps to answer some of these questions.

Several comments were made about whether this approach is too comprehensive, too inter-sectoral, whether one needs to have a big picture and not do individual street projects. When I started out this morning on the macroeconomists, I was saying that they did not see the composition, the elements of development strategy. From a policy point of view, what we were trying to do was not define a framework to do projects, we were trying

---

30 *National urban policy study: Egypt* – prepared for the Advisory Committee for Reconstruction, Ministry of Redevelopment, by PADCO Inc. with Engineering Consultants and Sharif El-Hakin and Associates, Cairo, 1982.

to define a framework which would justify how the sector relates to overall development strategies. I was not trying to say to my project colleagues: this ought to be the real interest rate in the operation, these are the plot sizes. We were talking first about an overall framework, without necessarily pre-judging the outcome, the content of projects, how much housing, how much social services. The next step is in helping in the translation of the policy work through that selective framework. It may be telecommunications we ought to be doing in a particular place; traditionally the Bank would say the Infrastructure Division does not do telecommunications. But nevertheless, that is what we ought to be doing if that comes out of the discussions.

In practice, the notion is to respond in a concrete, selective way. The question then becomes: if we are going to be selective, selection according to whose criteria? In the 1970s and the 1980s, criteria were in the briefcase. I could do a site and service project anywhere. Now in the age of word processors, if you push a couple of buttons, you produce an appraisal report; that is not difficult. Without preconceived criteria you have to listen, to study, to make a commitment. That implies a very different approach on the process side, and I am not going to get into the trap of trying to say what would be the outcome of a particular project. Somebody will ask what is the Bank project of the 1990s: I do not know and we are not going to pre-judge the character of these things, except that we believe that these individual operations have a macro-implication, a macro-consequence, that they are strategic in their choices and they respond to the criteria to improve productivity at the city level. It also relates to the poverty agenda. Simply to pursue growth without thinking about equity is not defensible. At this point I know there is one thing I can be fired for: doing a project and not understanding its environmental implications. So I had better be sure about the environmental implications of a project. These become general criteria by which one orients these operations. It does not mean we have to do it all but we do have to think about some of these criteria.

Mr Gu made a reference to Regional Planning and someone else to decentralization. My reading of this debate and particularly as it relates to the issues of productivity and environment, is that we have tended collectively to ignore the regional development issue in the past ten years or so. It was perceived as being overly complicated. We have ended up focusing on individual sectoral projects, and the urban economists have encouraged us to believe that big is better. But then environmentalism hit with a vengeance at the end of the 1980s and now I think we have to look again, more seriously, at the city size question, at regional development, at metropolitan framework issues, at the secondary cities questions. Countries have been doing work on secondary cities, but I am sceptical. Somebody in Bombay last time I was there, said: "We know we are going to have 200 million more urban residents in the next generation in India. We are not going to pour them all in to Bombay, Calcutta, Madras and Delhi.". I think this applies more generally. There has not been a lot of good analytical work in the Bank on this question. We are going to have to pick it up, at least from a research point of view.

A point of fact: there was a comment made about population growth being higher in the cities. It is not true. Population growth seems to decline with more female labour force participation and that is higher in the cities. In one case growth may be higher, but that is not what the worldwide experience is.

Let me end on the point about being selective, and that translates back into what we should be urging governments to do in terms of incentives. There is a need to look at where the strengths are but more importantly, there probably is a need to understand what government priorities for reform are, the strategic opportunities. Somebody yesterday mentioned Zambia, in a political transition, a new approach, or the Indian situation, thinking about infrastructure. If there is a moment to do infrastructure carefully now, let us try to do it and not get bogged down in lots of other things.

Discussion resumed
CHAIRMAN: Kenneth Watts
PARTICIPANTS: Jaya Appalraju, Arif Hasan, Theo Kolstee
Michael Parkes, Jonas Rabinovitch, P. S. A. Sundaram

Several issues arose for **India** in considering the two policy documents which required further elaboration. The first concerned the basic pattern of urbanization. Given the enormous numbers involved – India might have the dubious distinction in the next thirty or forty years of having the largest urban population – what ought to be the direction which urbanization should take?

Second, what ought to be the balance of urban population between large and small cities? This had been a continuing issue of controversy in India. Third, what was the nature of urbanization? Was India 'overurbanized' and, if so, by how much? This had been a political issue for a lot of people who had seen cities as parasites, feeding off the rest of the economy. How far could urban development be seen as supportive of rural development; was agricultural prosperity related to the type of urban infrastructure introduced? In the present workshop, there was little discussion of the rôle of linkages, of regional development encompassing both agricultural and industrial growth. In that context, there was a case for promoting some urban development.

The documents also said too little about employment, both urban and rural. The Bank document had a sectoral bias. There was a limit to the number of jobs that could be provided in agriculture, so urban employment had to be promoted. This then raised questions of the balance between employment in formal and informal sectors (and how was 'informal' to be defined?). The issue of employment related closely to questions of poverty, economic status, supportive services, safety nets, etc. Nor was infrastructure provision simply a question of promoting efficiency, productivity and an equitable distribution. There was also the problem of existing deficiencies. Infrastructure was needed in the informal sector to establish self-support systems.

Efforts were being made to assess the costs and benefits of infrastructure. Here the type and level of charges for services became important. Related to this financial question was the problem of capturing the increase in land values from the development costs of private developers who gained from the external economies of the city without paying for them or generating other economies.

The Bank also needed to define the different levels of urban management. Urban management could cover a metropolitan region, a group of cities, districts, a group of villages forming a township and so on. The level at which urban management could be effective was different for each case. Building in a democratic element into a single framework of administration that linked government to the political leadership was also important.

So far as productivity was concerned, the important question was whose productivity was under discussion and who gained? There was no single solution for all cities since they were all different. Different cities needed different solutions.

A speaker described **South Africa** as a train travelling at top speed, with the driver, feeling the engine room was too hot, deciding to jump off while the train hurtled on.

The country's relevance to the workshop discussion lay in the rôle of Community Based Organisations (CBOs: Civic Associations or Civics in the South African context). There were close to 1,000 in both urban and rural areas which had organized themselves over the past three or four years, both locally, regionally and nationally. The whole now constituted a sophisticated piece of administrative machinery at the local level in the face of a crumbling State apparatus, both heading on collision course with each other. The CBOs had succeeded in making effective their slogan: Make the cities ungovernable. They were forming themselves into agents of development.

Local government would have liked to draw in the Civic Associations to negotiations in parallel with the continuing national negotiations. Simultaneously, the Central Government had decided that issues of urban development should be decentralized, be the responsibility of local government. As a result, there now existed a wide range of extra-parliamentary groups, highly cohesive, representative and democratic, discussing issues of rents, transport, sewerage or city government with city administrations that had lost any legitimacy – and were hanging on to the discussions as a kind of last justification for their existence.

The second mission of the World Bank had been in South Africa the weekend before the workshop to define an urban agenda for the post-apartheid situation. The Civic Associations had been very suspicious of any Bank mission since it was an initiative coming through the existing State which lacked all legitimacy. The mission had been grappling with the problem of what to do with the inherited divisions which apartheid had left. Cities were divided in almost every feature – socially, economically, politically, physically. A sophisticated industrial economy in the metropolitan areas had been divided in all respects.

At a meeting of 850 representatives of local government, the private sector, construction industry and consultants, the Civics were asked to make a presentation on the future urban housing development of the country. There had been no consensus, but someone had suggested that the experiences of the Third World might provide lessons. It was decided this was too complicated, but a simple question was then set: assuming the ANC were part of a new democratic government, what should be undertaken with the existing staff? In Zimbabwe, people had started to leave overnight, and replacements had to be imported. A gentle response might be to ask the staff not to leave the country but remain and see the transition through. The group had rejected this and proposed instead that all local government officers should be summoned to a meeting where a chart of all institutions involved in local and regional government would be put up on a board. In practice, no board would be big enough to include all institutions and all the linkages. Each local government officer would be asked to explain the diagram – a real spaghetti junction – and anyone who could do so would be sacked; anyone who said they had never been able to understand the diagram would be hired.

There was no clear perception of what was needed. There had been many initiatives from abroad and locally, but the general feeling was opposition and an affirmation of the need for self-reliance. In the end, the group had settled on the demand for an urban strategy that stressed social issues, that there should be differentiated responses because there would be heightened expectations as well as severe shortages. The special position of the poor posed a quite separate agenda. It was a start, and a start was vital in such an explosive situation where seizing the opportunities had to be reconciled with severe constraints. That could happen only if the hidden agenda was clear – what were the existing patterns of subsidization in housing, the appropriate standards, housing costs and available resources?

Another speaker stressed that while governments might need a view from below, NGOs needed a view from above. Few NGOs or CBOs that were actively engaged in development had any awareness of what the World Bank was, within what parameters it operated, or what the UNDP was, what its mandate permitted it to do. If there were to be increased consultations, much greater awareness would be needed at the base for CBOs to participate.

Comment
Michael Cohen

When I hear Sivaramakrishnan reviewing our contradictions, I feel great admiration and a certain frustration, because I know that most of what he says is absolutely right.

He spoke about a number of definitions, about the importance of formal and informal and also the definition of productivity: whose productivity? Where do the efficiency gains come from? What do we expect from that? Who captures the benefits from productivity, etc? In the urban paper of the Bank, we have tried to duck that question by saying that there are a lot of productivity gains to be achieved, but there are a range of types. For example, Sivaram made the point about taxation pricing associated with the cost of bus transport versus individual car transport; cars are paying on the tax side two pence per kilometre and the buses are paying 53 pence. This comes back to the definition of subsidies. There are a whole series of contradictions in the allocation of benefits that are occurring in cities that need to be understood. When we talk about productivity, it's not just a question of the individual household or where they are in the income distribution. For a lot of productivity gains, the poor can benefit. There needs to be a redistribution of some of the costs. The Bombay case is a good one. In transport, the unintended implications for the environment and the overall physical situation are enormous. We hope that by introducing the question of productivity, we can begin to get at some of those things.

We are not suggesting by any means that we are ruling out subsidies. I think that the notion that the Bank was formally against subsidies is absurd. There are a whole lot of good reasons why we would want to subsidise things. Things like environmental education of the kind that produced results would be very well worth subsidizing; that is, producing a set of behaviours which would make sense on a social basis. We are certainly not against that but I think the point about definitions is extremely important and needs to be followed up.

In many societies there is such a thing as directed credit, subsidised credit for particular purposes. As long as you have that, you do not know the true price of money. Sectors should be competing with one another to get credit for various purposes. At a macro-level, what a lot of people in banking are saying is absolutely correct: there needs to be a better allocation of credit for various purposes. It seems that whenever we look at who benefits from directed credit, once again we come back to the ones who are doing very well thank you. Rarely do you see directed credit benefiting the poor, whether it is for agriculture, agricultural machinery or housing finance or a variety of things. There are some distributive implications in thinking about credit in a more neutral way – this is a longer discussion, but I think it is also an important issue.

Two specific things. Jaya was talking about South Africa,

referring to a comment I made this morning. We are trying to enter the debate in South Africa with a full awareness that virtually anything that we do will have an unhappy outcome for one side or the other. The question is how does one proceed in a professional, technical way and use data? One of my colleagues is there and has done some analysis of the housing sector. He has managed to desegregate housing indicators by race, and one of the conclusions being brought out is that the white sector is not doing very well either, because of the results of apartheid policy as it operates in housing and urban services. There are some important ways of demonstrating that reform and changes are to be to everyone's advantage, but politically this is going to be difficult. I do not have any difficulty in being regarded with suspicion – that's the way it goes.

The final two points, for those of you that do not know the Curitiba experience. In our judgement Curitiba is one of the most exciting places in the world. There is a move towards a better integration of policy and practice than in virtually any place we have seen. It is worth understanding and following up.

Around any policy, there is politics and what has come out today is that the political assumptions and consequences of policy need to be explicit. However, I am not sure if, in South Africa, we lay out the political implications of the policy change, that this is necessarily an advantage. We all come from institutions where if you are too explicit it will blow up in your face. There is an interesting problem here. As I said this morning, we have not laid out the political economy of our policy paper, but I am delighted to talk about it.

Summing up
Shabbir Cheema & Mark Hildebrand
Chief, Technical Cooperation Division,
United Nations Centre for Human Settlements

Shabbir Cheema

I would like to make several observations. The first question that has been raised is, why do projects, that are the building blocks of development in the developed countries as well as in developing countries, not reflect an integrated approach? Our colleague from Indonesia made an important point as a regional planner, concerning the institutional issue, the question of the organisation of government machinery. If you look at regional planning literature in the developing countries, regional planning did not fail because there was a lack of regional economic models to translate strategies into different policy options, nor because the trade flows between region and country did not reflect what was happening. The reality of the situation was – as I assessed in my ten years at the United Nations Centre for Regional Development in Japan – a basic institutional issue. In Indonesia we prepared about ten provincial plans, and found exactly the same issue which is repeated country after country. That is the issue we need to recognize and that is where opportunities for intervention come. The sector Ministries are so powerful that planners do not have the resources or the political power to enforce an integration. The world is as it is, not the way we want it to be, so looking for the right opportunities becomes very important. Let us see where the opportunities are to bring in an integrated approach. Governments are organised along sectoral lines, so there is no reason to give up regional planning. In my understanding from the Bank's paper and our perspective, there is no excuse not to take an integrated approach. There are opportunities where that is feasible.

The second observation I would like to make concerns urban research and its utilisation. In addition to the need for research, one of the issues in developing countries is access to the research, as well as its utilisation. Access becomes important in systems where communication is not very open. Several years ago, I was invited by a Minister of Local Government and Rural Development on a mission as an adviser for three weeks. The Minister required a paper on Resource Mobilisation Capacity of Municipalities, and gave me ten professional staff. I provided the framework; they had collected the data before I arrived. Even with that kind of political support, it was only after two weeks that the Department Secretary opened his locked desk to get one or two of the reports which were critical for my use. You can imagine the administrative culture involved. It is critical that research on developing countries is not monopolised by international agencies like UNDP, or other agencies. It should be led by the active participation of institutions in developing countries, using internalised skills. So often wonderful analytically sound studies of a country are known in that country by not more than ten people.

Another issue is the question of small business and its success. We can keep talking about urban poverty in a conceptual model, we can have alternative hypotheses about the determinants of poverty, alternative policy responses, but the fact remains that the opportunities for action to effect change are present and must by grasped.

There are a set of propositions on which there is general agreement, global level issues, whether embodied in the World Bank's policy agenda or the UNDP strategy. We need to translate these into action; and in order to do that we need to be clear in our own organisation. The strategy paper of UNDP is in some ways an internal document, to bring issues to the attention of our own senior managers which show them what the implications of not doing something are. For example, I was in Bangladesh a couple of weeks ago. It was interesting to see the five projects that UNDP is supporting there. One project was started by one Ministry, and six months later another project started with another Ministry, without the programme designers talking to the other Ministry. These two Ministries were not communicating with each other. One year later there was another project and then there were another two projects which provide technical support to World Bank lending programmes. So there are five projects and each of those five projects is operating in a policy vacuum. In the last two projects, with UNDP technical support, only 5 per cent of the loan had been dispersed, but 90 to 95 per cent of the technical assistance had already been spent. Something is wrong. We decided to use the Urban Management Programme – the inter-agency collaborative effort of the World Bank, UNDP and Habitat – as a means of country consultation to bring different actors together.

The issue of putting this agenda into operation requires action on both sides – on the part of the developing countries, our counterparts, and on the part of bilaterals, multilaterals as well. I do not expect the international bureaucracies to change overnight and for everybody to say: "Great. From now on we are only going to do integrated work". Similarly I do not expect the bureaucracy in the developing countries to change quickly; the Ministry of Public Works is never going to let the Ministry of the Environment call all the shots. But in between these two extremes there are a lot of opportunities and that is why I feel there is room for tremendous optimism in the ideas that collectively we are promoting.

Mark Hildebrand

We start with two recently published policy papers, one entitled *Urban policy and economic development*, the other entitled *Cities, people and poverty*. From the discussion this morning, it is evident that these two papers present us with two somewhat different perspectives on what is nearly the same agenda. There is a little more of a human development perspective in one and a little more of an economic perspective in the other. I would like to begin in this summary by going back to the challenge posed by Mr Lancaster as he opened this morning's sessions: on the one hand there seems to be a very real consensus on the need for better government, but why is so little being done on the ground?

In introducing the Bank's policy paper this morning Mike Cohen punctuated his comments on each section of the paper with what the Bank proposed to do differently as a result of each of the paper's policy topics. In this meeting I believe we need to try to address the same question but in a broader sense – what the international community of donors and what developing country governments need to be doing differently. We have some consensus on our broad objectives, but much less so on exactly what to do, and how to do it. I also want to strongly endorse the suggestion that has been made by several people this morning on a need for modesty as we look for new solutions, while we acknowledge that our past approaches to urban development have to a great extent had only limited impacts. But although it can be said that our urban development agendas in the past decade have failed to have the desired impacts, there are so many other failures around us, that we cannot get people's attention: communism has failed, the BCCI failed, the Savings and Loan industry of the US has failed, and that has had an impact on the whole US financial sector which is still not over. The failure of the savings and loan industry has indeed shaken confidence in the US economy. Therefore as we think about new paradigms in how we approach the urban agenda for the 1990s, let us not lose sight of the fact that we are standing, modestly dressed, on a rocking boat.

This morning there were many references to the political dimensions of urban issues. Indeed, in my view, it is clear that our success in implementation will depend to a great extent upon our ability to take into account and address these political dimensions. In this respect I would like to recall three comments which I have noted over the past several days, both here this morning, and the day before yesterday, across the Channel in Paris, at the Annual Review Meeting of the Urban Management Programme. Jorge Hardoy asked us: "Who are the policy makers that we want to talk to?" He proposed that they are not necessarily Ministers and Mayors, to whom we normally address ourselves, but that the policy makers are the people and community leaders who are actually building cities. He described the man who led an invasion of several thousand people in

Lima, as being more of a planner than the city planner of Lima (who happened to be the man's brother). Cities are being built by people who are living on the edge of the cities and surviving on a daily income. They are being built from below. Similarly Mr Luiz Edmundo Costa Leite, the Brazilian city manager noted: "We do not manage things; we just react to pressure". That point was disputed by some other urban managers, but to a great extent, everyone does concur on the need for better governance to help city managers get beyond "running around in some kind of misguided fire brigade mentality". The advantage of our coming together today and looking at these policy papers, is the opportunity to begin to see if we cannot find an approach which will help us to get out in front of these issues.

Arif Hasan mentioned earlier today that much of our discussion had been focused on a dialogue with policy makers, but that these policy makers have less and less control over what is happening. He noted that while government by-laws have increased, government's ability to implement them has often decreased, and that where communities have incorporated the functions of government, there is a more equitable relationship between communities and government. In referring to NGOs, Mr Hasan stressed that we need to go beyond NGOs giving us a view of the bottom, by helping NGOs get a better view of the top, of what is going on in the policy dialogue. These thoughts offer us another important challenge for rethinking.

In the discussion today many dichotomies were used as points of entry. One of the dichotomies that we struggled with in the early 1980s that both of these policy papers go well beyond, is that between urban and rural. We have looked carefully at urban/rural linkages and we now understand that modern agriculture is an urbanizing process, that there is a need for urban functions in a rural economy to ensure that the agricultural sector operates efficiently. But there are now a number of new dichotomies that keep coming up: municipal versus central government, local versus provincial governments, multilateral versus bilateral points of view, donors versus recipients, private versus public sector, community, versus local government, and even projects versus programmes. In my view there is a danger in us getting stuck with these dichotomies and we need to adopt a rather different perspective. If we are going to listen the way that we should and achieve the ability to respond to what we hear, we need to commit ourselves to a more open ended, consultative approach and to bringing in all the stakeholders. A precondition to implementing our new urban agenda may well be that all the parties are committed to a consultative approach that will bring in all the actors who are involved, or who will ultimately be effected by the changes that are being discussed. Right now, this usually does not happen.

The United Nations Commission on Human Settlements (Habitat) met in Harare in May of this year, and in discussing the importance of urbanization it set as one of its two principle themes for the next session in 1993 – municipal management. We have been brainstorming on how to approach this theme with Mr Sivaramakrishnan (who is here with us today), and during these brainstorming sessions he came up with a concept, or a way of describing this consultative approach, which we rather liked. He talked about "participatory organisational arrangements". We have learned that it is not usually constructive for external support agencies (ESAs) to try and establish new institutions, and we are still learning that it is likewise often not effective for ESAs to try to change institutional frameworks. But ESAs can often play a useful rôle in getting institutions, both formal and informal and across cities, to talk to each other. As a neutral outside force we have the potential to help these different urban actors into a mode where they see how they can take advantage of each others agendas.

We have also talked a lot today about the concept of co-ordination. It is a word that I find to be pretty useless in this business. Nobody likes to be co-ordinated. Institutions will not allow themselves (if they can help it) to be co-ordinated by other institutions, and governments do not want to hear about somebody outside of government co-ordinating their actions or commitments. Sometimes even inside governments, there are good reasons why they do not want to co-ordinate things. In my view the only way we can begin to achieve co-ordination is through a commitment to collaboration. If we are committed here to discuss policy issues to see if we can reach some kind of intellectual understanding of the usefulness of the arguments, then the next step is to go through this exercise in countries at the level of both national and local governments. We have to hear their agendas which may be very different, and we have to respond to these agendas. If each of us does this, one by one, we are obviously going to create a real problem. We must make a serious commitment to working together in this regard.

I referred earlier to the annual review meeting of the Urban Management Programme (UMP) which was held in Paris at the beginning of this week. The UMP started out as a partnership of UNDP, the World Bank and Habitat, but is now a partnership which includes eight bilateral external support agencies. During its next phase the UMP will be implemented at the country level through a mechanism of country consultations. The point of entry for the next phase of the Urban Management Programme at the national level will be the urban issues that governments themselves present for discussion in the country consultation.

The programme is structured in such a way that sustaining and nurturing this dialogue over the long term with all the relevant public and private sector actors is its *modus operandi*. The primary product of this effort is not new programmes or projects designed for support from the World Bank, UNDP, UNCHS (Habitat), or other external agencies, but a new consensus at the local level around how to tackle a particular urban issue or set of issues. Of necessity this involves a long term commitment to an informed dialogue, since experience has taught us that the windows of opportunity for lasting policy changes present themselves according to the evolution of internal political forces, not according to our own agendas or in response to the pressures for change which external support agencies often try to exert at the national level.

I would like to conclude this summary with two related aspects of how we need to change the way we do business, to achieve better results on the ground. The first is about our ability to listen and is very much related to the above-cited interventions. While our own consensus on the strategic elements of an urban agenda for the nineties is terribly important, so that we don't send mixed signals, or even work at cross-purposes with each other, our implementation strategy must begin with a much greater commitment to listening, so as to understand and better respond to local urban agendas. If we are going to be truly receptive and responsive to local agendas, we must also find ways of ensuring that we are more modest concerning our own models and proposals for solutions.

The second aspect of how we need to change the way we do business is to commit ourselves to investing in and taking full advantage of the intellectual capacity in developing countries regarding urban issues. We have taken the attitude over the years that there is nobody who really understands a particular urban development issue, in country X or country Y, as well as our consultants who are truly expert on the issue. We have convinced ourselves that we need to bring in these consultants if we are to get the job done right. In so far as we all keep working with our own rather small stables of consultants and experts, we reinforce the problem. As a manager of Habitat's technical co-operation programme, I have found that I just cannot support this approach any longer. In 1990 we started, within the framework of the Urban Management Programme, to develop a roster of expertise in every developing country initially in the following areas of expertise: land management, municipal finance and administration, infrastructure management, urban environmental management and urban poverty. As a matter of policy we have also started to do more and more of our work (now over 60 per cent) by using this in-country expertise.

As a number of you have mentioned today, the same approach must also be applied in the area of urban research. We must work much more with developing country research institutions to strengthen their capacities, not only to undertake research, but also to enable them to better disseminate the results of their research and to implement these results in a dialogue with policy makers. We should help these local institutions become the new "think-tanks" on urban policy issues to which their governments turn to develop policy options and to monitor progress in the sector. There are also a number of newsletters and other dissemination vehicles used by existing networks of regional research institutions in Africa, Asia, and Latin America. Many of them have been around for a number of years. Yet to a great extent, we still are not providing them with resources. We are instead duplicating their efforts from our side by more top down dissemination strategies. In my view we need to make a much bigger commitment in this regard. In Latin America, in Asia (there must be at least six urban research institutes in India alone), and even in Africa such institutions and their networks already exist. There is an unevenness in their capacity but there is something to build on. We cannot keep telling ourselves that we have got to do it ourselves.

CHAPTER THREE
Urban development strategies
EXPERIENCE FROM THE PAST

Opening
Kenneth Watts
Development Planning Unit

Yesterday, Tim Lankester asked why, if the main lines of urban policy are now more or less agreed upon, very little appears to have been happening on the ground. On the surface, this certainly seems to be the case: in this week's *Economist*, for example, there is a survey of Asia's Emerging Economies[31], which analyzes the factors for success without a single mention of urban development. Yet the success of these "Asian Tigers" has been a product of urban growth, and it seems no accident to me that work has long been going forward in many of them – certainly in Korea, Taiwan and Singapore – to review the spatial implications of development, and in general to attempt to put their urban house in order. In all three countries, powerful centralist forces are still at work; as Hendro pointed out yesterday, the prevalent practice in most countries is still to

---

31 "Where tigers breed": a survey of Asia's emerging economies, *The Economist*, November 16th 1992.

handle development through sectoral ministries. But as we have also seen, structures of government are changing, bringing about increasing power sharing with local levels of administration; and in the light of these trends, it seemed to me to be an opportune moment to review past experiences in **national policy formulation**, in order to reach some preliminary conclusions on the directions such work might in future take in other countries. Although some of the earlier of these studies tended to be somewhat theoretical in approach and over-ambitious in scope, they have brought to light issues which I consider important.

What should the objectives of a national urban study be? The first and most obvious objective is to gain an understanding of the urban processes in the country. Although world-wide research can point up issues and propose solutions, we must never forget that urban structures are always unique to each country, and that some knowledge, however sketchy, of the way they work is essential as a prelude to policy formulation. The paper I have written tries to summarize the efforts that were made in the different countries under review which seek to give structure to this most general concept.

It strikes me in reading the studies that each country has its own problems and particular ways of doing things, its economic, social and political background. It is very difficult to apply solutions from one to another without, as it were, going through a kind of prism of thinking which will translate what is applicable in the country concerned; and what each country study has sought to do is to provide a preliminary understanding of what is happening. That is what we should start off with, regardless of whether or not the inferences from the work (the proposed urban futures) provide us with a solution with which we can agree. I would emphasize this very strongly. If, for example, you look at two of the "Asian Tigers", or those that are approaching "tiger" status – Thailand and Taiwan – each is well linked in to the international economic order, but urban development has taken different directions in each one. In Thailand there is a highly centralized pattern based on Bangkok, whereas in Taiwan the pattern is much more dispersed. Each has developed in its own way, and generated its own unique problems. As a result each has addressed the problem of urban development, and hence of growth in general, in a different way.

This brings me to the second objective of urban studies: having developed an information base, the second is to consider the effect that general policies – those that are devised by governments to stimulate a country's economic and social development – have on the patterns of urban growth. We had quite a lot of discussion yesterday about this, and in my paper I have sought to review such policies as seen in the different perspectives of the countries concerned. One thing became clear: that similar policy prescriptions for different countries gave rise to different outcomes. We can all applaud the approach of the Bank in trying to analyze within the context of the urban scene the effect of different policies in specific countries, for example the work that has been done in Nigeria on comparative costing of electricity, or the point raised yesterday about comparative pricing on the roads of Bombay. But while conclusions of a general nature can be drawn on these points, we must never forget that they touch on issues that are specific to the countries concerned; and these have to be reviewed and amended with care and precision.

This brings me to a point that came out very strongly yesterday: that it is essential to embed urban policy in the development policy of the country as a whole. It is part and parcel of the way in which a country develops and cannot be put aside as a separate sector, to be treated as an adjunct to development policy, or indeed a separate sector, as tends to happen today. In the discussions yesterday we heard of a number of different ways in which policies can affect urban development. Part of the thrust, part of the importance of the urban studies is to highlight that.

The third way in which urban studies are important is to come to specific measures which are designed to upgrade cities. The main concern would appear to be whether it is possible for central government to take measures that will at once enhance the capabilities of those cities that are already doing well – and so enable them to contribute more to the nation's wellbeing – while at the same time mitigating the plight of those places which lack the basic needs of life. These seem to me to be the twin objectives of urban policy.

In quite a number of the cases, the emphasis is on upgrading urban infrastructure. Now, I know that Mike Cohen has drawn our attention to the fact that this should not be, as it were, a knee-jerk reaction to city up-grading; and that cities may lack other facilities – more cars in São Paulo than telephones! – and that these might well have to assume a higher priority in urban investment than what we normally take to be urban infrastructure. But the point that I think has been understood is that in the vast majority of cases it is by constructing urban infrastructure that you can register very quickly a physical effect that people can see. In political terms this should not be ignored. There are many ways in which you can tackle this, to involve people or not to involve them. I believe strongly, with John Turner, that unless this is done with the full involvement of the local community it does not mean very much, and we are learning how to do this from a number of different places in the world. Nevertheless urban infrastructure is a crucial issue which can determine the way in which governments, through financial direction can influence the development of cities.

I concluded from this review that national urban studies were worth while as a prelude to urban policy formulation, though certain limitations must be borne in mind. The effectiveness of local government is one highly important issue here, and one that was much talked about yesterday. Yesterday, Shabbir Cheema spoke of a case in Bangladesh in which a loan, which the World Bank had entered with two local administrations to undertake major urban works, had been disbursed only to the extent of 5% over a period of some four years, whereas the UNDP project, which was supposed to provide technical assistance to local governments in implementing the loan, had been substantially used up. In addition to the very valid point he made about the lack of policy, there is another: that the assumptions made both by the Bank and the UNDP on the ability of local governments to administer such loans were wrong, and their need for technical assistance was greatly underestimated. Before such policies of decentralizing loans are implemented, it seems clear that very careful appraisals have to be made of capabilities, as well as levels of commitment.

As countries develop, so the capability to undertake this kind of study is developing too. As we go through the progression of these different studies we see that the Thai case (which is done entirely by Thais) is a good study which somehow underlines the fact that such urban studies are undertakings which outsiders cannot do. We may perhaps help from the outside by bringing certain perspectives to the work; and I suspect that you get at the truth more if the people themselves are concerned with it.

Problems and issues of implementation
Nigel Harris

The workshop, as Ken (Watts) and I originally conceived of it, was to assess whether the two documents identified what people thought were the key priorities, and if they did, how could they be made operational at the national and local government levels and in terms of the activity of other agencies, bodies and groups, within the urban areas: how could anybody do anything about it? Yesterday's discussion opened up a range of considerations which partly superseded my paper, so I am not going to bother with the paper. You can read it if you like, but in one sense it has become slightly redundant, because we have opened up many new issues.

I should also say I start from a set of assumptions. I do not find the problem of productivity difficult. We are speaking of total factor productivity in the urban area and since we know that at the most general level, the skills, energy and ingenuity of the labour force are the key to a city's prosperity, then the issue of labour productivity is fundamental, the productivity of the work force.

Secondly I do not see a conflict in the pursuit of social or cultural aims and economic aims. I do not see productivity as in collision with ballet. Ballet is a part of London's attraction to people, means to attract and hold capital and skilled workers. Quality of life is part of the economy and any economic policy which ignored the fact that the social existence of the city is a pre-condition of its economic performance is clearly on auto-destruct. It is an auto-destruct policy to pursue one element in isolation in economic growth. So while there are collisions, they should fundamentally be part of the same process.

Speaking now of the city level – Ken has been dealing with the national level – what then do we want to come out of these discussions? Simple, robust, practical programmes for sets of people who are running cities and are trapped in an extremely active political context. That is, the demands on their time are considerable, the burdens of their daily life are extreme. Somehow or other we want to slide in this little word, "productivity" with its association of poverty, environment and so on, so it actually changes their behaviour. It is not unfair to say that if you were to confront the Mayor of a big city of a developing country today with "productivity", his eyes would go glazed, and you would know that he was thinking about what to say to the Minister when he came, about the by-election tomorrow, the demonstration the day afterwards, this afternoon's committee meeting and so on; ie. it means nothing, and until we can translate it into something that he/she can do something about, it remains an empty word.

The danger, which I explore in the paper in terms of Bank documents, is that the gap between strategy and implementation becomes enormous. The implementation is an old programme to do with the management of land, household services, housing and so on. That old agenda has an amazing persistence. I am reminded of the terms of reference of the Madras Metropolitan

Development Authority in the early 1980s. This included: to alleviate the condition of the poor, pay special attention to employment, and the improvement of the informal sector, etc. Did they do anything about it? Nothing at all. They were back to managing land, land use controls. In the title, the Madras Metropolitan Development Authority, the "development", I presume, meant land development, because it certainly did not mean economic development. There was a disjuncture between the strategy that cities ought to be concerned with economic development, and what was actually being undertaken. I think that is true for almost all the donor and government programmes in the urban field. There has been a failure to connect the issues of economic development with the issues of how you run cities. The two have gone off in different directions. If we are not capable of spelling out what productivity means in terms of practical issues in the city, it will just be the old agenda, except that when the Mayor boasts of what he has been doing about sanitation in the city for the last 30 years, he will slip in the word "productivity" from time to time, the new fashionable word to describe old things.

It is a danger because the undertow is powerful in terms of the traditional issues and projects. Why do people like projects? Because they are politically visible. What is special about the political context of the city? It is politically very visible. You can get away with all sorts of murder at the macro economic level, but in the city, it is there, it is visible. If you build a new conference centre, a new highway, you can boast and show it, so the project at the city level becomes terribly important and very distorting if you are trying to do what Mike is trying to do, influence policy which cannot be seen and therefore does not affect the political context. The Mayor is worried about his political future and therefore has to play his cards in order to maximize the political return.

The danger exists therefore of slippage between the proclaimed aim in the two policy documents of the Bank and UNDP and what actually happens, unless we can define effective action. There is a threefold problem – how to translate these aims into practical city-specific action programmes, and how they relate to what the city does at the moment; secondly, how to create a national enabling, facilitating context with appropriate powers vested at the level of the locality, because at the moment productivity makes not a lot of sense since many cities do not have the power to do anything about it; and thirdly, how can local authorities gain the political incentive to do anything about it, because if they do, they will get the skills, create institutions, do all that is required to pursue the aims. At the moment there is no political incentive, it does not mean anything in terms of what people are voting for, how cities are managed, etc.

The risk in what I am saying is illustrated in the anti-Irish joke: "If I wanted to go to Dublin, I would not start from here". It is not a helpful comment on the agenda document, but it is also true that the Bank agenda document does not start from the preconditions for enhancing productivity. What determines urban productivity? Then we can judge what ought to be the priorities for tackling it. We do not have a sense of key priorities for action. What are the different rates of return – whether they are social or political returns, rather than simple financial returns – on doing different kinds of things? How do we balance the economic cost of traffic congestion, getting goods off the dockside, inputs into the factories which relate to the goods imported? How do we balance traffic congestion with the cost of contaminated water supply, with the cost of not educating women, of workers arriving exhausted to work because they have to travel on a terrible transport system?

Unless we can begin to add some rates of return and order these priorities, we are not going to be able to come up with a programme which does and can affect cities.

There are several levels here. I hear no discussion of what are the factors at stake in forcing and sustaining centralization. These are obviously key issues. Unless we know why governments centralize, we do not know when they will decentralize. We do not know whether we are pushing at an open door or whether the door is forever a bombshelter that we will never break into, because the forces of centralization are too powerful. They have been in certain circumstances. Macro economic policy, structural adjustment, forces a considerable concentration of central economic management. Fierce international economic competition forces centralization. Military competition, the insecurity of a State in a competitive system of States, forces centralization. Is it the case that these factors are weakening in some cases and not in others? There is an argument to suggest that they are weakening at different speeds and in different places, but we require that weakening in order to talk credibly about decentralization.

Second are the constraints that the Bank agenda document identifies in terms of the existing operation of the city. We do not know how serious these issues are, in terms of regulatory regime. For example, East London, 1840, average expectation of life of 30, no regulatory regime: wonderful! That is to say the simple removal of regulations is not going to produce an end to poverty. It is not that there is a Promethean poverty stricken person waiting to break out if only the chains of constraints can be removed. It is unfortunately more complicated than that and at the moment we do not have a clear cut set of costings. The one thing we do know, thanks to Kyu Sik Lee[32] is that Nigerian manufacturers can spend up to 35 per cent of start-up costs for new plant on making up for deficiencies of public infrastructure. That is an important conclusion, but it is one of the few we have in terms of quantifying what the priorities have to be.

It is time we had some environmental economics in the city. I do not mean by that valuing the environment but assessing the costs of unrequited labour power. How much does it cost to have women queuing for two hours to get water, for people to be drinking contaminated water and being off sick for so many days per month? We may find the productivity of cites is much lower than we think if we really added up all the costs in terms of the unpaid labour inputs into the system.

There is a national level, there are issues of improving the

---

32 Kyu Sik Lee and Alex Anas, op. cit.

efficiency of the city as it exists; and then there is dealing with the real economy. When we speak of urban productivity, we are speaking of the way in which the city labour force produces the goods and services of the city. That includes the emerging function of the city, not as a place for producing goods but as a junction for flows of people, commodities, finance and information. The city of 2010 is likely to be essentially a junction point and the speed, ease, and cost of movement will become vital in terms of the future prosperity of the city.

In the paper, there is a discussion of some of the factors shaping city output and how local authorities can seek to anticipate bottlenecks, facilitate economic change and exploit opportunities. Exploiting opportunities goes beyond what either of the documents speak of. It is a positive rôle for an entrepreneurial local authority rather than one which is simply enabling or facilitating. Such a rôle entails special attention to the crucial spatial configurations of the city economy: central business district, downtown, transport junctions, wholesale markets, specialized industrial areas and so on.

If we ignore all the other issues, the resources for producing an entrepreneurial local authority already exist in big cities. The local authority lacks the skills, but there are a lot of academics in the local University. There is a disassociation between the academics and the local authority and the Chamber of Commerce. If these three forces can be put together, if this is what we mean by "urban management", then we can see a recipe for creating an entrepreneurial local authority as the lead sector in this coalition. Such a coalition could lead to an increase in the sophisticated advice which is going into city management as well as sectoral studies and so on. It needs a data base on which a more coherent approach can take place. The coalition also can constitute a pressure group on the national government to change matters affecting the city: the import licensing which restricts city production, the national tariff on transport which affects the local system, and so on.

There is a lot of discussion that the decline in economic barriers between countries, the liberalization of the world system, is making the locus of competition that between regions and cities, so that this question of strengthening local authorities' economic capacity is likely to become more and more important. In that context, in a week's time the first study of London in the 21st century will be published and will attempt to assess the city's competitive capacity *vis-à-vis* Tokyo and New York[33]. Where will London be in the year 2020 in relationship to New York and Tokyo, and Frankfurt and Paris in the European context? The work is trying to move towards an economic perspective for the metropolitan area of London, in the context of competition of other cities, not between Britain and Japan, France or Germany.

This relates to the question of research. I agree with Mike that sophisticated research is needed but we also need cruder research on a bigger scale for there are thousands of cities at stake, far beyond the capacity of aid donors to facilitate. We need therefore a way in which cities themselves are going to become more systematic about gathering the basic data, understanding the local strengths and weaknesses of the economy, what opportunities occur in the world and regional economies, what are the effects and changes of national macro economic policy upon the city. There is a whole agenda of issues here which are not being dealt with but have to be undertaken by cities; they cannot be undertaken by outsiders, by aid donors and so on. The rôle of aid donors has to be very much more suggesting the kind of institutional framework which might make this effective, the kind of methodology which is involved, what things to look for and helping with the training of staff in order to build the local capacity to develop an entrepreneurial local authority.

The underlying problem is that we can discuss various more or less Utopian schemes of this kind, but it does not touch the underlying issue: What gives an interest to the local authority to take the economy seriously? We know historically that national governments took the economy seriously when they saw the

---

33 *London: world city moving into the 21st century: a research project*, commissioned by London Planning Advisory Committee and others, from Coopers and LyBrand Deloitte and others, London, Nov. 1991.

relationship between economic activity and their own revenue. They realized in 17th and 18th century Europe that they could not fight their wars without worrying about agricultural output. Agricultural output was fundamental to the ability to kill other people. That connection became clear at the national level and macro economic policy was born. I suspect that the same may be true of local authorities – not in terms of the capacity to kill, at least I hope not – when they understand that their own political power, standing and revenue, their political survival depends on taking the economy seriously. In a representative context, in which local governments have to fight for votes and the voters include the poor, then perhaps there may be a chance local leaders will begin to take the economy seriously and institute the drive to create the skills for this end. It is not an either/or issue: we have examples today of local authorities which have been able to build the kind of coalitions which maximize the exploitation of the opportunities.

Mike mentioned the mission to the Mexican border earlier this year and that was fascinating. Mexico has a highly centralized government but Ciudad Juarez, its business group and its local authority, were able to exploit opportunities of national government policy to build the base of 135,000 manufacturing workers. Juarez has the biggest concentration of manufacturing on the border. That is partly the result of active promotion, development, going out to attract business, bringing it in, constantly worrying about it and so on. So there is a lot that can be done by local authorities even in highly centralized systems. There are other examples in a text from USAID[34], the redevelopment of central Kingston, Jamaica and a city in Brazil. There are scattered examples without great changes in the centralized administrative structure.

In the cases that are mentioned, certainly the ones on the

---

34 George E. Peterson, G. Thomas Kingsley, Jeffrey P. Telgarsky, *Urban economies and national development*, Office of Housing and Urban Programmes, USAID, Washington DC, Feb 1991.

Mexican border, and the others in South China, (in Guangdong province), what has led to the administrative transformation and made it possible for a local authority to begin to worry about productivity, is the opportunity of economic growth. In terms of the programme of making entrepreneurial local authorities, decentralization is important, local accountability and elections are important, but growth is vital.

Note, incidentally, that the more democratic the system, the more politicized the issues of urban development, so that if any aid donor thinks it can put up a position of being non-political technical adviser in an increasingly democratic system, that is a contradiction. Increasing democracy means increasing politicization of the issues of urban development.

There is then a third issue: the need for economic growth. In a stagnating system, centralization is almost inevitable and sleepy local authorities, pestilential heaps of corruption and inertia are also inevitable. There has to be the wind of economic growth for local authorities to begin to be entrepreneurial, to worry about productivity, to worry about the poor and the productivity of the poor and to worry about the environment. The environment is increasingly becoming a component of economic growth. If you have a lousy environment there will not be economic growth: no one is going to want to live in that city. It is a circuit. Economic growth is the character which has to be introduced into the equation which is why the possibility of worrying about productivity is greater on the Mexican border, or Guangdong Province in China, it is greater in Malaysia, in the high growth sectors at the moment. That does not mean to say we should not be trying to generalize it, but we should do so with less optimism. Rising expectations have the capacity to galvanize both local governments and populations, and as we saw from Sivaramakrishnan's remarks yesterday, it also leads back to the government changing. If we need to get more shirts and pants out of the port of Bombay, because the United States is taking more of them, how do we change the port of Bombay, the railway infrastructure, the customs regulations which prevent containers being taken off Bombay docks, and so on? Economic growth rolls back into a programme which ultimately will assist the drive to local decentralization. The possibilities of manufactured exports have been crucial in the 1980s in encouraging some measures of decentralization in Asia and Latin America, (but not in sub-Saharan Africa). In that process a national government policy becomes decisive. If governments do not wish to exploit the opportunity of exports, then they can stalemate the system down to the base.

I return to the starting point, unless we can convert the documents into prioritized practice, simple and robust programmes of action, backed by a clear conception of why cities politically should do anything about it, then there is a danger that the important step forward in identifying the macro economic significance of the urban areas will get swamped by the old agenda. It will just become a new language, new wine in old bottles.

Discussion

CHAIRMEN: P. S. A. Sundaram & Hendropranoto Suselo
PARTICIPANTS: Paul Ackroyd, Fitz Ford, David Leibson, Desmond McNeill, Steffan Mildner, Elsadig Mahmoud Musa, Eduardo Rojas, K. C. Sivaramakrishnan, Paul Syagga, Emiel Wegelin,

The first speaker argued that implementation was the key to what could be done rather than the policy itself. Specific instruments at the city level and economic policy at the national level predetermined what could be accomplished. It is here also that research must begin, otherwise the attractive approach of encouraging an open policy dialogue and asking questions rather than imposing conditionalities would degenerate again into projects.

A second speaker reflected, on the basis both of the London

workshop and the preceding Paris review meeting, on what urban management was and why it was now important. He offered initially three propositions which were apparently inconsistent with each other:
  (i) The application of basic economic principles had recently become important in the urban field. In the new housing policy paper which the World Bank was about to produce, one of the main arguments was that economic efficiency was important, especially relative to the conditions of the poor. Excessive regulation of housing had supply side effects which entailed higher costs to everybody, but disproportionately high for the poor.
 (ii) The poor were also the ones who suffered most severely when policies were not properly targeted. On the other hand, relative to poverty, there were a number of people who argued that unfettered private enterprise had not proved to be a solution in the past and was unlikely to be so in the future. Government intervention was required to protect the poor.
(iii) In a recent World Bank review of municipal finance, the author had summarized the politics rather succinctly: bad policy was good politics.

Thus, on the one hand it was important to be concerned about the traditional market issues of efficiency and ensuring equity; on the other hand, it was precisely market failures which had promoted the increasing rôle of government. Furthermore, the context was such that governments found it convenient to ignore what was economically sensible for short term political gains.

Where did that leave people in terms of trying to devise an approach to the management of urbanization? The speaker suggested an organic paradigm in trying to conceptualize the issues. Cities were growing, living, changing and, in some cases, dying. Hitherto people had been concerned with pathologies and how to get better housing, infrastructure, not destroying the environment etc. This was the approach of aspirin, surgery, antibiotics. But perhaps the approach ought to be in terms of urban management, keeping the body healthy: preventive rather than curative medicine. A body remained healthy because there was a continuous communication system or a set of systems encompassing the body, ensuring no part was starved of oxygen, that wastes were removed and exchanges took place between different parts to ensure survival.

However, the method of discussing governmental institutions and urban management implied parts which were not interconnected. An earlier speaker spoke of the fact that the poor were excluded from involvement. Another discussed the need for policy dialogue; care was needed here since, for example, the average life in office of a Minister in Latin America was eight months. If dialogue took place with intermittent actors, and the more continuous elements in the situation were ignored, it would not go very far.

Management ought to be a process that continually involved all participants, and this related to the idea of markets. If markets functioned, there was an efficient exchange based upon information and participation. There were however goods that did not fit this market paradigm – the classic "public goods". Here political decisions were important. But if the decisions made were limited to a narrow set of interest groups, it was unlikely that exchanges and the allocation of resources would be satisfactory. Concretely, for example, that would take us directly to the problem of persuading people to pay for services when they would have had no rôle in deciding what services should be provided and at what standards. To be effective in making better decisions about the provision of public goods, mechanisms were needed to involve all parts of the body in a dialogue on what was to be provided, who was to pay and who to manage.

Participation was thus not simply an afterthought or no more than an idealistic question. It was central to efficiency, to the issues discussed in the workshop. Only with participation could one deregulate, otherwise incompetence would increase. Public managers were asked to survive on a day to day basis on inadequate incomes. Being rational beings, they would look for means to increase their incomes; corruption was built into the structure. The framework of policy should not pretend that public managers were either lesser or superior beings in their ability to survive on less than others with the same levels of competence. Managers had to face this issue, and the public at large had to do so as well. Participation was the means to ensure accountability and curb corruption – but it was also a means whereby people could assume responsibility and realize that jobs could not be done on inadequate pay.

There had to be continuous negotiations between the actors. No-one from outside could predetermine the outcome of these negotiations. All that outsiders could do was to provide the tools to help clarify the issues and facilitate trade offs.

Another speaker drew attention to the paper by Ken Watts (see Ch. 21) and the link it proposed between urban strategies and national development policies. It was interesting that Ken found that all the studies reviewed had served some useful rôle. The speaker agreed on the basis of his involvement with two of the studies, one in Pakistan and one in Indonesia. But there were two qualifications. Sometimes the monumental amount of work involved had been used as an excuse for not starting any practical work until the strategy document was completed. That was to be avoided. There were many obvious things governments could and should do while refining the analytical framework.

Second, such studies were only useful if conducted at the level of national economic policy making, whatever that agency was – the National Planning Agency, the National Economic and Social Development Board in Thailand, Bappenas in Indonesia. They could not be undertaken in a sectoral agency if they were to have any impact.

There was another important feature. To have maximum impact, the studies should be carried out in a participatory manner. There were considerable differences in the ways the different strategy documents were drawn up. The Indonesian National Urban Development Strategy was a consultants' exercise, lacking much interdepartmental, government-plus-private sector or other working groups. Having an impact meant also creating awareness at the national development policy level that urban issues were an essential ingredient.

Even if the four studies reviewed were not the ideal model, the need to link closely urban development policy and national economic policy remained a key matter. The links needed much more work to spell out with precision the interactions.

The speaker was troubled by the practicality of some of the ideas in the second paper (by Nigel Harris). Local authorities were very overburdened. Was it sensible to increase the burdens with another set of agendas? In Indonesia, the Integrated Urban Infrastructure Development programme with its emphasis on integration and decentralization involved a quantum leap in local authority responsibilities. The programme started in 1985 and was not yet one third of the way along the road. It did not make sense to increase the load further.

This related to the issue of strengthening local government. Much more work was needed here, again bearing in mind the great limitations. The paper's suggestion of the establishment of an economic intelligence agency at local government level was probably a useful innovation, provided there was a constituency for the idea. There was great variety in this. On the one hand, the Karachi Metropolitan Corporation was nowhere near ready for such a thing; it was hardly able to take care of the operations and maintenance of classic municipal services. On the other hand, there were cities with a growing awareness that local government had a function to play in selling the city and facilitating economic development, but innovations needed caution.

Another note of caution was needed over the paper's account of the experience in Madras, that as implementation grew nearer, the agenda became increasingly narrowed, and economic aims fell by the wayside. But many agencies were limited by their mandates which did not enable them to undertake economic development. How was this to be changed? Was it suggested that local government should obtain new mandates or that new agencies were relevant?

There were also severe manpower constraints at all levels. The quality and quantity of manpower needed to be raised. That topic had not been sufficiently noted in the discussions so far.

Another speaker raised the issue of the inefficient operation of land markets – pricing gave the wrong signals, so distorting infrastructure planning. There were also many implicit subsidies to some groups involved in infrastructure provision, as also in the housing market. Some of these issues then distorted reforms. For example, in Santiago de Chile, the results of decontrol in transport had been a significant increase air pollution: 35 per cent of air pollution was generated by the 16,000 public transport vehicles.

There was a great problem, a speaker argued, with physical planning now since it was accused of seeking to fossilize the city. A long time would be needed to reshape the planning tradition and relate it to the dynamic forces of economic development. But still new mechanisms of development control were needed. How were urban planners to be induced to take economic issues into account? The problem was not eased by the fact that urban staff were usually the worst paid, and their posts were least desirable.

A further speaker raised the issue of conditionality in aid. The conditions were now coming to include decentralization, accountability, even elections. Furthermore, decentralization entailed accepting wide (and possibly growing) disparities between local authorities. In sub-Saharan Africa, towns were managed politically, so that introducing efficiency as a criterion of performance was difficult. How could you have efficiency in such a politically charged atmosphere?

Comment
Michael Cohen

In his paper, Nigel throws back the challenge to us, appropriately: "Have we raised more expectations of the framework than we are able to deliver?" In a sense these are some of the questions framed now. One ought to stop a moment and take note that in these sessions there is almost no discussion of housing. That is a positive step forward in that part of the purpose in the policy paper was to change the terms of the discussion, to broaden it out. From the urban sector, we are looking higher up in terms of macro questions and more broadly. Bringing in more actors and talking about participation and process is extremely important. In the past we have defined ourselves into a narrow box and spent a generation on a few projects without broadening the issue.

Having said that I do not think it fair to assume that tomorrow practice will change. One has to assume there are time lags, processes that have to go on. If we are to respect the issues of participation and process, one cannot be too greedy. We can be intellectually dissatisfied – as I think you are when you say that the productivity issue is insufficiently specified – but it is quite another thing from a process point of view to assume either that governments cannot develop new ways of thinking and act on them, or that we in the external community, whether it is the universities or donor agencies, cannot also respond.

In the World Bank, we have a process of doing sector studies first, which leads to operations. We have already seen the substantial increase in the number of studies. My point here is: do not be too greedy; things will change, but not overnight.

Nor am I anxious that they do change overnight. I think that if there was an immediate reaction and a new cookie cutter came into action, we might want to do something elaborate. But that does not make any sense, nor does it adjust to the need for tailored responses and support of the negotiating process. After all, using the health analogy, there are many individuals and, for example, Nigel does not want a prescription that my doctor gave me. One needs to be discriminating.

You are being a little too demanding with regards to rates of return for different kinds of investment. The economics profession has never been able to tell us how much transport versus how much telecommunication, so let us not assume here that when we talk about a broader picture we are going to be able to be so methodologically accurate as to discriminate priorities in quantitive terms. I would rather learn a little bit more about the political: what in Bombay are the opportunities if infrastructure has become inadequate for export promotion. If that is really a possibility, let us see what kind of progress we can make there. But I am not going to wait for the economists to tell me what the rates of return are on these various things.

Another point about enabling conditions and whether one can only talk about productivity in the context of growth. I would say that's the soft option. Certainly, the Mexicans are talking of productivity, they are growing again happily, but take Peru or other places where things are not going very well, and ask the question: for example, was the cholera epidemic in Peru a random event? Or could this be attributed to the last ten years of economic deterioration and collapse of infrastructure? I think good sense would suggest it is not random event.

Summing up
Nigel Harris

I found Fitz's (Ford) contribution valuable. Each time government intervenes for absolutely legitimate purposes, rent-seeking is implicit in what it does. There is no way to escape it. In the past people did not see that rent-seeking was so much implicit in the perfectly valid interventions of the public sector, that the more discretion was available to government officers at any level, the greater the possibility of corruption and rent-seeking. Discretion and rent-seeking go together. That is one of the lessons that has emerged in recent years and something that has to be built into any strategy for urban development and its relationship to national government.

Mike Cohen reproached me for talking about economic growth, saying that was one of the easy ones. What we need to do is approach the difficult cases. I agree, but I think we do have to understand the relationship between growth, the national government and the urban, without saying that the norm is the Pearl River delta of Guangdong, or the Mexican border. It is not, but it is fascinating to see that despite centralization, local authorities there were able to seize the initiative. We need to stress what the most important national government urban policy is: the promotion of manufactured exports. That is a fundamental urban policy. In the case of the Mexico/US border, the US government, in its wisdom, introduced tariffs 806 and 807; the Mexican government, in its wisdom, passed the *maquiladora* regulations. As a result, the townships of the border took off, seized the initiative, despite the centralized structure, the distribution of finances and so on. It was the opportunity which led them to expand. If we come back to asking the question: what are the preconditions for decentralization, we can see there what it was.

In the Soviet Union it is not decentralization; the central government has been stripped of powers and it became the smile on the Cheshire cat's face when the cat disappeared. It was not something they decided or wanted. On the contrary, they would have gone in exactly the opposite direction. I suspect that is how decentralization is going to happen, not as a unilateral decision by central government to decentralize; one cannot see any reason why they would want to do that, it robs them of powers, the power of patronage, all sorts of other powers, robs them of political significance. The process of decentralization has to start at the base rather than the top. Local authorities will seize power rather than central governments conceding it.

On the points that Emiel (Wegelin) made, I do not know whether responsibility for the "urban" should be sectoral or cross-sectoral. The environment is the same. You can make a separate environmental agency and it is weak. Each time it approaches the Minister of Finance with "green issues", the Minister says we are dealing with more important things. On the other hand if you try to make the urban issue cross-sectoral, there are real problems in terms of making it a serious question in the Ministry of Finance as opposed to the Ministry of Development.

There is another issue on this question: the importance of government in shaping what happens in the city. Government does not know what happens in the city. The importance of strong local government is that it plays back; when national policy hits it, it squeals loud and the national government is obliged politically to respond to the city. So there is an interaction here. The national government is important, but cannot know the costs of its policy unless the localities are willing to shout loudly.

Are there manpower constraints? This is like saying is there a shortage of investment in developing countries? We always thought there was, the problem of development was capital shortage. If only we could expand the capital flows, development could take place. I think it is doubtful. If interest rates are low, there is a capital shortage. If interest rates are high, there is no capital shortage. There is an enormous mass of unutilized resources in developing countries which do not come to market because the return is so low. It is not worth entrusting it to the market. The same I think is true of manpower constraints. It is not an absolute constraint. As Sundaram pointed out, pay rates are crucial. If pay rates are so low then there is a manpower shortage. The reform of pay rates, conditions, status and professionalism of local government employment is fundamental in determining whether there is a manpower shortage. I do not think the issues can be separated.

Similarly with the burdens on local authorities. The burdens are in part the result of the structural organization of local government and its financial basis. Implicit in what I have been arguing is a transfer of national government attributes to city government. If that is the case, there has to be an expanded resource base, in which case the whole quality of local government has to change. It is not a question of imposing new responsibilities so much as reorganizing the way that local governments operate.

I was interested in what Señor Rojas said because one of the things in the urban environment issue that comes out clearly and links economic efficiency to the environment, is that the issues are ones of extravagance. The mark of a poor society is that it has to be extravagant in all possible areas. This is the paradox: it takes twice as much gasoline to drive a vehicle or to produce power and so on. This is grotesque extravagance, the mark of poverty. The poorer the person, the more they are forced to be extravagant in their expenditure, which makes them even poorer. So in the interests of economic efficiency, the environment is not a side issue or a zero sum game. Increased efficiency of the urban area will produce an improved environment. We have to underline that because otherwise what happens is, it seems to be an alternative. When that happens in the Ministry of Finance or Industry or Planning they say on the environmental question – get lost. Whereas we need to say the bad environment at the moment depends on the importation of twice as much oil as is used to produce energy. Without an energy policy in the city, you cannot relieve the balance of payments. That is the connection and it is part of making the city more efficient.

CHAPTER FOUR
Issues of urban management

Opening
Mark Hildebrand & Patrick McAuslan
United Nations Centre for Human Settlements

Mark Hildebrand

This morning's presentations set the challenge for this afternoon very well by focusing on the problems and issues of implementing urban development strategies. However, we are still missing a concept of the whole. The same knowledge gap became apparent as we presented the Urban Management Programme at our Annual Review Meeting in Paris earlier this week. I believe it would be useful for our discussion this afternoon to clarify some of the issues raised in this context.

The Urban Management Programme was initiated five years ago by the World Bank, Habitat and the UNDP. We have since been joined by approximately eight bi-laterals and the UMP has now become a major programme of collaboration. The strategy for Phase 2 of the programme, beginning in 1992 and covering the next five years, is to focus on implementation and to do so at the regional and national levels. The Municipal Development Programme (MDP) which Patrick Wakely just mentioned is one of the first regional initiatives of this context. It will serve, among other things, to focus on building capacity in sub-Saharan Africa on urban management issues. The MDP has two programme units, one in Harare, Zimbabwe and another has been set up in Lomé, Togo with the support of GTZ. The MDP will provide both a vehicle for the dissemination, application and further refinement of the products created under the Urban Management Programme, and also valuable feedback from the region regarding requirements for further applied research and related technical cooperation activities in sub-Saharan Africa.

The issue of a vision of the whole, or at least of how the various components of the two policy papers before us fit together has been raised in a slightly different context within the framework of the Urban Management Programme. But the concern is very much the same one we are facing in our deliberations today – how do these various policy issues connect with the critical problem of how to manage what is happening at the local level? How do we translate our broad policy objectives into action and help create both national and local level enabling strategies? What are the political incentives in this process?

While we do not need to wait for national urban development strategy as a prerequisite for action, as Mr Ackroyd (ODA) was quick to observe there is a real concern over fragmentation. The danger remains that we may take piecemeal approach. This again brings us back to this question of a vision of the whole. In the past, we hoped that this vision would be provided by a master plan, but the process of the preparation of master plans has now been very much discredited by experience. However, we have yet to address what the rôle for planners *should* be and what are the retraining requirements.

We also have serious problems in changing our practice very fast. Most of the institutions with which we are associated, intergovernmental or governmental, with the exception of NGOs, move very slowly. The problem is that the reality we are facing is changing very rapidly. One of the underlying premises of these two policy papers is that our programmes in the 1980s became more and more marginalized – at least the impacts of these programmes were clearly on the margin. While recognizing that we have not had much to do with the fundamental changes taking place in response to rapid urbanization, we also need to recognize that Governments themselves have often not initiated these changes. People have. We have seen this in the rapid political changes taking place in Asia, Europe, Africa and Latin America over the past two years. As I mentioned yesterday, this should help us to retain a sense of modesty as to the potential impact of our work. Yet this is not a time to slow down, but rather a time for us to quickly change the way we do business.

This morning Fitz Ford asked the question: "What does it mean, better urban management?" And in responding to Nigel Harris's presentation, Fitz noted that the key issues need to be addressed on the basis of country specificity and a process which is highly participatory. Indeed while the question of "How does this all fit together" remains unresolved it needs first and foremost to be addressed at the local level. In the context of the Urban Management Programme it has taken us some time to understand exactly what we are doing in each of the Programme's components; it has taken us some time to come to grips with the question of how these strategies fit together. After the Paris meeting I discussed this issue rather intensively with Patrick McAuslan, Programme Manager of the Urban Management Programme team at Habitat (Fitz Ford is the Programme Coordinator based in Washington). To give you a sense of our embryonic thinking of how it all fits together from the perspective of the city level, I would like to hand the rest of this discussion over to Patrick.

Patrick McAuslan

We were challenged at the Paris meeting of the UMP to try and spell out what we meant by urban management. The programme had been started by focusing on three topics, land management, municipal finance and administration and infrastructure management. In 1990, a fourth topic, urban environment and in 1991 a fifth, the alleviation of urban poverty were added. So perhaps there was something missing in not providing an outline of the whole. Although one can state fairly clearly what the objectives of urban management are, all sorts of problems begin to arise. For instance, we could say the objective was to enhance the information available to, and the capacity of, those responsible for the provision of services in and government of towns and cities, to be more effective, responsive, accountable and transparent in their work. The minute we say that, we have to ask: "Who are those responsible, what sort of services are we concerned with, what do we mean by government and how can we enhance the capacity?" In order to be able to answer these questions, it seems that we have to go back another stage and say what is our vision of the city. We have to try and match in our management process, the vision of the urban which has been produced in the policy statements by the World Bank and the UNDP. Until we do that, I think, it is a fair criticism to say that we are really groping in what we are trying to do in relation to urban management. How can we locate our specific tasks of the Urban Management programme in some kind of general set of ideas or approaches about the nature of the city?

It is a truism to state that if we get out of the Central Business District of cities in the developing world, get out of our cars and walk around, if we use the means of transport of the people, we discover a tremendous engine of creativity and energy. We find too what I would call a natural democracy, people working together, sharing resources, discussing what to do with very little hierarchy. We find also amongst the urban majority a very well understood notion of the concept of sustainability, the reuse of resources, recycling of materials. What we have then is a city of creativity, of energy, democracy, sustainability and that is the city of the majority.

Yet the whole process of urban management of those cities is derived largely from models of the north, especially for the metropolitan countries, Britain, France, Portugal, etc. This is a model of containment, of suppression and of waste. The model of the city exported to the Third World was based on the industrial revolution of the nineteenth century Europe and there is one characteristic of that city: fear of the masses, of their diseases, their unpredictability, their power and their numbers. Urban authorities were established to tame and control the masses and a superstructure was erected which could only be operated by professionals or by those with education, whether they were elected or appointed. Techniques of management were invented, finance, planning, law, medicine, public health, etc., which were controlling devices to enable the minority to rule and govern in their own interests and to forget about the majority. This model of urban management was transferred to developing countries, in some cases being imposed upon existing urban centres. In the Indian subcontinent and parts of Nigeria and Southeast Asia, this model was imposed on existing urban centres; in many parts of the world, in particular Africa, this was a model which was created for the new colonial cities and towns. This model has had a disastrous effect on the growth and management of cities. City governments were designed to control and contain, to keep the masses separate. Government was not in any way democratic. There were no controls on the way the operation of government worked, and indeed, the whole philosophy of government was that it should be a top down notion.

The structure of government, the administrative arrangements, the rôle of professionals, the legal frameworks, these paid no attention to the needs of the urban majority, and there was no attempt to involve them. I will give a simple illustration. I did some work on planning systems in Trinidad and Tobago a few years ago and I should say that if I was looking for a model of a planning department that I would take people to, in order to demonstrate professionalism, commitment, enthusiasm, intellectual vigour and probity, I would take them to the planning department of Trinidad and Tobago, a department entirely run and controlled by women. But the one blind spot was the notion that planning was a professional activity, and neither councillors nor people should be involved or expected to have views about what to do. They had been trained as planners and their job was to plan, and the people's job was then to comply with the planning. There was one small town called Ariba which had been planned to have 7,521 new jobs over the next five or six years; one felt that if the 7,522nd person turned up, they would be turned away and told to wait for the sixth year.

Even where the urban majority began to get the vote and to assert themselves, they found the institutions of local government were promptly changed and altered to take away the powers which had previously been allocated to them. Urban development authorities and corporations were established to which people could be appointed by central government; local authorities lost the power of urban planning and development. They began to find public corporations set up to manage the infrastructure, water, sewerage disposal and whatever, and so they lost those powers and in some countries they even found electing local government was taken away from them.

So really to echo a point made earlier in this workshop, one finds that many cities are governed by the minority, in the interests of the minority, with the majority totally shut out of any involvement in urban management. We are faced with a structure and functions of urban government which are really not appropriate for dealing with the issues, concerns and problems of the urban majority. They are positively hostile. One of the problems when we look at the Urban Management Programme is that there is a danger that if we just try to improve the management of existing structures and functions of municipal government, all we are doing is trying to improve structures and functions that have no relationship to the lives of ordinary people. Indeed they are designed to have no relationship to the lives of the ordinary people.

Our vision of urban management has to try to embrace the cities of the majority, to try and structure our efforts to assist the energy, creativity, democracy and sustainability that exists within the urban majority. In other words, we have to have a strategy, to persuade the professionals, the urban minorities, that it is in their interests to move away from the old style of urban management towards a new style and a new approach. We have to assist the professionals and urban minorities to come to terms with the city as it exists and try to adapt their processes and their functions of management. Only by doing that is there the slightest possibility that the policy statements that have been produced will begin to be effective in the day to day functions of management.

What then are the tasks that urban management has in the future? The diagram sets out some very tentative first thoughts. There are four boxes which indicate the kind of functions which are involved in what might be called the new forms of urban

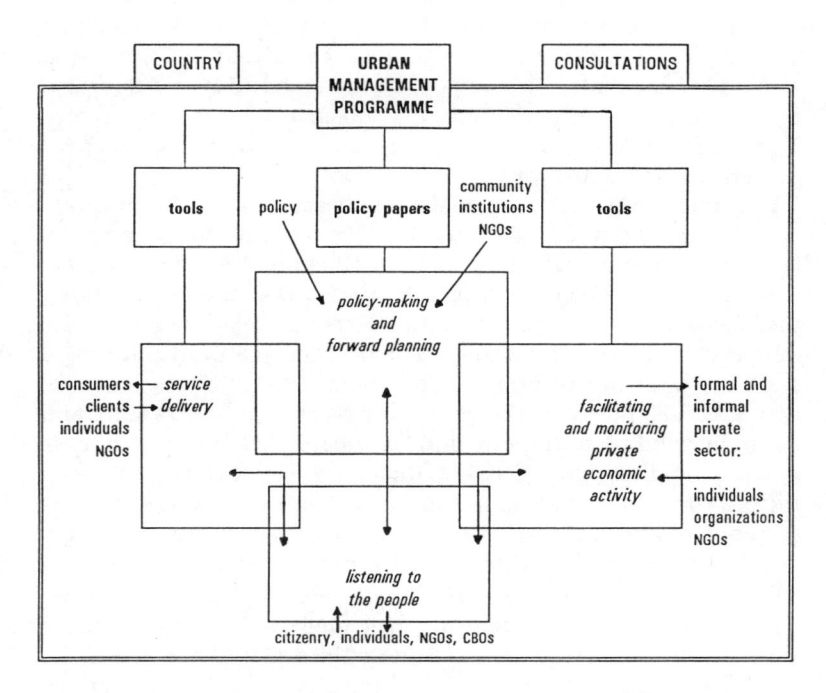

```
┌─────────────┬──────────────────┬─────────────────┐
│  COUNTRY    │  URBAN           │  CONSULTATIONS  │
│             │  MANAGEMENT      │                 │
│             │  PROGRAMME       │                 │
└─────────────┴──────────────────┴─────────────────┘

           tools    policy   policy papers   community      tools
                                             institutions
                                             NGOs

                              policy-making
                                  and
                              forward planning

   consumers ← service                        ─────────   formal and
   clients   → delivery                       facilitating  informal
   individuals                                and monitoring private
   NGOs                                       private       sector:
                                              economic
                                              activity    individuals
                                                          organizations
                                                          NGOs

                              listening to
                              the people
                         citizenry, individuals, NGOs, CBOs
```

management. What we have is the function of policy making and planning for the future, the development of ideas, the continued maintenance of the vision of the future; some institution within urban government has to think about the future, though not necessarily through the production of master plans. Then we have the box that deals with monitoring and facilitating private economic and productive activity. This includes the notion that the urban authority should be concerned with productivity, trying to increase and improve the economy of the city, and with the monitoring of private services, whether it is the delivery of land or infrastructure or whatever. Parallel to that there will still be some services that are delivered by the local authority itself. The fourth box is listening to the people both directly and via NGOs and CBOs, community based organizations. These are the organizations that really have to be seen as central in the future management of the city. The city can no longer be managed on the basis of the old council, the councillors, mayor-in-council and structures like that; cities have to be managed, run and operated by or in association with community based organizations which have in fact taken over a lot of the functions of management at grassroots levels anyway.

The four boxes are inter-related with each other. Community based organizations are involved in monitoring, possibly assisting in the private delivery of goods and services, and there are discussions between those deliverers and the CBOs. Again the CBOs are involved in discussions in relation to service delivery. Policy and planning are concerned with the delivery of services, both in the public and private sector. There are two-way linkages between the community based organizations and the policy and planning functions of the local authority, whoever is carrying that out. Outside those boxes we have the four sectors of the outside community to which the local authority is relating, monitoring, assisting, dealing with the private sector. Policy and planning deals with the policy community, that is liaising with universities, policy institutes, liaising with international organizations and central government to both feed in ideas and get ideas to assist them in their future thinking about the city. The main people with whom local authority service deliverers are concerned are their customers – the consumers and the CBOs have contact with the citizens who are feeding in ideas and the CBOs are discussing matters with the citizens.

This is very much a first step and no doubt it can be refined, but it gives an idea that we have to get away from the more traditional forms of local authority which try to do everything and compartmentalize everything into neat little divisions of parks and gardens, finance and planning, and think much more in terms of the inter-relationships between different parts and activities of the local authority. The advantage of this approach is that one can begin to see where the Urban Management Programme has an input into new forms of urban management. The Urban Management Programme is concerned to produce policy papers, research, engage in forward thinking, discover what is happening about forward planning, and similar approaches.

Documents, publications and activities from the Urban Management Programme feed into Policy and Planning for the future in towns and cities of the developing world. The Urban Management Programme is also concerned with producing tools, design guides, ideas about how to do things. One takes the general policies and tries to turn them into much more down-to- earth guides for the managers of particular activities. Here the tools that feed into both the delivery monitoring of the private delivery of goods and services raise fundamental and tricky issues in relation to, for example, the regulation of the private delivery of water services, environmental health services or whatever they happen to be.

Setting out the framework, one can see where the Urban Management Programme has some kind of gap. We are concerned about trying to decentralize management institutions, to decentralize delivery of services and the development of ideas about the management of cities down to the CBOs, and yet the Urban Management Programme has had no impact on the function of listening people and the rôle of NGOs and CBOs in urban management other than people in CBOs who might read the policy papers and the tools. I am not suggesting that these would be irrelevant to CBOs, but in terms of trying to develop some kind of approach and assistance of conceptual ideas to assist CBOs to begin to play a much more fundamental rôle in the management of urban areas, here the Urban Management Programme does seem to have that kind of gap.

It has been mentioned several times that the approach of the Urban Management Programme and the partners in it is increasingly to engage in a consultative process rather than coming in with the idea of saying: this is what you need, take the loan and get on with it. We want to develop a consultative process in which we bring together all the actors in the country or the city, sit down with them and say: what do you see as the issues? what do you see as the problems? what can we bring from the Urban Management Programme which will assist you in facing these problems?

So we have surrounding the whole of these four boxes and also the outside – consumers, citizens, private sector, policy community – the country consultation to indicate that, when there is a consultation from the Urban Management Programme, it brings in the community, both the community of the local authority and the wider community of the outside. The fundamental aim is to bring together people who might not otherwise talk to each other from the private sector, the public sector, the popular sector, or whatever. To give an illustration: when we had a country consultation in Ghana on man-management, we persuaded the military to attend as major land owners in Accra. Indeed it was with some difficulty that the General Officer Commanding was restrained from coming. It was thought that if he came, no one would say anything, so the senior officer in charge of land and maintenance attended and he played a very active part in the discussions. We felt that if the Army was a major land owner, we could not discuss land management problems without bringing them in.

These are no more than suggestions for opening up the discussion as to the functions and rôles of urban management. We want to suggest that the Urban Management Programme should continue to get away from traditional approaches of urban management, should try to encourage cities, towns and national governments of the developing countries to move away from their traditional notions and structures of urban management. If this means reviewing legislative frameworks, administrative arrangements, methods of financing, then this is something that will have to be addressed. This brings us back full circle to where we started off yesterday with Mr Lankester when he said that thinking about changing institutions would be a very fundamental and important part of any attempt to address the issues of urbanization in the developing world.

The boxes represent functions of urban management. Immediately outside the boxes are the principal constituencies of the particular functions. The arrows are channels of communication. The double lines represent the UMP and its assumed channels of communications and influence.

At the moment the UMP publications are directed namely at the urban management community (the boxes) rather than the constituencies. Country consultations aim to embrace both the urban management community and the constituencies. No or very little UMP work has yet been done on:
- listening to the people, a neglected *function* of urban management because it is assumed to take place;
- crossing the boundaries, i.e. getting NGOs and CBOs, etc. into the management process or delegating or transferring functions to them.

Does the UMP have a rôle there, if so, what?

Discussion

CHAIRMEN: Jaya Appalraju & Sherif Hassan Kamel
INTRODUCTION: Mark Hildebrand & Patrick McAuslan
PARTICIPANTS: Arif Hasan, Theo Kolstee, Desmond McNeill, Jonas Rabinovitch, P. S. A. Sundaram, Paul Syagga, Pervez Tahir, John Turner,

The discussion was mainly preoccupied with two issues – the elaboration of the diagram and the significance of NGOs and CBOs.

One speaker wondered whether one's perception of the circles depended upon which circle you occupied and whether the circles were expanding or contracting. Communication between the circles would be a problem since the relative power of different elements was very unequal. Another comment was that all participants in the diagram except the CBOs earned their living from urban management – and perhaps that was why there was a gap in the Urban Management Programme (UMP). The diagram was a political map and negotiations would be continuous between the circles so that the diagram was also lines of continuing consultation-negotiation. Did the international donors have any rôle in this pattern of dialogue? The emphasis now was heavily upon the importance of the country consultation, and this should be formalized as a permanent institution, a continuing forum. So far as the local level was concerned, efforts were needed to change the style of donor relationships so that they could be more effective. The World Bank had undertaken a special assessment in the urban field to test how far past collaboration with UNICEF had made programmes more effective in the community; in then reassessing the 150 projects of the Bank in the pipeline, it was possible to identify the twenty or thirty projects where collaboration with UNICEF would enhance base level effectiveness.

One speaker felt that the diagram was misleading. Communities and mayors varied very widely, and many were very selfish. A different approach was needed for each of them. All however needed to be able to answer the question as to where their city was going, how did its inhabitants ensure their survival? Without answers to these two questions, they could not enter into discussions and a dialogue about the future. Energy, water, soil were the three key areas on which they needed to have views. Countries and cities needed to be able to develop their own agenda if they were to be effective. Brazil, for example, had no urban agenda, which left political leaders free to respond to political demands rather than what was technically appropriate.

The UMP would take a long time, another contributor felt, to get to the level of the CBOs, even though they were growing in numbers and power. They were proving increasingly effective in overcoming the problems which governments faced in dealing with the mass of the population, but their experience was insufficiently reflected in government policy. Some CBOs had become influential in influencing official policy; for example, in Karachi, the CBO-initiated programme, the Orangi Pilot Project, had been adopted by the government and other agencies for replication elsewhere in the country. But there were still great resistances and, as the UMP suggested, more research was needed from below to assess how serious they were.

An opposite view held that there was too much romanticization of NGOs, much as self-help had been idealized in the nineteen 1970s. Many NGOs were foreign-based and could have no representative rôle for local communities. Not a lot was known about CBOs – finding out who they were and how they operated was a high priority for research.

Another contribution drew a sharp distinction between NGOs and CBOs in South Africa. CBOs were intermediating between the population and government, were local, indigenous and evolved in response to very specific circumstances. They were highly political and sophisticated with usually a good understanding and rapport with their communities. The question was how could they be related to the processes confronting the workshop since there were no models or examples available from past experience.

This was not so, someone replied. We were in danger of reinventing the wheel. In the 1960s, urban programmes had been based upon needs as articulated by the community. The Urban Basic Services programme that had been in operation for many years – first with UNICEF support, and latterly in some cities, taken over by ODA – was essentially concerned with identifying and facilitating local organizations which could articulate needs.

Another speaker maintained that there were many areas where NGOs or CBOs did not exist. Recently in Pakistan, the government had asked communities to create organizations with which the government could discuss issues, and matching financial and technical assistance was made available. But there had been no response. It was denied by another intervention that this was the standard case; in Zimbabwe, attempts to forge working alliances with CBOs had been wrecked not because of a lack of CBOs but because of their multiplicity. All went down together, both the good ones which represented communities and the bad self-serving ones.

But there were an astonishing number of CBOs in cities, another speaker argued. A recent conference had shown quite extraordinary numbers and rapidity in growth. But mutual learning was constrained because of the lack of communication between them. Changes for the better in official policy depended upon CBO pressure and demonstration, but the CBOs found it most difficult to learn from each other, to pool their experience. This ought to be a priority for aid.

The UMP had had a great deal of contact with NGOs, another contributor argued. Discussions and workshops had been continuous as efforts to get to know them, identify their needs and the means to help them. Of course, there was a difficulty since NGOs did not earn a living from talking to the UMP, so it was difficult for them to make the time for discussions. Nonetheless, efforts had been made even if it could now be seen that they were not sufficient. The UMP commitment made this year to address the issues involved in the alleviation of urban poverty would make it necessary to increase involvement with NGOs.

Summing up
Mark Hildebrand & Patrick McAuslan

Mark Hildebrand

The interventions are basically green concepts, in the sense that they are fresh in our minds, they are embryonic. The idea in the UMP was to put something forward that would be thought-provoking in the sense that there is a need for a vision of the city and it has to be created at the city level. Thinking about this diagram as a political diagram – because that is what it is – begs the question: where do we fit in? What is our action agenda?

Regarding how the CBOs support themselves and how we support them, there are obviously a number of programmes designed to do that. We have to approach this with a lot of care in order to be strategic. It is a question of having an understanding of how the community is working, how we do consultations, if in fact the dynamic is not working well, if there is no commitment to consultation. You do not try to change this necessarily because there is so much of a demand for what we do. Habitat has expanded threefold in the past five years and the

Patrick McAuslan

I would like to take up Mark's (Hildebrand) and Arif's (Hasan) points, in suggesting that one concentrates on CBOs. They already exist, we are not trying to create something. There are a myriad of organizations which exist, they are already doing things, and we want to try and work with them and use them as a basis for introducing new ideas, new approaches in cities.

Paul's (Ackroyd) comment with regard to NGOs and CBOs is a very valid one. But it is worth making the point that when we use CBOs, there is a difference. Some NGOs can be used, but a lot are international and come with their own agendas. There was recently a rather sceptical article about NGOs, basically saying look out for them, they are no better than other international organizations, they have their own agendas, they are funded by their own governments and we must be careful of them.

But there are many community based organizations, in many cities, even in sub-Saharan Africa. Mabagunge's paper which he did while a Research Fellow at the Bank, was on home-based voluntary organizations and the need to make use of them. This has been a source of inspiration to our thinking about the use of CBOs. He based these ideas on what has happened in the cities in Nigeria, looking at the way that local organizations are developing an agenda on the urban environment. So I think there are a lot of locally developing CBOs in many cities around the world.

So, to answer Mr Sundaram's point, yes we know there are CBOs, they have been in existence for a long time. What has happened in the past is that urban management has neglected them all too frequently. In the early or middle 1960s, there was a major reorganization of local government in Calcutta and the journal *Nagarlok*[35] ran a special issue on this. The new approach to the government was the creation of a mayor-in-council. I hope I don't offend anyone here by saying this was rather like trying to rearrange the chairs on the Titanic. The problems in Calcutta are not going to be solved whether there is a Mayor-in-Council who is able to give orders or a Mayor not in Council but who has to pay attention to the committee structure. Although there is no need to engage in fundamental legislative reform, clearly in some countries there may be the need where it is thought necessary to do that before you can engage in changed policies.

Final statement
Michael Cohen & Shabbir Cheema

Michael Cohen

One of the questions that I came into this meeting with, knowing that we were going to be talking about implementation, was: what would constitute success, that is, success from a variety of points of view for effective urban assistance or urban development? We have been through quite a few criteria. Mark (Hildebrand) referred to the dichotomies and the dichotomies getting away. There have also been a great many analogies and metaphors used in these discussions. I would like to draw on two of them as a way of summarizing my reaction.

I think the comment of Fitz (Ford) about the organic health analogy was very interesting: the question of the process, the inter-connectedness, the notion of changing health status and the way in which there is mutual interdependence in a lot of the things we have been talking about; later there was an effort at graphically presenting it. With that metaphor there are a couple

---

35 *Municipal Affairs Quarterly*, Indian Institute of Public Administration, New Delhi.

of points I would make. In this particular case we have to come out with views on how healthy the organism is. My sense is that in a lot of places where we are working, there are contradictions and all kinds of problems. I do not think there are too many places where, if they were organisms, they would get too far down the road in their current health status. To use the same analogy, they are a little like us, they do not quite have enough sleep, do not eat all the right things and there are a number of ailments which are affecting them: whether they are pricing those resources correctly, let us say water, whether the environment is indeed sustainable, are we subsidizing certain kinds of behaviours that are not going to be able to continue? So my question is how healthy is the present situation, in terms of cities? I think we have got to invest in operations to keep the main organism going and also keep the organism learning and growing. In each one of these areas there is a tremendous set of policy opportunities and areas for investment and we do not want a narrow view.

The issue of the environment and of decentralization and political empowerment are things that in the urban sector were not treated in the 1970s and 1980s. They are out there now and if we cannot figure out how they are related to some of the concerns, we are not taking advantage of opportunities.

Finally, Hendropranoto (Suselo) made a comment yesterday about the policy people and the operations people. This comes back to the point with the DPU; we are here and the DPU is not necessarily operations. But they are reflecting about policy and directions to go in.

There were some interesting points about intervention from the outside, that we should not have preordained outcomes in mind. We know what this has meant in, for example, the proverbial sites and services project in the briefcase, brought out to order. Yet I do think we have to have a normative view. We do have to have some criteria and principles that we believe are important, whether they are stated as baldly and generally with things such as equity and efficiency. We cannot avoid the issue of professional responsibility by saying what we think about some of these things. In some cases that may lead to open conflict and disagreement with some of the partners. But that is part of the professional game. One needs to engage and that is maybe where the policy people put a little more out there than the operational people. But the operational people have to deal with the real world. There is room for policy here and maybe it is the process of going back and forth as we have done in the past two days which gives us insight on how to go.

Shabbir Cheema

I would like to start with the political factor in implementing the urban agenda. Many of you have seen UNDP's *Human development report 1991*, in which we analyze data on health and on education for selected developing countries. In each of the sectors, there is a detailed analysis of the data and the investment we have made. The main conclusion of the Report is: it is not lack of resources but lack of political commitment which is the real cause of deprivation and poor human conditions in developing countries. This is not a sweeping statement. It is validated by comparative data in all sectors of almost all countries. So it is not correct to talk about undertaking urban policy analysis and implementation, without talking about the political factor, and I think we need to recognize that.

When we talk about poverty alleviation, the rôle of communities and of NGOs is important. We understand that through the government institutions, benefits very often do not go to the deserving, and we are all trying to find mechanisms to reach them. So the political factor is critical. In our agencies we have relative freedom to focus on that, but in all the papers I have seen it becomes very clear that the political factor is a dimension.

The second point is that many colleagues have discussed the question of decentralization. It would be contradictory to say that you want participation in urban development, but not decentralization – it does not work. At the same time the whole international agenda, without decentralization in developing countries, will become a meaningless exercise. We recognize constraints in the implementation of the decentralization programme. The way we need to look at this is that decentralization evolves from pressure from below, from the grass root level. At the same time decentralization often cannot take place because not every country is like the Soviet Union with 70 years of communism; and no decentralization can take place without financial and technical, as well as political support and commitment from the central government. It is wrong to assume that the centre is a homogeneous set of actors. You have people at the centre who strongly support decentralization, but at the same time you have to accept that there are constraints on the centre. Furthermore, when we are talking about deconcentration, delegation, devolution, transfer to NGOs, decentralization of population, decentralization of industrial activities – for each of those six phenomena many people have the tendency to use the word "decentralization" – we need to recognize that each of the six is different.

The third point is to recognize the integration required for local relationships between local government, NGOs and CBOs. If you talk about CBOs you are talking about only part of the phenomena. If you talk about NGOs, many of them tend not to be indigenous. One thing we are missing in the relationship is the municipality. People say that municipalities are full of corruption and incompetence, but I would say the same of many central governments in developing countries. It is wrong to generalize from one element of local relationships and eliminate the local government from the scene.

I do not see any contradiction in urbanization strategy between a policy perspective approach and an opportunity approach. If you have a policy or a strategy in a country, you then have opportunities to implement part of that strategy. This is not fragmentation of concepts. It is possible, however, to take an opportunity to do a wrong thing, or to take an opportunity to do a right thing, within a conceptual policy framework.

Finally, how can these agendas be made operational? What are the avenues? I think each of us has a part in our respective rôles in implementing these agendas. The critical rôle is that of our government counterparts. Of course we are limited in facilitating that process and UNDP, within these limitations, has four mechanisms to implement the agenda. One is that from now on focus will be on programme support, linked to the government's ongoing programme. In Thailand, for example, we asked our counterparts to be the leader, to commit themselves to the government programme. Secondly, we have a very clear commitment to rely on local institutions, Ministries, departments, etc., and that will be a more meaningful way to deal with these issues. We are shifting from technical issues to institutional and managerial issues, and to achieve that we have to rely on the national institutions. A further mechanism is that we are going to have a process approach, no more one-time intervention. It will be a long term commitment to a programme. Finally, the focus in UNDP is going to be on country-based impact, and that is where the rôle of the Urban Management Programme becomes very critical. It can provide the intellectual input, tools and policy packages; that is the context within which we look at the Urban Management Programme.

Final address
Al Van Huyck
Independent Consultant
(former President of PADCO, Washington)

I have been a prodigal son. I have spent the past year out of the field, running for political office in local government in the United States. For me, coming here is catching up on the state of the art and direction. There has been some substantial progress made in the World Bank and UNDP papers that we have been discussing. The focus on productivity and economics is vital, while still addressing some of our fundamental concerns with poverty, the rôle of women, the environment; Nigel's remarks that the environment is now part of the economic process in an important contribution. The discussion of decentralization waxes on. We are still discussing it, and still supporting it, and still waiting to see action. And of course urban management is still a priority. So the issues have been joined and developed.

We have had plenty of discussion so I will take just a few minutes to draw upon my experience as a defeated politician. I lost 58 to 42 per cent. I now know why politicians pay no attention to planners because I tried to run my campaign as a professional planner addressing the issues of my local government, Loudoun County. It is a very large geographic area and in rapid transition between urban and rural values. It has a budget of 220 million dollars split between education and local government services. It is the largest employer in the county with over 3,000 employees so it's not huge by Cairo or Karachi standards, but it is still significant. It is local government, and I think we can learn something from it.

Just to illustrate it for fun, I was thinking today as I was listening, what would this session be like if indeed it was an American local government political campaign and we had two candidates, the UNDP paper and the World Bank paper. Now we, as professionals, have been discussing this from the point of view of seeking clarity and understanding. We have been adding our own perspectives and values to enrich the shared dialogue. We have noted similarities and explored in a professional way, the differences between them, and the field. But if this was a political campaign we would have ultimately to vote for one paper or the other. We could not have both. One would be defeated and the other would win. Our group would have come here already divided up to support one paper or the other, for a variety of reasons which might not have much to do with the paper. For example one might say: "I have a better chance of getting contracts if the UNDP paper gets in", and another might say, "well when I was Minister of Housing, the World Bank screwed me over and I'm going to get those guys".

Let's assume the DPU students are the voters. How would it happens. We would be seeking to exploit differences, not similarities and we would try to polarize. For instance Nigel (Harris) might have started by saying "Mr Cohen of the World Bank has insulted the intelligence of every person in this room, with his suggestions of increased decentralization. Surely he must know that such a policy would cost millions of jobs in the central government?" Desmond (McNeill) meanwhile, working for Michael, would have been out with the students (voters) and would come back and say "Look Michael, that productivity stuff went real good, they liked the environment but we're in trouble with decentralization because 75 per cent of those students are from central government ministries". So Michael would have come in this morning and said "Well I support decentralization as a long range policy objective, but I want to stress my commitment to the many millions of central government workers who are doing wonderful work and furthermore I am promising a 5 per cent pay-raise".

Of course Shabbir Cheema (UNDP) is now in trouble. It is late in the afternoon and they are going to vote in two hours. His group would say, "Well there is still a chance, because 80 per cent of the DPU students are Muslim". He would say "While I'm totally against negative campaigning, but I have searched my heart, and I feel compelled to say that I saw Michael Cohen drink wine at lunchtime. Can we trust the future of urban policy to a man who drinks wine at lunch?". At that point we vote, and who knows? But that's what happened to me. This campaign was the most extraordinary experience because the issues were clearly not important.

I want to draw a few conclusions briefly. I prepared a platform, 16 pages long, single spaced, of what I was going to recommend for Loudoun County. All of you would have been proud of it. It addressed the issues. After having started with a 16 page platform that seriously addressed the issues, my very last piece in defeat said my priorities were: put education first, cut government spending, bring jobs and investment to Loudoun County and provide real growth management. I still lost.

We have to learn, if we are going start addressing our issues in the political agenda that our language is totally wrong. I used the term "comparative advantage" in a written answer to a question, i.e. Loudoun County's comparative advantage over Fairfax County (next door). I found out the next day that no one knew what comparative advantage meant. I used the word "life-cycle" costing for our capital improvements, and again no one understood what I meant. We have got to learn if we are going to be effective in the political arena, to get our message across in political terms.

One of the things I have always been mystified by, is why can't people see the problems of the poor, the problems that need to be addressed. The answer is that all people have their own agenda of demands and grievances. I talked to thousands of people, the campaign was a year long; people have their agenda of grievances with government and they have their priorities of what they want addressed. This explained to me – which should have been self-evident in retrospect – why it is that, when you speak to an upper income person in a developing country and ask them what is the most important problem in their city, they say "Traffic". The reason they say traffic is because you can internalize water supplies through your own system, sanitation, recreation, electricity with your own generator. The one thing you can't take care of is traffic.

The reality is that people have their own agenda at all levels and they want their own agenda addressed first before you can move on. I got into trouble on affordable housing. I thought that affordable housing would be my issue, but I discovered what many others had found: that affordable housing is really a code word. Loudoun County does not want affordable housing. They want to address a narrow segment of the housing market that had not been well served by the private market, for school teachers, policemen and others working on civil service salaries who want to live in the community and not further out. They do not want to address truly affordable housing for the poor. What they had in mind was how to write down a $120,000 town house to $70,000 which is what these people could afford. You will not be surprised to know that they wanted subsidized interest rates. They got $2 million of 5 per cent money which is going to build 20 homes. They also have, as developers, to write down the cost of the land for affordable housing. The developers are all for this because in Virginia they have a system where they have to contribute school and other infrastructure needs and by putting affordable housing in the mix, they are able to take raw land, at cost and then write down the retail cost of the lot. So it becomes a bonanza for them to provide affordable housing. So I discovered that people didn't want affordable housing per se.

Another thing that is important. We are all believers in markets and market efficiency. Well I am now totally convinced that at the political level everyone is working against efficient markets. Nobody wants them. We're wrong, guys! Many private businessmen I talked to in the course of the campaign were really looking for special privileges, special deals and special things. They did not want efficient markets. We've got another big problem there.

Another important thing, as we press for decentralization in local government. American local government is well advanced. It introduces a whole set of interesting new problems that I was forced to think about. First we are talking about the property tax. Twice in the World Bank paper it mentions that only 1 per cent of revenues are raised from property tax. The property tax is the main thing in local government in the United States and it has some very pernicious results in meeting needs. It makes a battle between whether you get non-residential development which has lower requirements for services and is therefore considered profit, or whether you get housing. Within the Washington Metropolitan area, which this community was, you would be talking about creating housing and jobs and so on at the metropolitan scale. But it becomes a fractured debate at a local level as you want to push low-income housing on your neighbour to get the jobs. So you begin competing in ways that are interesting politically but not very successful if we are talking about efficient development of metropolitan areas.

Small area local politics in a metropolitan area have all sorts of ramifications. Tremendous problems of equity are introduced when your primary vehicle is local government, equity in the general sense. For instance, one of my opponent's big issues was Loudoun County tax yields. For each tax dollar sent to the State, Loudoun County got 63 cents back. Naïvely early in the campaign I thought that was a pretty fair deal, because there are an awful lot of poor people in south-west Virginia that are in desperate poverty. If our rich Northern area (our medium household income is $54,000 a year) were not helping them, who would? But I found out that's not it. Later in the campaign the

State Transport guy came up to give a speech on a separate issue and he made a big deal that in Virginia for each dollar sent to the federal government, they only got 78 cents back. This whole idea of equity becomes very difficult when property taxes are the major vehicle for financing local government.

Finally, a couple of quick notes. It was fascinating to get away from talking with you (planners) and go to talk to lots and lots of other people. It really is interesting and you find tremendous innovations going on. I suspect this is true in every country not just the United States. We need, in these policy papers to begin to think about the global economy. I started out thinking that my international experience would be a turn off politically so I talked about being in economic development and planning, my background, but didn't stress the international. Then I discovered that Loudoun County is heavily involved internationally in an incredible variety of ways, from sending out frozen bulls' semen overseas for cattle production to people running international management training centres, which bring people from all over the world to a farm where they have training sessions. People are doing all sorts of things internationally and the global economy, global interdependence, is important even at the local level.

If I were going to criticize the policy papers, it would be because the city is treated as if it was a self-contained economy. It clearly is not and we've got to think about the fact that we are in a world capital market, and world labour market. The telecommunications revolution is huge. Business itself is losing its national characteristics; many of the large multinationals are no longer American firms or British firms. They are in fact global firms with managers and subcontractors, registered in different countries. The economy has gone beyond our previous thinking and we must adapt. We are beginning to see a bifurcation, particularly in some African cities, where part of those cities has got to be ready to compete at an international level, a global world, with high-tech communication and flow, whereas the mass of their population is at a quite different level. I do not know how that is going to be bridged and how you treat with fairness these two things that are both growing, but it's very exciting.

Secondly, I think we are going to see a new definition between agglomeration economies and diseconomies. The diseconomies are proving to be much more serious because in fact the agglomeration economies are going to be less valued because of telecommunications.

We are seeing a breakdown of traditional thinking. It is now possible in the new economy we are living in, to begin to run economic activities which just ten to fifteen years ago had to be close together. One of the implications that needs to be brought out particularly in the World Bank paper, is that there is no reference to national networks of cities. I think it is really important. Countries now have to look at the whole settlement hierarchy system in new ways – not with our old paradigms. We are thinking about new ways that cities could interact to the benefit of both rural and urban poor through innovative new technology. We have to address how these networks of cities are going to be interacting in these policy statements.

All of us are excited about the newly emerging concepts that are represented in the policy papers that we have been talking about today. But we are pulling away from our institutional moorings here and we ought to be aware of it. There must be all sorts of discussions going on in the World Bank about the implications of this paper on their institutional relationships and the way things are done. That is just one agency. When we begin to think about bringing the urban policy work out into the field, then we get a geometric increase in the complications of moving into the new institutional relationships. In the groups we have worked with in housing – the old national housing corporations – client relationships were well established. Now we are talking about reformulating our approach. The reason that national urban policy studies, the precursors to this work, did not go anywhere, did not have the impact that they might have had, was because there were no clients for them. I know PADCO's in Egypt had no client. The Ministry we were attached to was really the Ministry that was heavily involved in the new towns, which was only one aspect to which we brought a lot of bad news – correct, but bad news. We have to think about that and it may be that the next phase that we should be looking at in the research mode is how to pick up on using national urban policy in the indicator sense. We are doing this now through the UNCHS-World Bank housing indicator project. If we could begin to think about how to get indicators to guide whether cities are becoming more or less efficient, more or less productive, then I think there would be ways to guide without having the heavy hand of a NUDS. I would hope in the research agenda we could begin to think about that. It is going to be difficult and complex, but I think that is going to be the next methodological problem to be addressed if indeed we are going to get the benefit of our much more complicated but promising concepts about urbanization that we have discussed here at the DPU.

PART II
Policy experience

CHAPTER FIVE
National urban development policies and strategies: a review of country experience
KENNETH WATTS

Synopsis

Urban policy studies have been undertaken in a number of countries in recent years, and this paper reviews some of the more important issues raised in them. These are broadly of two types: those which are concerned with the effect of fundamental economic and social policies on the process of urban development, and how these policies may help or hinder the ways in which cities contribute to a country's economic and social wellbeing; and those of a more tactical nature by means of which governments may seek to target investment in such a way as to maximize the benefits that can be derived from urban development, and minimize its negative effects. One principal conclusion is that although urban policy studies are of value in providing governments with a general understanding of urban dynamics in their own country, and therefore with a framework for action on a countrywide level, there are limits to the ability of central administrations to affect direct changes at all levels of society. The rôle of local authorities in reflecting peoples' ambitions and needs at the township level is crucial to ensure the implementation of the practical measures necessary to achieve success.

I. Introduction

As the world becomes increasingly urbanized, so is it more and more recognized – though this is not yet universally the case – that urbanization is not a process that is detrimental to a country's wellbeing, in spite of its often chaotic and uncontrolled nature and the desperate plight visited upon so many of the urban poor. On the contrary, urbanization plays a necessary and crucial rôle in a country's development, and one which, if successfully managed, can lead to economic success.

With this recognition has come an increasing realization of the immense complexity of the processes that create cities, which are the outcome of a huge range of both public and private endeavours taking place within a limited and highly congested space. Indeed, it is perhaps because of this very complexity, and the difficulties involved both in understanding it and in imposing a measure of order upon it, that urbanization still has not attained the degree of priority on the world agenda as that enjoyed by, for example, the environment. Never-theless, major international agencies such as the World Bank, the UNDP and the UNCHS have started to reformulate agendas listing the many courses of action open to the world community in general (and countries in particular) in their attempts to meet the challenges posed by rapid urbanization: to render cities more economically efficient, to mitigate the all-too-evident sufferings of the urban poor, and in general to create conditions for the future economic and social wellbeing of all urban dwellers.

At the heart of the discussion lies the question as to whether governments can, by various means open to them, bring about changes in the ways in which urbanization is taking place, which are of a kind that will better promote its efficiency and mitigate its ill effects. The possibility of intervening in this process at the national level has only recently been considered at all seriously in most countries. Although *economic* planning and/or management has long been undertaken by governments at the central level, *spatial* or *physical* planning has usually been the prerogative of the local levels of government. The former, being largely a product of centralized economies, often had a counterpart in the ambitious national physical plans of Eastern Europe; but in the market economies, many fewer attempts have been made to do this.

Furthermore, as a recent paper has put it: "nowhere in the discussions of the linkages between national and local planning is there any reference (beyond the usual reasons of better local knowledge and improved coordination) as to *why the local component of planning is important and how economic planning (mainly national) and physical planning (mainly local) ought to interrelate* (Peterson et al. (a),45 – emphasis mine). And there is perhaps a wider issue at stake here: the dichotomy between economic and physical development – the one concerned with expanding output, the other with the organization of space to achieve optimal efficiency – has somehow to be resolved at the national level, where all important policy decisions are taken.

During recent years, a number of countries have been attempting to fill this gap by undertaking comprehensive national strategy or policy studies of urban development. The objectives of such studies have broadly been to analyse the dynamics of the urban process in their respective territories, and to examine the options open to them in coping with the challenges of urbanization. Although each study is unique in its scope and content, the following elements are typically found in all of them:

- An economic, demographic, social and functional analysis of the urban structure of the country;
- An identification of the problems and development potentials of the different urban areas in the country by undertaking a range of studies into such matters as the extent of urban poverty, the inequities in income distribution, unbalanced growth, poor access to services, problems of urban management; and also an identification of urban areas with high growth potential;
- An analysis of urban policy alternatives designed to overcome, or at least ameliorate the identified problems, and to assist urban areas with high potential to function more efficiently. Also an identification of specific programmes

relative to certain types of city, and recommendations for major secondary cities;
- An identification of overall investment needs and of priority urban programmes, with specific reference to the need to integrate sectoral programmes at the local level.

II. *The paper's purpose*

The purpose of this paper is to review and discuss a selected number of these studies. The first part of the paper reviews in broad terms the work undertaken in each of the studies of the analytical background of urban development in their respective countries, in accordance with the first point in the paragraph above. Secondly, the paper will examine the nature of the relationships that the studies have sought to establish between general social and economic policies and urban development; and it will discuss the extent to which changes in general policy can induce, either purposefully or inadvertently, both adverse or beneficial effects on urban life. It will also discuss the various policy proposals made in the different studies to optimize the effects of urban change. Thirdly, it will continue by reviewing a number of specific issues, such as the use of investment in urban infrastructure as an instrument of urban policy, the need for reform of local government structures and finance, that are highlighted in the studies mainly in response to points three and four above. A final part will sum up the issues that are raised in the paper.

III. The national character of the urbanization process

Urbanization is a worldwide phenomenon, and it is possible to identify similarities in the ways it manifests itself in different countries; but it is unwise to assume that a set of policies that are appropriate to one country will necessarily be successful in others. Thus the importance of these country studies lies in the fact that in *every region, and perhaps in every country, the process of urbanization is a unique phenomenon with roots in the social and economic life of the area concerned.* The applicability of different elements of the international agendas, and the priorities to be assigned to them, will vary from country to country; and a comparative study of the work that has so far been undertaken in a number of countries reveals the nature of the issues brought to the surface by the urbanization process, and the measures thought necessary to deal with them.

However, although a few countries instituted these urban policy studies, the fact is that in most of the earlier cases, their effect on national development policy has been very limited, or virtually non-existent. An important reason for this may have been because they tended to be theoretical in their approach, not addressing practical issues of immediate concern to policy makers – a criticism that cannot be levelled in the same measure at the more recent studies. Undoubtedly, these earlier studies were also unrealistic in their assumptions on the capability of central governments to execute policies and programmes of the kind that they prescribed. Indeed, bearing in mind the unstable economic environment within which all governments operate, is it Utopian to imagine that they can undertake the kinds of sustained actions that city development demands?

In spite of these criticisms, the earlier work certainly highlighted important issues, and suggested ways of dealing with them; and as such they provide useful pointers to the directions that subsequent studies took. It is in this context that these national policy studies will be discussed.

IV. The analytical background for national strategies

The commissioning of national urban strategy or policy studies did not start in earnest until the early 1980s, when the first of them – the National Urban Policy Study (NUPS) for Egypt – was undertaken. There had been previous attempts to prepare national physical *plans*, which although long on multi-sectoral physical analysis, were usually rather short on economic analysis. The same was true of the large numbers of regional plans that had been prepared during this period, very few of which provided a basis for development policy. In any case, by the end of the 1970s, the end-state planning techniques of the 1950s and 1960s had become discredited. Furthermore, the realization had gained ground that the character of urban development owed much more to the operation of economic forces in general, and of the market in particular, than had previously been taken into account; and that an understanding of the working of these forces must lie at the heart of urban development policy.

What were the reasons for this burgeoning of interest in national urbanization studies during the 1980s? In the first place, there was a need for policy makers to find out what was actually happening. The data on such matters as population trends and movements, on the evolving patterns of industrial location, transportation and trade, as well as social indicators on health, education, the incidence of poverty, were all available, and sectoral analyses were abundantly available. What was lacking was an attempt to analyse all these data comprehensively, in the urban context.

Governments were starting to perceive that it was costing them increasingly large sums of money to service cities, with consequent deleterious effects on the exchequer, and some say, on foreign borrowing; and at the same time, larger and larger numbers of destitute poor were congregating in the cities, bringing with them social and political consequences of a potentially explosive character. Looked at positively, an analysis of urban trends could be used not only to gain an understanding of the dimensions of the problem, but also to assess urban rôles and functions in the context of national development, and thereby establish a basis for policy.

Possibly the most ambitious attempt at trying to assess urban rôles and trends was undertaken in the Pakistan study, with the object of determining the growth potential of all cities with populations of 100,000 and above in the country. The more interesting of the proposals involved the application of various criteria to assess cities' potential. The first of these involved the adjustment of population trend estimates according to whether they were generating a higher or lower value added per capita, a model which would necessarily give emphasis to cities such as Karachi which are already large. The second model sought to modify this by introducing the concept that higher value added would be attributable to the presence of a higher level of infrastructure using the existence of telephone connections, electricity consumption and banking services as indicators. A third variant had cost minimization as the criterion, under which the total investment costs per capita for each city (job creation plus infrastructure costs) are compared. In each case, the estimates reached are necessarily arbitrary, and in any case, the data upon which these estimates are based are not available in all countries; but the methodology may be worth studying as a basis for providing broad brush estimates of urban futures in a country. Further reference is made to this study on page 150 and footnote 51 below.

This kind of analysis is also a feature of both the Indonesian and more recent Thai studies. It is most clearly articulated in the terms of reference of the latter study, the initial objective of which is to "assess the implications of improving urban rôles and functions in order to support the long-term development of the country, particularly in terms of the increasingly rapid internationalization of the Thai economy." (T, p.1).

Central to this analysis is *the concept of urban hierarchies*, and the present and possible future functions of cities in the whole pattern of a country's development, about which there is, of course, a considerable literature. In the NUDS study for Indonesia, the urban areas are classified according to their functions, and a broad typology is proposed according to the degree to which they perform a "hinterland service" (i.e as administrative/social/market centres for the surrounding region), serve as centres for inter-regional communications, or are centres for goods processing (manufacturing). Cities are then ranked hierarchically into national, inter-regional, regional and local development centres, and general packages of government actions and policy orientations are discussed for each type of city. Population projections are made for each city on the basis of its possible future potential, and a data base is established, providing basic information on all aspects of a city's present physical and economic status, together with its future needs and potential. This data base is intended to give *general* guidance for future government policy and for the targeting of urban works programmes in particular, but it is stressed that in order to be useful, it would have to be continuously updated, a point that is discussed later in this paper. (I, pp.131–70).

A somewhat similar approach was adopted for the Thai study. The methodology is described as a process which relies "on regional socio-economic data to assess the potential of specific areas and sectors, to identify those urban centers with the most economic potential along a number of dimensions and select special areas which represent opportunities for growth, such as border towns, or require additional investment assistance, such as lagging regions. In addition the process can identify the specific rôle cities should play in relation to hinterland development . . ." The methodology eschews what it calls "abstract, generalized 'rôles' for cities", and rather adopts a system of classification based on an "index of socio-economic performance" constructed by using twenty different variables associated with per-capita gross provincial product. This analysis gives rise to a classification of cities into six levels of potential, and is used in turn to provide the analytical basis for the design of a general investment programme extending beyond that of public works alone.[36] In Korea too, the study on national physical development proposes a regional division of function, whereby large cities have central and comprehensive functions, and smaller cities have "specialized functions according to their own potential and specificity."

A hierarchical model is also used in the Malaysian study "to help structure the analysis of interrelated urban areas." A detailed study was undertaken to assign rôles to each urban area based on certain characteristics such as size, administrative rôle, commercial function and degree of industrial development. This analysis was then used to "guide service provision by indicating the level of facility that is appropriate for each level of centre". In general, the resultant analysis showed that urban rôles are as yet somewhat weakly defined, with equally weak linkages existing between secondary and tertiary towns; but by the same token, the basic structure provides a satisfactory basis for future urban development. (M, p.13).

Discussion

The purpose of these various methodologies is to identify where the problems and potentials lie: the problems (apart from those associated with the major cities) being predominantly in what the Thai study calls the "lagging regions", and the potentials are in those places which already possess a capacity for growth which, if supported by a variety of means, can contribute more to the national economy. The Malaysian study identifies the latter goal very well: "an urban policy has as a key objective the release of this growth potential but this objective needs to be pursued in coordination with other development policies." (M, p.26).

While certainly useful in identifying cities where great problems exist (and quantifying those problems), and others – such as

---

36 This description, necessarily summarized for a paper of this kind, does not do adequate justice to the careful work described in the study in Thailand, op. cit., pp.110 et seq.

administrative and market centres, whose status in the hierarchy is comparatively stable – the question is whether such national studies can succeed, as the Pakistan study sought to do, in identifying all of the potentials that exist in urban areas within a country. Or, to put the matter in a different way, whether a single study of this type can be expected to provide more than a "snapshot" of what is happening in a country at the time when the study is undertaken, while perhaps overlooking the almost imperceptible, yet vital stirrings of new enterprise in unlikely places. This is certainly a matter that is discussed in many of the studies, including the Thai one, and is a theme that will recur in this paper: studies such as those under review may well be of value in creating a general overview of trends at a particular moment in time, but unless mechanisms are set in place that keep the centre advised of events in the country at large, opportunities will be missed.

Furthermore, it must never be assumed that such national studies can take the place of detailed local knowledge, which only a properly organized local authority can have. Indeed, in their recent study on *Urban economies and national development*, Peterson et al. (b) lay much more stress on the need for local authorities themselves to take initiatives in developing local potentials. Although cautioning against the dangers implicit in such devices as local tax incentives, they consider that:

"Local governments will do better to think of themselves as long-term investors in development. They can identify the region's potential competitive advantages, then build on the strengths through public and private investment, flexible business regulation, and efforts to control the local cost structure". (Peterson et al. (b), p.57)[37].

However, as they admit, urban areas are part of a national and international economy, and even the best designed local strategy cannot overcome market – and other – disadvantages. It is perhaps in this respect that national strategies can play a rôle; and the need is stressed later in this paper for mediating

---

37 For a full discussion of the latter, see chapter 2 of Peterson et al. (b).

mechanisms to be established so that local enterprise can be recognized and supported from the centre.

V. *Urbanization and national policy issues*

Having established an analytical basis for urban policy, there are divergent views on what the elements of such a policy should be. The complex forces at work in creating urban development are even now only partially understood, hence the proposal by the World Bank that more research should be undertaken to create a greater measure of understanding of urban dynamics. However, the world cannot wait, and the question still arises as to where one should start: should one seek to affect the operation of those fundamental social and economic forces that energize the growth of cities; or, recognizing the difficulty of understanding, far less controlling, such forces, concentrate upon tactical measures designed to enhance the general wellbeing of cities and their inhabitants? From a review of the work undertaken during the 1980s, it appears that while some attempts were made to define the nature of the former, the more productive outcomes were from the second. In this part of the paper, an attempt will be made to examine the different national urban studies in the light of national policy issues.

From a very wide-ranging discussion on this aspect, it is very difficult to distinguish those elements of national policy that have the greatest impact upon urban development, and should receive most urgent attention. However, as a starting point, it is proposed to take the following *ex-cathedra* view expressed by Renaud in 1979. While conceding that every nation should take a different approach, he wrote:

"The proper formulation of a national urbanization strategy requires the systematic discussion of three main policy areas affecting patterns of population distribution and national settlements. The country must examine in turn: (1) the implicit spatial effects and biases of national policies; (2) the

appropriate policies to deal with such problems of large cities as congestion and pollution; and (3) the problems of regional inequality and the direct (explicit) policy instruments for the redistribution of economic activities. Of these three clusters of spatial policy instruments, the best known is the third, though the first two often have greater impact." (Renaud, p.98).
Evidence shows that some of the national studies undertaken during the 1980s did attempt to address some of these concerns. However, because urban affairs had not yet attained a sufficiently high degree of priority on national policy agendas, little was done to implement them, or at least the first two of them. Each of these three elements is now discussed in turn.

The effect of national development policy on urban development

The interaction between economic policy and urbanization has long been discussed in the literature. In Egypt, the NUPS study had noted that "many of the most important influences of government on the settlement system are policies and practices of the government that are not necessarily thought of as urban policies. A policy of rapid industrialization, for example, produces increased urbanization and concentration of population in major urban centres, expansion of public sector employment fosters growth in major government centres, subsidies for low income housing in high cost urban areas increases the rate of migration to such areas, and so on"(E, p.58). The study proposes that the effect of these and other similar policies should be reviewed in the urban context. In parenthesis it may be noted that this cluster of policies is by no means universally applicable, thus emphasizing the degree to which urbanization varies in its dynamics from country to country: for example, in some countries such as Taiwan, industrialization has been associated with dispersal, and in others with the growth of primate cities.

In the case of Indonesia, the National Urban Development

Strategy study (NUDS) reviewed a range of national development policies, and discussed their impact on spatial development. The study listed the following national macro/sectoral policies as being important in this respect (I, p.8–9):
- Sectoral policies: e.g. agriculture, manufacturing, mining.
- Other implicit policies: e.g. consumer subsidy policy, taxation and service pricing, credit/monetary policy, regulatory policy, development of government institutions, population policies, human capital development, and composition of government investment.
- Other policies considered were national spatial policies including direct government investment in employment-generating activities, in infrastructure and general locational incentives.

To this list might be added a whole range of other issues: the effect, for example, of credit policies in general and higher interest rates in particular on activity in such sectors as the construction industry; of exchange rates, the effect on the export performance of industry; and, most recently, the effect of the whole range of structural policies which have as their objective the reduction of market distortions such as commodity subsidies of all kinds (including those benefiting urban dwellers), and a shift away from import substitution to export-led industrial development, which greatly influences industrial location decisions.

In the NUDS report, it was concluded that while the general statements of policy as set out in the national development plans were consistent with each other, and supported change in the Indonesian economy favourable to more decentralized patterns of settlement, "it is recognized that a number of these policies represent major shifts from past directions taken by the government and that it will be difficult to bring about many of these changes in a short period of time" (I, p.103).

Although not specifically discussed in these terms in the Thai study, there is an all-pervading sense in it of the interlocking nature between the strong performance of the Thai economy and the pattern of urbanization in Thailand, with specific reference to the domination exercised by Bangkok, a point that is discussed further below. However, the study recognizes that there have been certain policies in the past that are biased in favour of Bangkok, "such as heavy taxation of rice, implicit and explicit subsidization of import-substitution activities and the centralization of political and administrative decision-making authority within Bangkok" (T, p.6). As the study states, the country is indeed at the beginnings of a fundamental change in the nature of its economy, and this boom and the increasing integration of the Thai economy into that of the world at large are factors which must lie behind any discussion on urban futures.

Malaysia is a country which has already moved to an export-orientation in its industrial policy, linked to the development of high technology; and it is recognized that this will lead in turn to concentrations of activity in certain areas which will benefit from agglomeration. Although the emphasis in past plans has been on the creation of job opportunities in the rural areas by crop diversification and the opening up of new lands, this will have to change in future. (M, p.27).

It is not possible to assess how many of the propositions set out above may well be susceptible to proof, and indeed how many of them are susceptible to general application. There appears to be a need for more research into many of the "shibboleths" that are so often set up as guides to policy; and in any case, the particular nature of every country's problems has to be studied. Even when "proven" to be beneficial (insofar as it is possible to do this), the extent to which such policies can actually be put into effect depends upon the degree of acceptance that they acquire with policy-makers and politicians; and here one comes up against the manifold political, administrative and financial constraints which affect, and some say impede, policy implementation in urban affairs. The fact is that there is seldom an "urban lobby" as there is a "farm lobby" or a "manufacturer's lobby". *But the question has perhaps to be asked with increasing insistence as to whether in future the importance of the urban agenda is such that the implications of policy decisions on such strictly non-urban matters as agricultural and trade policy, which have long been having a bearing on urbanization, should now be evaluated in the light of urban policy.*

Congestion and pollution in big cities

Turning to Renaud's second point concerning the problems of big city congestion and pollution, reference is made to aspects of these problems in virtually all of the studies under review, and in at least two of the countries concerned, Egypt and Thailand, the authors consider that the problem of capital city primacy is such as to cause concern. However, all studies appear to be realistic in their assessment of the importance of big cities to the future economic development of the country as a whole, and none proposes active measures to restrict their growth[38]. Nevertheless, thought is being given to the possibility of relieving congestion by spreading economic growth away from such cities, an issue that is discussed in the next section. As to the relief of general conditions in both large and small cities, the policies proposed are mainly concerned with improving urban infrastructure, with the aim of both rendering it more efficient and of creating a better urban environment.

The need to improve the urban environment in general has only recently arrived on the urban agenda, although parts of it have been tackled in piecemeal fashion with the implementation of water supply, sewerage and sanitation schemes. Only in the 1991 Thai study do such considerations gain more than a peripheral mention, the references in previous studies being more to the need to improve the general or natural environment. Indeed the environmental proposals in the Thai study might well

---

38 See for example NUPS: "Efforts to prevent industrial expansion in major metropolitan regions are likely to result in reduced rates of economic growth in the nation." (E, p.75). NUDS: "The strategy recommends some moderation of growth rates for Indonesia's dominant metropolitan areas, but recognizes that these areas remain vital to the national economy. Their growth should not be restricted by regulation". (I, p.141). Similarly, the assumption in the Thai study is that Bangkok will continue to grow.

be considered to be a starting point for work on this aspect in the future. At the core of the proposals is the prospective creation of an Environmental Impact Fund, based on the single payment of "environmental impact fees "at the time of development approval. These fees are calculated to be proportional to the cost to the environment of the proposed development[39]. Other recent initiatives include the enactment of the Environmental Management Act of 1982 in Indonesia under which detailed environmental assessments (EAs) of all major projects should be undertaken. But, as a recent World Bank study reports, much remains to be done to make the Act operationally effective[40].

The quest for regional balance

The third of Renaud's policies concerns that of dealing with the problems of regional inequality, and whether it is possible to devise viable policies aimed at the redistribution of economic activity within the country, often from the capital itself, and at what cost or net gain to the wellbeing of the nation as a whole. An examination of the national policy studies shows that this subject is considered to be of great importance, and to have a direct bearing upon the political wellbeing of a country. However, it is recognized that if active regulatory steps are taken to relocate economic activities away from the capital city – which in many cases is the primary producer of a very high proportion of the country's wealth – the economic wellbeing of the country as a whole will suffer; and that even in robust economies, far less those of a more fragile nature, it is unwise to attempt to

---

39 In the Thai study, it is mentioned that this practice has been successfully employed in Taiwan and Korea, particularly for water and sewerage, and in the rapidly expanding urban areas of North America.(T, p.162–7).

40 *Indonesia: a strategy for infrastructure development*, World Bank, 1991, p.110. For a much fuller treatment of this whole subject, see Nigel Harris, *Environmental issues in the cities of the developing world*, DPU, 1990.

disturb this relationship between location and economic activity.

The studies register increasing concern over the fact that a very high environmental cost is having to be paid for the advantages gained by the "excessive" concentration of activity in these major cities themselves, and that this has also resulted in the maldistribution of the social benefits of economic growth. Measures of a practical nature aimed at overcoming such inequalities are therefore proposed. It should be stressed that these attempts do not constitute a return to the old anti-urban case which regarded cities as being bad, but a realistic attempt to ensure that the benefits of development are more evenly spread amongst the population as a whole[41].

The degree of regional inequality[42] varies greatly between countries, even between those with similar levels of economic development. Renaud's researches show that the degree of "primacy"[43] – that is, the degree of concentration of economic activity within a single primate city in relation to that of the remainder of the country – tends to diminish as the national per

---

41 One country where anti-urban propaganda has been active in the political debate is Cambodia. *The Economist* has recently pointed out that the Khmer Rouge has always argued that cities were parasitical, and that unless the government tackles the problem of rural poverty, the same issue will emerge upon the political agenda (*The Economist*, 26 October 1991, p.82).

42 The concept of regional inequality is extremely difficult to define. Crude measures based on comparisons between the regional GDP will always conceal pockets of extreme poverty in the most prosperous regions, and be distorted by the location of high revenue producers such as oil fields within otherwise poor regions. Other indicators such as the relative incidence of poverty are likewise not easy to define. These problems are recognized in the studies themselves, but the general concept of trying to achieve a measure of equality within the country (however defined) has to be accepted as a basis for discussing proposals. The concept itself is discussed further below.

43 In the Renaud analysis, primacy is defined as the ratio between the population of the largest city in the country and that of the total urban population (Renaud, op. cit. p.109). However, this rough measure tends grossly to underestimate the economic significance of the "primate city": Bangkok, for example, contributes some 40 per cent of the national GDP, Jakarta more than 11 per cent, Lima 28 per cent, Manila 25 per cent and so on, out of all proportion to their population size.

capita GNP increases; but there are also other differences as well, due to the size of the country, its geography and even its political evolution. In all of the countries for which national urban studies have been prepared, regional inequalities exist to a greater or lesser extent. They are indeed a fact of life, and also tend to conceal the underlying problem, which is that the degree of heterogeneity within each region in this respect is almost always greater than the difference between regions themselves. The studies attempt to deal with this problem realistically, and demonstrate a certain evolution of thought on this subject.

Starting with the NUPS study for Egypt (1982), the importance is first emphasized of establishing an effective relationship between spatial and industrial location policy, and two general principles are enunciated[44]:
- that "priority should be given to programme choices and spatial locations for investment in programmes and locations where economic efficiency can be demonstrated"
- that industrial investment and spatial policies "should be based on the principle of conserving the amount of public investment required . . ."

With these principles in view, the study asks whether it is possible to achieve the major national objectives of a high national economic growth rate while maintaining social justice through interpersonal and inter-regional equity. In Egypt's case the report concluded that the best strategy would be to place *"primary emphasis on seeking national economic growth and gains in inter-personal equity, and less emphasis on attempting to achieve the convergence of regional incomes across all regions of the country during the next two decades."* (emphasis mine). The implications of this conclusion are that the general dynamics of the urban process in Egypt should be accepted as largely unalterable, but that every

---

44 These principles and the discussion on them are in NUPS, op. cit., pp.59–70. Renaud discusses the concept of economic efficiency in this context in his book, which is concerned with the creation of a physical and economic environment within which the urban economy can function in such a way as to provide maximum benefit both to the nation as a whole, and its citizens in particular. See Renaud pp.108 et seq.

attempt should be made to mitigate its less efficient (and less humane) aspects by alternative spatial policies; and the inference is that specific urban areas outside the primate city of Cairo should be identified where investment is likely to be efficient, and then invested in. Insofar as government is concerned, this would be mainly in infrastructure, an issue which is treated later in this paper.

It is worth noting that in all of the scenarios adopted in the Pakistan study described on p.126 above, which are concerned with efficiency of investment, Karachi is projected to increase at a rate higher than the historical trends would suggest, and thereby increase its primacy.

In Indonesia, the emphasis was somewhat different. In the first place, the character of the country, being an enormous and dispersed island system, is utterly different from that of Egypt. The imperatives of achieving a measure of inter-regional equity may therefore be much stronger than in Egypt. Nevertheless, the NUDS report (1985) summarized the general objectives of the economic development plans as seeking to achieve the twin goals of *spatial balance and integration both between and within regions*. Putting on one side, for the moment, what is meant by "spatial balance" (a point discussed later in this paper), in terms of urban development this was taken to mean encouraging the growth of effective urban centres in all regions and the avoidance of extremely skewed hierarchies (the emergence of single dominant cities) within regions. Under such a policy, increasing emphasis might be given to using cities to strengthen regional economies outside Java; but at the same time, the goals of national integration would be achieved by supporting "both activities and physical improvements that will facilitate outward linkages in all cities."

The degree of success achieved by the Indonesian government over the years in this respect can be gathered from a recent World Bank report on National Infrastructure Strategy for Indonesia, which commented on the fact that "economic growth has taken place at strikingly rapid and relatively uniform rates in all regions of Indonesia", though "considerable differences persist in the per-capita incomes and the incidence of poverty across the regions . . ." To pick up the point in the NUDS analysis on the need to promote integration, the report comments that despite wide differences in the levels of regional distribution of infrastructure, "a major accomplishment . . . over the past two decades has been the provision of basic infrastructure to all regions of Indonesia."

The study next asks how these imbalances should be addressed. Dismissing, as other studies have done, all regulatory approaches to addressing these inequalities for reasons already given, the report nevertheless acknowledges the need to achieve a measure of regional balance. It suggests that this may best be done through the elimination of a number of biases that presently favour investment in the metropolitan areas of Java, including: the modification of the present nationally uniform pricing policies for electricity, fuels etc, which (the report states) reduce infrastructure investment in remoter and less densely populated areas; the elimination of restrictive trade policies (e.g. for rattan and a number of other agricultural products) which cause much of the trade to move through Javan ports; and the decentralization of investment decision making, which would obviate the need for firms to maintain Jakarta-based presences. Above all, the report concludes, there is a need to strengthen local government, a point which is taken up further below[45]. Although one might debate certain of these issues, particularly on the advisability of modifying the uniform pricing of energy, the general drift of the argument is familiar from other studies.

Similar themes are encountered in the Thai study (1991). In Thailand, however, Bangkok's dominance is far greater than that for any comparable country: even in 1980, almost 70 per cent of all urban population lived in the city region, and in the late 1980s an equally high proportion of all investment took place there. Strategy during the 1980s sought to promote the dispersal of economic activity away from the Bangkok region, without too much success. But whereas policy in the early 1980s had emphasized public investment and spatial development as the

---

45 World Bank, op cit. (footnote 40 above), pp.114–19.

main instruments for promoting change, the more recent methods were of a fiscal and financial nature – for example, to promote greater efficiency in tax collection and property tax adjustments, designed to relate the rates charged more closely to social costs.

Faced with the consequences of Bangkok's dominance within the present urban hierarchy – a dominance that has nevertheless been the main driving force towards Thailand's current economic success – the writers of the report have come out with a new enunciation of policy, which is worth quoting in full:

> "Although uncontrolled urban development may, on its own generate its own spatial dynamics, public policy initiatives will be required to assist much of the momentum behind urban growth for two reasons. First, the ability of private citizens and industry to continue to locate in Bangkok without paying full social costs – increasing traffic congestion, environmental degradation and other negative externalities – is likely to continue for some time even with the adoption of improved management policies. [Second], the benefits of locating away from Bangkok are highly underestimated by the private sector. In addition, the concentration of higher order amenities in [the city] is probably unparalleled by any other Asian country. *Without a decisive lead by the Government to create both the economic and social infrastructure in regional clusters away from Bangkok, the attraction of industry away from [the city] by market forces alone is likely to lag far behind the actual potential.* (T, p.110 – emphasis mine).

The conclusion is reached that, since Bangkok will certainly retain its present pre-eminence in Thailand's urban hierarchy, its future growth must be better managed, by infrastructure led development in towns elsewhere, as well as by appropriate cost recovery and cost sharing strategies for both government and the private sector. Insofar as the outlying regions are concerned, the proposal is to target investment to a system of "regional networks" or "clusters", rather than single cities. The purpose of this is to "link a number of regional settlements into a tight network of interaction which, as a totality, has a greater potential for generating agglomeration economies than focusing on a single growth centre." (T, p.116). This concept is discussed further below.

Although single city primacy is not yet an issue for Malaysia, the study foresees the possibility of high growth taking place in Kuala Lumpur and other selected cities, and it expressed concern that this may bring a weakening of the somewhat fragile urban hierarchy in Malaysia as a whole. However, the conclusion reached is that "a broadly facilitative stance is appropriate for an urban sector policy which assists in the achievements of agglomeration benefits and efficiencies of scale in infrastructure use" (M, p.34).

A similar conclusion has been reached in the case of Seoul. A 1990 Korean strategy study concluded that "although the Seoul metropolitan region enjoys important agglomeration economies, it also has huge social cost in the form of transportation congestion, housing shortage, rapid increase of land value, environmental pollution etc. Regions other than Seoul suffer from lack of economic and social opportunities for self-realization of residents." The study goes on to recommend a number of measures to rectify these imbalances[46].

Discussion

In order adequately to summarize and comment on this discussion, one must first seek to define a number of terms that recur: what is meant, for example, by "regional equality" and "regional balance"? If one accepts the argument that it is difficult, if not impossible, to achieve a state of affairs where everybody enjoys equal benefits from national development, what should be the objective? Going beyond the time-honoured "growth v. equity" argument, should the objective be to enable all citizens at least to enjoy a minimum level of service provision, as has

---

[46] *Basic strategies for the balanced regional development in the age of decentralization* by Y. H. Park et al., quoted in *Abstracts in human settlements*, Korean Research Institute for Human Settlements 1991, Abstract 2.1.

been attempted in Indonesia; or should it perhaps aim at providing equal opportunities for all to achieve a measure of prosperity, wherever they may be located? Is the latter too Utopian a concept, and if not, how is it to be achieved ? There are many cases where government intervention has exacerbated inequalities rather than resolved them, but is this an argument for nothing to be attempted?

One of the most formidable arguments against active intervention is that ideally the location of economic activity should be dictated by the logic of the market, and for a government to compel an industrialist (for example) to locate in a place where he or she cannot make money is self-defeating. As one recent study has put it: ". . . it is the rate of return to capital in alternative locations, corrected for externalities, that is critical. A policy of trying simply to minimize the capital costs of job creation makes no sense." (Peterson et al. (b), p.16). But while accepting the general thrust of this argument, the studies show that, in the words of the Thai study, freedom to choose location has been costly in terms of the provision of infrastructure, and that the imposition of limitations on the location of certain types of heavy industry is essential, not least in the interests of the environment.

The studies also show that in reaching decisions on location of enterprises, an individual entrepreneur will often be influenced by a range of non-economic factors in favour of certain locations. This particularly applies to the primate cities, where the presence of all the paraphernalia of government is concentrated, and where, as a consequence of preferential treatment, standards of life are better, in spite of the environmental hazards of life in major tropical cities. This suggests that measures taken to correct such biases in favour of other locations may have an influence on location decisions by individual industrialists and others.

Another set of questions concerns the so-called congestion costs of concentrating activity in large cities. There is evidence at least from the Thai study that the full social costs of locating an enterprise in a large city are not being met, and it is proposed that measures should be instituted to correct this. There does indeed seem to be a need to establish appropriate pricing policies, not only for infrastructure but also in relation to staple foods, permits for the operation of polluting industries and so on, so as to even out incentives. Yet, bearing in mind that (for example) Bangkok contributes 40 per cent of the national GDP, at what stage does one risk meddling with "the goose that lays the golden egg" of national development, so that it is tempted to move elsewhere? And, with the same important statistic in mind, should not all efforts be made to improve conditions in the big city at whatever the cost?

The broad conclusion that can be drawn from the above discussion is that although the general consensus is that the promotion of economic and social equality within the regions of a country is a desirable political goal, it certainly cannot be achieved through regulatory means. Doubts must however exist about the capacity of governments anywhere to achieve it, and there is in any case empirical evidence to support the theory that such inequalities will even out in the course of time. However, the consensus seems to be that central governments certainly have a rôle in seeking to further such an end – present political realities demand no less – and the studies discuss a number of different approaches; a variety of administrative, fiscal and financial measures have been put forward in the different studies. *Discussion could well centre around the extent to which these measures have been tried in the different countries represented at the workshop, and how successful they have been in achieving the objective of regional balance.*

VI. Specific issues and measures

The studies explore a number of specific issues and measures that have as their objective a more equitable life for all. Before entering this discussion, it must be admitted at the outset that many of the matters that are discussed below are, in reality, all parts of a package of measures necessary to institute reform into systems that are often at present highly centralized. Thus the first of these measures – that of using investment in urban infrastructure either as a stimulus to economic development or as a corrective to environmental inadequacies in deprived urban areas – is in reality only achievable if other of the measures are also implemented: for instance, the reform of local government, to ensure that sufficient power, responsibility and capability is created at the local level to carry through such programmes; and the reform of fiscal and financial arrangements to enable local authorities to become financially more independent[47]. Nevertheless, from the standpoint of *national policy*, there is perhaps some merit in treating these subjects separately, as the studies have done, though the interconnected nature of the subjects is referred to throughout.

Investment in infrastructure as an instrument of urban policy

In most developing countries, both political and financial control has in the past been highly centralized, and this has meant that decisions on the use of national revenues for all national and local development projects, particularly those concerned with the construction and upgrading of infrastructure, have been taken in central sectoral ministries. One of the more sophisticated arguments used is that of ensuring macroeconomic stability in the country. As a recent World Bank report has it:

"An essential prerequisite for formulating an appropriate infrastructure development strategy is the analysis of the availability of external and internal financial resources. This in turn requires a review of the aggregate resource envelope and its distribution between public and private sectors, based on [the country's] target for a sustainable growth path. [The country's] main macroeconomic task for the 1990s is to sustain a rapid pace of growth without jeopardizing financial

---

[47] For a general discussion on these issues, see Emiel Wegelin, "New approaches in urban services delivery", *Cities*, August 1990, pp.244–58.

stability."[48]

While the argument has some force in general terms, the difficulty arises when the need for financial control is extended into project planning and implementation as well. There is a valid point that macroeconomic control over a country's finances is more easily achieved when central sectoral ministries are given complete control over its distribution. Nobody can deny the rôle of the centre in the location and design of national infrastructure projects; but when this central control is extended to the choice and location of local as well as national projects, the outcome locally has often been a plethora of unrelated projects, which frequently do not respond to local perceptions of need or local priorities. Moreover, the concentration of technical capability in the central offices of government has deprived local administrations of the technical knowledge necessary to manage such work.

There is a growing body of opinion that it is far more effective and efficient to enable local authorities themselves to plan and implement projects, particularly in infrastructure, in spite of the possible economies of scale that may accrue if the job is done nationally. The first and most important issue here, which none of the studies raises as such, is that of deciding what the most appropriate functional distribution of taxation powers should be as between central and local government. Most studies assume that local authorities' tax base will remain the same, though making it clear that improvements should be instituted to make the process more efficient. If this is to be the case, the next question is how to channel resources in appropriate amounts from the centre to the local authorities, in the most efficient and equitable way[49].

---

48 World Bank, op. cit.
49 In a recent report for the World Bank, Davey argues the case both for and against transfers from central to local government, and in the process reaches the conclusion that "effective municipal government in growing cities needs access to a *buoyant* revenue base, [emphasis mine] usually involving taxation of income or expenditure . . .": and that although local taxation is important at the margin, such buoyancy is only really achievable through the medium of

Some writers stress the need to encourage enterprising local authorities towards self-reliance by rewarding them financially, and compelling others to move away from complete dependence on central government funding by stimulating local revenue-raising – the "carrot-and-stick" approach described by Wegelin. Such an approach is exemplified by Davey's dictum that:

". . . in conditions of population growth and economic change, the requirements of effective city management have much in common with those of modern industry. Demands are great, resources heavily limited. There has to be a sense of strategic priority, both financially and spatially . . ."[50]

This matter is further discussed below in the context of local government generally.

One way of achieving an equitable distribution of funds is to establish general criteria for their apportionment, as has been recently done under World Bank auspices in Ecuador. A formula was agreed to, whereby 60 per cent of the national grant was to be apportioned on the basis of population levels in each urban area, 30 per cent in accordance with a generally accepted poverty index in each one, and the remaining 10 per cent on the basis of the degree of "fiscal effort in relation to fiscal capacity". The advantages of this method are that there are specific built-in biases to target the poor and to reward enterprising local

---

central government transfers. (The Chinese case reported in the next footnote is certainly an exception here!) Davey, *Strengthening municipal government*, para 2.176 p.46.

50 Davey, op. cit., para 2.90, p.26. The case of China is also instructive here, as recently reported in *The Economist*. Although mainly concerned with reporting China's industrial performance, the article noted that "the provinces and, in turn, local governments do all the tax collection. The provinces then make deals with the central government about how much of the haul they will turn over (as do the local governments to the provinces). The burden varies wildly [from place to place]..." (*The Economist*, 1 June 1991, p.20). According to other reports, the result for provincial and local governments – at least in some provinces – has been to release a flood of energy which, though somewhat anarchic in character, has on the whole had a beneficial effect on local development.

authorities, combined with simplicity of application, and a reduced likelihood of prolonged negotiation having to take place between the centre and the local authorities over grant levels; and although it cannot protect local authorities from national financial crisis, it is at least equitable. One disadvantage may be that it imposes on the authorities the necessity of ensuring the frequent updating both of population and poverty surveys.

A similar generalized arrangement was proposed in the NUPS study for Egypt, where it was estimated that the national government subsidized some 82 per cent of the budgets of the governorates in the late 1970s. As an equitable formula for the distribution of this funding, the study suggested that it "could be based upon population, but also upon other available sources of income (the add-on taxes) and the level of income of the population . . . it should be increased as local revenue increases initially so that the local governments have an incentive to improve their revenue collection." (E, p.429). This is an instance of the use of Wegelin's "carrot and stick" approach. It is also strongly advocated in the Malaysian study, in which stress is laid on the need to stimulate the growth in self-reliance in local authorities in revenue raising.(M, p.32).

However, if the goal of investment is to be that of promoting the national interest, then other methods of identifying needs and priorities seem to be necessary. What seems to be called for is a method by which apportionment takes place in accordance with an assessment of each individual town's needs in relation to its potential contribution to the future development of the country as a whole. The first general attempt at such a broader methodology was in the Pakistan study already described in p.126 above. However, this analysis was to be used not simply to provide a basis for infrastructure investment as such, but to give general direction to investment planning in general, and in particular to make comparisons between global investment costs and the size of the so-called resource pool.[51]

Such an analysis was also attempted in the NUDS study for Indonesia. As already noted above, an information system was set up based on present and estimated future populations of more than 500 urban areas throughout the country, together with indicative targets for various infrastructure programmes such as water supply, waste disposal, drainage and urban roads. These had been based on analyses of both the needs and the potential of each urban area, and were recommended – but only partially used – as base line data for the newly established Integrated Urban Infrastructure Development Program (IUIDP). IUIDP itself has developed into an extremely ambitious and comprehensive programme set up originally under the Ministry of Public Works, which aimed at providing each of Indonesia's urban areas with the means to upgrade their levels of infrastructure[52].

---

51 This account, and the summary of the methodology on p.126 of the present paper, are taken from the summary contained in the Asian Development Bank Urban Sector profile undertaken in 1986, where it was described as a key input into evolving a long-term spatial strategy for urbanization in Pakistan.

52 The ideas underlining the IUIDP programme were first developed in 1984 and 1985 as an attempt at multisectoral planning, programming and implementation of urban works programmes in Indonesian towns and cities. It was based on the grant system operating from the Ministry of Public Works. The principle gradually evolved that decision-making in choice and priorities of projects should be devolved to local authorities. In its later more developed form, the IUIDP procedures were as follows:
- Matters of general policy were settled in an interdepartmental coordinating body (TKPP) on which sat representatives from the Ministries of Planning (BAPPENAS), Finance, Home Affairs and Public Works.
- Although Central Public Works maintained management control over the programme through its authorisation of grant aid to the local authorities and by monitoring both the planning and execution of project proposals, the decisions on choice of projects and their priority rested with the local authorities.
- The main instrument for central management control was an annual and multi-year programme budget (PJM) which all local authorities had to prepare based on rough physical plans (IDAPs) indicating location of the proposed works.

In the process of PJM preparation, possibilities for enhancing local revenue contribution to the programme were to be reviewed and proposals made on

The Malaysian study (1986) was not as comprehensive as the Indonesian one, but more directly related to investment needs. The emphasis in the advice given in the study is that because of limited resources, priority should be given to those projects that are likely to make "the maximum impact on the longer term directions of urban development and make the greatest possible contribution to the achievement of urban policy objectives" (M, p.59). Having undertaken a review of existing deficiencies and sector plans, the study lists urban infrastructure projects as those requiring most urgent attention. In fact the typology of these is very similar to those identified in Indonesia. Then, based on the urban analysis already described, the study identifies three groups of locations which deserve priority (M, p.61):
- those which require upgrading to provide basic minimum standards;
- those which are in the process of growing to an extent that requires standards above the minimum; and
- those that are likely to become the foci of growth in the future, where the emphasis should be the removal of bottlenecks to accelerate development, and in general provide the infrastructure needed to achieve their potential.

The general study was then followed by detailed studies on the main localities involved.

Using the regional networks analysis, the Thai study lists the infrastructure works of all types that are considered necessary to upgrade the status of Bangkok and the other major cities concerned. It is admitted that the lists are incomplete because data are lacking. At the same time, the study advocates the establishment of a system of regional development grants to provinces rather than cities "since an urban area cannot be developed in isolation without supporting development

---

this.
- A wide-ranging programme of technical assistance was mobilized to assist in the enhancement of both management and technical capabilities at the provincial and local levels to coordinate and implement IUIDP.

The system is certainly worth evaluating with a view to its application elsewhere.

occurring in the rural areas surrounding the urban centre". The basis for the allocation of grants is to be "(1) the degree of development urgency in terms of national development policy, (2) the type of development projects to be promoted, and (3) the financial resources for the activity or investment in the locality." (p.183).

Discussion

Any discussion on these methodologies must start by asking what problems arise when a central administration makes decisions on the apportionment of development finance on a fair and efficient basis. The proposition that such an apportionment should be made on the basis of both potential and need is a worthwhile starting point, together with the need to reward local enterprise in all its forms. But how is this to be translated into a reliable formula that will stand the test of time? The extent to which data bases in general can be used on a year by year basis for investment decision-making is clearly dependent on whether they are continuously updated, which is notoriously difficult to do. Population projections themselves have also to be continuously reviewed, because those for smaller urban areas are often unreliable; and trend analysis may well prove to be a poor guide because unforeseen local events can influence the way in which the population increases or decreases.

It is often the influence of these local events – the election/appointment of an unusually lively administration, the setting up of an industry which attains a measure of success more rapidly than expected, the influx of an unpredicted number of new incoming migrants for whatever reason – that should be closely monitored to ensure that investment decisions are taken in such a way that both the national interest and local equity are well served[53].

The conclusion must be that if, in the national interest, decisions have to be made at the central level on the apportionment of development finance, there is a case for doing this on the basis of the kinds of analysis that the studies exemplify.

Alternatively, there are certainly grounds to favour a formula-driven system, since this may be more reliable, predictable and, in the longer run, more equitable than an *ad hoc* year-by-year assessment. And in this case, there certainly should be a basic review every five years, in order to monitor change. In any case, this should be supported by a continuous process of mediation between the local and central levels of government so as to ensure that serious needs are met and local enterprise is rewarded. And that in turn requires the strengthening of local government to the extent necessary to act as an adequate partner in the development of the country as a whole.

Standards for the provision of public services

For the purposes of the present paper, this must be an item that is recorded as important without need to discuss it. All of the studies refer to it as an important issue, for it clearly affects the extent to which projects can be funded. In all too many cases, standards of construction, for example, still adhere to regulations that were established in pre-independence times, and there is a great need for a review to be initiated into the definition and application of all such standards.

---

53 An interesting case of this kind of phenomenon is reported from Korea, where the regional development plan for the island of Cheju, off the south coast of the country, has had to be revised after only two years. Because of the prosperity of the country as a whole, the use of the island as a tourist destination has been realised far more rapidly than expected, with consequent deficiencies in infrastructure. A new plan must now be drawn up, not only correcting this, but also using the tourist bonus to create a stronger general economic base.

The reform of local government

Throughout this paper, the importance has been stressed of achieving a new balance of responsibilities between central and local government administrations, giving more comprehensive powers to the latter over fiscal matters and the control of local revenue, and over decisions on the prioritization, planning and execution of projects. It features in both of the international agendas, and is generally considered to be a crucial element in government policy towards urban affairs. It is also dealt with comprehensively in the urban policy studies presently under review. And, as a recent international workshop put it "there is a marked trend, worldwide, towards the decentralization of responsibility for urban management and planning to the local government level. . . . This is because planning needs to be integrated into the decision-making process about resource allocation and service delivery at the local level, based on a proper understanding of local needs and priorities." (Devas, p.16).

But although much advocated, and often much supported at the highest levels of government, true decentralization seems to be very difficult to implement. Peterson et al. provide ten country case studies which demonstrate the problems involved in this process (Peterson et al. (a), Appendix B). The difficulties encountered in Kenya, which has been seeking to decentralize for more than 15 years, are typical of those that are generally met:
- shortage of government structures and skilled personnel;
- field agents (of central ministries) being concerned about the politicization of their "technical" activities;
- central HQs of ministries reluctant to give up authority;
- field agents retaining loyalty to their line ministry, not to the local planning agency;
- decentralization highlighting regional imbalances;
- centralization being considered important to the process of "nation-building".

Although these "facts of life" – among others – have to be borne in mind in reviewing the proposals in the studies, though the proposals themselves are of interest. These are concerned with central as well as local levels, and the review of urban policy proposals will start with a discussion on central government before local government.

Central government arrangements

Because of the political nature of the subject, this issue is infrequently discussed in a general way. Yet it is one that now requires very serious consideration. The general approach by governments to urban questions has invariably been fragmented. The comment made in the Malaysian study that:
> "a complex and fragmented institutional and financial framework applies in Malaysia to provide urban management and development. Centralized policy making works through decentralized operations management, maintenance and development control . . . etc."(p.22)

is by no means unique, but could be applied almost everywhere. Unless these problems of central management are clarified, the full advantages of decentralization of decision-making to local administrations will not be realized.

The issues here are twofold: what should be the rôle of central government in urban development, and how should it perform that rôle? These issues are succinctly set out in the NUPS project:
> "at the national government level the effective implementation of a national urban policy requires better coordinated policy planning and implementation of the plans that are adopted. Such coordination also requires better coordination between planning, programming and budgeting to set priorities for investment that are spatially as well as sectorally oriented." (E, p.426)

The suggested solution was first to set up an Office of Urban Policy Affairs in the office of the Prime Minister or the Deputy Prime Minister for Economic and Financial Affairs, having responsibility for urban policy development and monitoring; and second, in order to achieve better inter-ministerial coordination, to establish an additional ministerial committee concerned with urban policy, on which were represented ministers of the main development ministries.

In the NUDS recommendations, it was proposed that a National Urban Development Coordinating Board be established, to formulate urban and regional policies, and generally to oversee the approval, funding and monitoring of the plans and policies concerned: "in short, [to institutionalize] strategic urban planning capabilities within the government". In the event, a coordinating body was constituted, comprising representatives of the four main actors in urban affairs: planning, finance, home affairs, and public works (see footnote 51).

The Thai study states unequivocally that "in the longer term, urban management in Thailand will require either a wholly new or significantly modified institutional framework", and debates the alternatives of establishing a National Urban Development Policy Committee, with a sub-structure of implementation committees, or of combining all central government offices that are concerned with urban affairs under a new Ministry or Office of Urban Development. And in a recent study in Bangladesh, the need was expressed for an "Apex Body" to formulate urban policy.

Discussion

Because, as stated above, these questions enter the political arena, and the political configuration of every country is different, no paradigm can be proposed that would be universally acceptable. Even among states with similar forms of government – federal or unitary – there are different degrees of power exercised by the centre over local administrations. Furthermore, as witnessed in the Soviet Union, we are in a period of rapid change. And for all forms of government, as any student of government will be aware, the prospect of adding another coordinating mechanism or cabinet committee, this time dealing with urban affairs, to the already over-burdened structures of central government, will be anathema to many administrations.

Yet the proposition has to be made: that when the vital importance of this sector to the future social and economic wellbeing of each country is so amply demonstrated, and at a time when the negative effects of urban growth are so much in the public eye, should the urban sector not now assume an equal importance with other high profile portfolios such as health, education and even economic affairs? To affect a change in the present structures of government will undoubtedly be politically difficult and administratively complex, involving the relinquishment of powers by powerful ministries and the setting up of procedures that will somehow ensure better coordination, both spatially and in terms of budget allocations. The urban strategy studies raise these issues and propose solutions, and although there is evidence that action is being taken in certain countries to rectify this, it is doubtful whether many governments have fully confronted them.

One issue that does not receive much attention in the studies is that which is concerned with the distribution of functions between national and local administrations. While the involvement of central government departments in local project work is usually considered to be dysfunctional, there is a whole range of infrastructural activity which, in the national interest, has to remain within central government preserve; and, to an increasing extent, to be the preserve of private enterprise. A re-definition of the functions and responsibilities of each level of government in the widest sense is necessary in this, to take central ministries out of the business of project planning and implementation, and more into policy formulation and the monitoring and evaluation of work at the local levels[54]. The example of Indonesia may once again be cited in this respect, where a major area of debate over the past five years has centred

---

54 Davey has proposed a prescription of the functions that should be vested in municipalities, which he calls a "critical mass of functions": town planning, roads and footpaths, drainage, water supply, sanitation, preventive health (including garbage collection and street cleaning), open spaces and public transport. These may be undertaken directly or by hiring the services under supervision (Davey op. cit.).

on the functions of all tiers of government in the delivery of urban infrastructure, and indeed all aspects of the delivery process. This has been done under the auspices of the TKPP, the co-ordinating body noted under footnote 51 above.

The decentralization to local authorities

This subject is being dealt with at length under another agenda item of the workshop (see Ch. 4) in which the UNDP/World Bank/UNCHS Urban Management Programme is discussed, and for this reason it will not receive lengthy treatment in this paper. However, it must be touched upon because it is such a critical issue in each of the studies under review.

Many, but not all, of the studies distinguish between two levels of local government: the provincial or regional level, and the local city or municipal level, and an active debate is being entered on the relative importance of each. Two main questions arise. Firstly, leaving the primate cities on one side, is there a rôle for the middle levels of government, or should there be delegation of all powers directly to the local level? And secondly, what should be the rôle of the decentralized offices of the central government departments, which in every country act as the agents for the central ministries?

In the NUPS study for Egypt, the importance of the middle level – the governorates – is emphasized both as the place where most urban management functions should be located, ".. with policy made by coordination between the governor and the concerned national ministries for such urban development functions as preservation of arable land, industrial location, the preparation of plans and the provision of basic infrastructure" (E, p.427). But, it is stressed, this is not enough: the need is recognized for "increasing participation by the local councils at the city and urban quarter level in the formulation of budgets and the expenditure of funds for urban services in the area under their jurisdiction". This formula seems to prescribe the delegation of many central government powers to the governorate, whilst giving local authorities greater control over budgets. The main advantage seems to be that better coordination can be achieved in a whole range of policy matters such as infrastructure development, the location of economic activities, and agricultural development.

This prescription also perhaps has some advantages in relation to another problem, which the study discusses: that of staffing local offices with adequate numbers of professional and technical people required to ensure the satisfactory performance of those services that are delegated to local authorities. The fact is well known that this problem will not be solved simply by training an adequate number of people; career prospects have also to be guaranteed, adequate levels of remuneration have to be established, and conditions in general have to be created that will ensure the commitment of trained staff to the aspirations and needs of local authorities. It may well be that these considerations argue the case for building up staffs at the middle levels of government in the first place, where such conditions are more likely to be provided, rather than attempting a wholesale decentralization of all functions immediately. This emphasis on building up the regional level is also a feature of the Thai study (see below).

The discussion of local government structure in NUDS concentrates almost entirely on the need to upgrade administrations at the local level rather than at the province, though the coordinating function of provinces is recognized. But in Indonesia (as in other countries), there is a complex system of direct vertical decentralization – or rather "deconcentration" – from sectoral ministries to local administrations which complicates arrangements. Nevertheless, an active programme of decentralization is in train in the country, the IUIDP programme already described above being but one manifestation of this process.

NUDS also makes a significant contribution to discussion of one rather difficult issue: as Devas has put it, local governments "often lack both the required functional jurisdiction (i.e. they are not responsible for controlling some of the essential urban services) and the territorial jurisdiction (i.e. they do not cover the entire urban area, or the urban area may be divided between a number of governments)" (Devas, p.16). While the resolution of the former is a matter of political/administrative fiat, the latter often poses more practical difficulties.

The solution proposed by NUDS is to recognize that the areas over which a city extends can be "functionally" as well as administratively defined. "Functional Urban Areas" are defined as "contiguous areas which are consistently urban in character as indicated by levels of population density, economic functions and facilities"[55]. In the NUDS urban data file already noted above, details of these functional areas were worked out with the Central Statistics Bureau, and it was suggested that project planning and implementation should be undertaken within these wider urban areas. As the study states, "functional areas provide the only reasonable basis for assessing many urban needs." It should however be noted that the concept, though sensible in theory has created problems in developing IUIDP financing plans, since no local administration is particularly keen on sharing resources with other areas outside their administrative boundary.

The theme of devolution of authority and responsibility to local governments is also pursued in the Thai study. The study describes the present set up as "three orders of administrative bureaucratic power, i.e. central, provincial and local", each with its own representative committee structure, but needing to be strengthened by stronger and more effective institutional frameworks at the local levels. It notes that "more stress on a regional network approach will do much to justify and further the goal of greater local government authority. While the tasks of coordinating among regions must remain with the central government for obvious reasons, the actual investment selected for construction or funding must be selected by local residents with first-hand knowledge of existing economic and social

---

55 NUDS op. cit., p.56. In the text, functionally urban areas are more specifically defined as having:
- a population density of more than 5,000 persons/km^2;
- less than 25 per cent of its households engaged primarily in agriculture; and
- more than eight urban facilities.

opportunities." The stress here is more on the regional network approach than on local government proper, for the reasons already discussed above.

Discussion

Once again, prescription is impossible. The general message is that it is most desirable that effective decentralization should take place, in the sense of devolving project choice and execution to local levels of government, and granting them sufficient powers/resources to enable them to carry out their obligations[56]. But it is equally clear that this will not be an easy transition: as one study states: "it will by its very nature be extremely time-consuming and politically difficult." But in the thrust towards truly local participation in urban affairs, it is perhaps unwise to focus solely on the local authority as distinct from the middle levels of government. Although not as representative of grass root opinion as town administrations proper, the provinces or regions are an essential element in the whole picture, for it is there that the mediation takes place between central and local concerns. It is this mediation that is the most important element in development strategy, ensuring that there is a continuous exchange of information between the different levels of government.

---

56 In a more general sense, it is as well to be reminded of the features that may be said to comprise the *sine qua non* for effective municipal government, which Davey lists as follows (op. cit., p.68, para. 5.05):
"(a) responsibility for a hard core of functions, including roads and public transport, preventive health, water supply and sanitation, land use and building control; (b) responsibility for both capital construction and operation and maintenance of infrastructural services; (c) access to buoyant taxes on income or expenditure, whether by direct levy, surcharging or tax sharing; (d) regular accountability to the electorate; and (e) a clear focus of executive authority."

The financing of development

As with administration, so with the financing of investment, this forms an integral element of the Urban Management Programme. All of the studies under review deal with this issue to some extent, and have broadly the same prescriptions: if, as stated quite unequivocally in the NUPS study for Egypt, decentralization of authority is to be encouraged, it "cannot become a reality without decentralization of budgeting and of authority to make expenditures". The methods by which this can be achieved, and the pace at which it can take place, will vary greatly from country to country; but these are not issues that are discussed in detail in this paper. A very real issue in this emphasis on improving local fiscal performance is that of relieving the national exchequer by the tapping of local resources. Providing this is done in a controlled manner not calculated to distort national budgetary performance, this cannot but be beneficial to the country's development. As Wegelin has put it: "the increasingly recommended urban development path is to reduce the dependency of cities on national fiscal sources through increased generation of local revenues to finance more cost effective urban infrastructure/services development" (Wegelin, p.245). And indeed, in the Thai study, it is assumed that no more than 36 per cent of the required investment for cities other than Bangkok will be funded by direct central grant, the remainder being found from local authority or public enterprise sources (T, p.190). However, as already noted, Davey is, in the more general sense, more inclined to see this as being important at the margin (see footnote 49).

There are a number of issues in this connection that cannot be adequately dealt with in a paper such as this, but are nevertheless important: how budgets are prepared and approved (which vitally affects the pace at which projects can be implemented); why multi-year programme budgeting is so important (since it enables local authorities partially to escape from year-to-year financial planning); and why it is essential to incorporate operations and maintenance (O&M) activities into the whole process of budget preparation in particular and local authority management in general[57]. These are all issues that do not feature strongly in the studies, yet are of critical importance to the satisfactory implementation of a programme strategy[58]. No criticism is intended here of the studies themselves, which are after all more concerned with policy than with the actual machinery of government.

In these earlier studies, the main emphasis was on the need to expand local authorities' revenue base by various means, which is an obvious and important measure. However, from NUDS onwards, there was to be an increasing emphasis on other ways of extending the resource base available to local administrations, as well as on the need to explore other means of financing development. These subjects are discussed below.

The idea of a "municipal development fund"

At the time when NUDS was being drafted, the idea of setting up a Municipal Development Fund (MDF) was already under discussion between the Government of Indonesia and the World Bank, and the NUDS study endorses this as an important initiative in "providing long-term financial resources to local governments for the development, provision and maintenance of local infrastructure."

However, discussion has so far ranged around the possibility of setting up a Regional Development Account, which is envisaged as a one-window borrowing facility for local governments to borrow from the centre.

In Thailand, on the other hand, an MDF has been in existence

---

[57] The exception here is the World Bank's Infrastructure Strategy Study for Indonesia (qv), in which the need for a realistic O&M strategy is emphasized, making the obvious but often forgotten point that "in several cases, the need for new capital investment can be significantly reduced by improved O&M of existing infrastructure."

[58] The study of multisectoral investment planning by Peterson et al. (a) reviews all of these aspects very thoroughly, with examples from a variety of countries.

for some time, owned by the local governments themselves, and to which they have to contribute compulsorily by buying shares in it. This entitles them to borrow from the Fund. In the Thai study, there is a proposal that a new organization, perhaps called the "Local Government Development Corporation" should be set up, operating independently but under the supervision of the Ministry of Finance. It is stressed that this should be on a "strict financial basis", and rules are set up for its operation. It is proposed to be funded from a variety of sources, governmental, private and donor.

The judicious and well regulated use by local authorities of such independent sources of funding must be to the good, since it enables them partially to escape from the tyranny of annual budget exercises, with all the administrative hassles that they entail, and all the uncertainties that they introduce into local project implementation. The possibility of utilizing commercial banks as the administering agents for such funds, though advocated by some international agencies, does not seem to have materialized in many places as yet[59].

The concept of the "resource pool or envelope"

The resource pool concept appears in different studies. It arises from the perceived necessity to analyse the availability of a country's financial resources as an essential basis for constructing an appropriate infrastructure development strategy. In NUPS, for example, the size of the resource pool for investment was calculated based on certain assumptions, (including a 7 per cent growth rate in the economy), and this was compared with the estimated costs of implementing four possible strategies for the

---

59 Peterson et al. in their paper on MSIP, comment that the use of commercial banks as administering agents for such funds have certain advantages, since banks "must be convinced of the feasibility of market lending to local governments. . . .[Furthermore] commercial banks have been found to place just as much pressure, if not more, on upgrading local capital planning procedures [as government itself]"(Peterson et al. (a), p.33).

country's future development. The result was a serious shortfall (see Figs 1–8 of the NUPS report). A similar result was obtained in the Pakistan study, of which the AsDB report states that "the somewhat frightening conclusion . . . is that under all scenarios and even with drastic scaling down of standards of provision of services, resources available for urban development are only a fraction of the required investment funds."

The NUDS study takes the subject a stage further by comparing the proportion of the GDP that has been assigned to investment (the gross domestic investment or GDI), which was found to average 22 per cent over the previous 4 years. The actual development budget was found to be running at about 50 per cent of the GDI, and estimates of the resources pool were prepared on the basis of a 4.5 per cent and 5 per cent GDP growth rate. However, although indicative estimates of invest-ment costs were prepared for three alternative development strategies urban service investments, no direct comparison appears to have been made between these costs and the resource pool size. For the World Bank's Infrastructure Strategy, a much more complex analysis was undertaken; but it is interesting to note that, at the most basic level, the conclusions reached that the "prudent levels of public investment" should approximate to 10 per cent of GDP are not dissimilar to those of NUDS. The estimates are then compared with those investment requirements in the main sub-sectors of infrastructure to derive general conclusions on the feasibility of the proposed programmes.

In the Thai study, the whole approach is more pragmatic, relating investment costs to actual revenue estimates for each city (T, p.188).

It may be concluded that estimates of resources of this kind can do no more than provide a basis for discussion, rather than a precise measure of financial availability, to be used as a tool that will assist in reaching more general policy conclusions. In the real world, unknowable factors govern both the available funding, and the sectoral investment allocations from year to year, factors which in any case must be kept constantly under review.

The rôle of the private sector

An emerging theme in the studies is the need to consider possibilities of an expanded rôle for private enterprise in the provision of infrastructure. It is discussed at some length in the Malaysian study, where the conclusion is reached that "a much more systematic effort is required at federal, state and local government levels to examine the service provision options and ensure a cost effective and efficient level of local services". However, there are presently inadequate skills, especially at the local level in all but the largest municipalities, to examine the options properly and the information is frequently inadequate for suitable decision-making. The latter point, which is surely a general one, should be borne in mind before introducing any general programme involving private enterprise in the execution of projects.

The general issue of private involvement in investment also receives specific mention in the Thai study, and a long list of recommendations on this matter are made. But it is admitted that without a commitment on the part of the government to impose significant and economically rational user charges, private investors are unlikely to offer a solution to Thailand's infrastructure problems" (T, p.184).

Pricing policies also exercise the World Bank in their infrastructure policy study for Indonesia, and they discuss these issues under three different sets of circumstances:

- "For services for which a competitive market is feasible, and for which no subsidization is called for, there may be no need for any government regulation of prices. Price determination could be left entirely to market forces (e.g. a number of telecom services, the servicing of commercial installations).
- A mix of market determination and government regulation may be necessary for services which can potentially be provide competitively by the private sector but for which some subsidization of part of the service, for the benefit of the poor, may be desired. (e.g. transportation).
- In the case of services for which, because of 'natural

monopoly' characteristics, the public sector is the dominant provider, the price is fixed by regulation, but this should be done efficiently and in a transparent way (e.g. power generation and distribution)."

This attempt to codify issues in relation to the pricing of utility costs seems of particular relevance, not only to the private but the public sector as well. One may indeed aver that the ultimate objective should be that local governments are treated by central government as quasi-private institutions, able to manage themselves in the same way as the private sector does – though with the requisite safeguards to protect the citizens in their charge.

VII. Conclusions

The impression left after reviewing these studies is that they represent serious attempts to come to grips with the urban crises in the countries concerned; and that these attempts are rooted both in the spatial realities of the country, and the economic realities of the world in which each country exists. They are based on an underlying premise that although the logic of economic forces must to a very great extent govern the shape of urban patterns in a country – and that for the good of the country's economic wellbeing, it would be unwise to try to affect the workings of these forces – there are nevertheless a range of policies that can modify the workings of these forces to an extent that may enhance economic growth, and be socially beneficial.

The proposed policies are of two basic kinds: those that affect the ways in which the central government organizes its responses to the fundamentals of economic existence – its sponsorship of economic development in all its forms, its pricing policies, the terms of trade, and ultimately its management of the national budget; and those policies that are of a more strictly practical type that, for example, govern the location of industrial and commercial enterprises, and target investment into deprived urban areas and those with high growth potential.

As to the former, it seems from the review of the country studies that much more attention needs to be paid to urban concerns at the time when such general development policies are formulated. Although the context is different, this view seems to be borne out by the statement in the World Bank's Agenda document that "the performance and management of the urban economy should be introduced into country strategy formulation and economic analysis as a *macroeconomic issue* rather than as a purely sectoral issue" [emphasis mine]. In particular, the list of issues given by the Bank document – the level and composition of public infrastructure investment in support of economic growth, the contribution of urban to national fiscal performance, the impact of adjustment policies on the productivity of the urban economy and so on – are all of a kind that, one way or another, find their resonances in the country studies. But at the same time, much more research into these matters seems to be necessary. In this respect, the Bank's research item (e) on the rôle of government in the urban development process, of how (for example) the productivity of individual households and firms are affected by the political structure, and by the locus of decision-making in the structure, seems opportune.

As to the second of the two types of policy, those of a more practical kind, the underlying philosophy seems to be that it is possible to influence urban development into more socially benign channels by targeting investment into specific locations, particularly in infrastructure. This entails a process of distribution of national resources by the central to local governments, and the paper has explored the ways in which this has been proposed to be done according to the different studies. The conclusion seems to be that it is worth attempting to apportion resources according to some kind of methodology which takes into account both potential and need; but that there is a need to establish an active system of monitoring between central and local government, so that the information base upon which such decisions are reached is continously updated – or at least every five years.

Urban policy studies of the kind that are reviewed here are no more than position papers prepared at a particular point in time.

The trends that they register have to be continuously reviewed, and systems introduced to mediate the whole process.

Powerful arguments have been put forward, both in the studies reviewed here, and in the literature, for each government to continue with processes of decentralization of functions to local administrations, and this must surely be taken note of. National studies such as these do not take the place of local initiative; their purpose should be to provide a broad framework within which such initiatives can be fully exploited for the benefit of all, and within which private initiative can also contribute.

Underlying the whole argument is the question as to whether such studies are worth undertaking at all. The answer according to the evidence gathered here seems to be in the affirmative, and various reasons can be offered in the support of this contention.

First, and perhaps most importantly, since it is clear from all relevant studies that the urban sector contributes the lion's share to a country's economy – as well as making the most demands on its exchequer – it seems imperative for a government to seek some kind of an understanding of the way in which it works. Such an understanding should, in the second place, lead to an examination of policies that are in its power both to spread the development benefits derived from the growth of cities, and to mitigate the failings of the urbanization process. Thirdly, if, as stated in the above quotation from the World Bank's Agenda document, urbanization is a multi-sectoral process, it needs to be studied in the round, and not just in sectoral reports that may touch on certain aspects of it in the context of national development policy. Finally, it is only through such a heightened understanding of the whole process of city growth that a government can acquire the means whereby it can measure and guide its own activities.

VIII. Main sources used in the paper

A. National studies

National Urban Development Strategy Project (Government of Indonesia/UNDP/UNCHS), Final Report, Sept. 1985, (I).

National urban development policy framework for Thailand, prepared by the Thailand Development Research Institute Foundation for the National Economic and Social Development Board, 1991 (T).

National Human Settlements Policy Study, Pakistan (Summary in Asian Development Bank Urban Sector Profile: see Footnote 50)

Urban Development Policy and Programme Study, Malaysia, volume 1, *Policy and programme framework*, prepared for the Government of Malaysia and the Asian Development Bank by COWIconsult in association with Coopers & Lybrand associates and Rekarancang Sdn Bhd., 1986 (M).

National Urban Policy Study, Egypt, prepared for the Advisory Committee for Reconstruction, Ministry of Development by PADCO Inc with Engineering Consultants Group and Sherif El-Hakim and Associates, 1982 (E).

B. Other main sources

Davey, Kenneth, *Strengthening municipal government*, World Bank 1989.

Devas, Nick, *New directions for urban planning and management conclusions from an international workshop on urban planning and management in rapidly urbanising countries*, by University of Birmingham, September 1989.

Kahnert, Friedrich, *Improving urban employment and labor productivity*, World Bank 1987.

Peterson, George E., G. Thomas Kingsley, Jeffrey P. Telgarsky, (a) *Multi-sectoral investment planning (MSIP)*, UNCHS Urban Management Programme, 1990.

Peterson, George E., G. Thomas Kingsley, Jeffrey P. Telgarsky (b) *Urban economies and national development USA* 1991.

Renaud, Bertrand, *National urbanization policy in developing countries*. World Bank Staff Working Paper, 1979.

United Nations Development Programme, *Cities, people & poverty, urban development cooperation for the 1990s*, 1991.

Wegelin, Emiel, "New approaches in urban services delivery", in *Cities*, August 1990, 244–58.

World Bank, *Urban policy and economic development: an agenda for the 1990s*, 1990.

CHAPTER SIX
Productivity and poverty in the cities of the developing countries
NIGEL HARRIS
Development Planning Unit

The first part of this paper discusses what seems occasionally to be a divergence between the overall aims of urban sector policies and what is actually implemented. From this there follows a discussion of what productivity and the reduction of poverty might imply at three levels – national policy (the discussion is very brief since this is the theme of the other paper in this session), traditional urban policy, and policies that affect the underlying urban economy, as the basis for assessing the prototypical determinants of urban productivity and poverty and the means available to urban managers to do something about them.

There have always been people responsible for formulating and implementing urban programmes who have regarded urbanization as a favourable index of economic development. But beyond the affirmation that rapid urban growth is one of the effects of, and a contribution to, economic development, few practical implications have been derived for the programmes themselves. No criteria of economic potential have been developed to distinguish different types of urbanization, cities or urban projects. There has been apparently little attention to assessing precisely the implications for economic development of different types of project and programme. In a not dissimilar way, there have rarely been arguments about the different implications of different projects for alleviating poverty or meeting what the poor perceive as their priority needs.

Thus, a team recently assessing the institutional effects of World Bank lending in Madras, comments in exactly this light that:

"It is striking that these direct concerns with economic development and with human development are not counted in the core of Madras' urban development projects. The formal project objectives . . . seem only implicitly related. It seems these concerns are central neither to Madras' urban agenda nor to the World Bank's urban agenda. Each agency (involved in the programme, NH) has chosen to focus on less direct influences on the economy and on human welfare, on the physical environmental infrastructure that only indirectly affects economic and human development"[60].

In practice, Madras's urban development was reduced to a concern for shelter and infrastructural extension, without any precise vindication of the programmes in terms either of the economic development of the city or maximizing its effects in terms of the poverty amelioration. Indeed, no clear cut diagnosis of the economic or poverty problems of the city was advanced in order to allow the observer to see the remedial relevance of the programmes. The report notes that "in the absence of self-generating economic growth and self-generating economic development, loans for infrastructure and shelter will permit only short term amelioration"[61].

These observations concern Madras, but they could be applied equally to possibly the majority of urban programmes[62].

---

60 Melvin M. Webber, Anna Haines, Chelan Vaidya *Urban projects in Madras: a review*, UDD Discussion Paper, World Bank, Washington DC, April 1991, para.3.10, p.16.
61 Ibid, para. 4.3, p.24.
62 The authors of the Madras paper speculate that the inconsistency between macroeconomic or social objectives and particular projects or programmes may arise from a preoccupation with the purely visible aspects of the city, citing in this connection the observation that:

"the evils of malnutrition, illness and ignorance are less visible than the

For example, two of the World Bank's latest draft infrastructure reviews[63] provide excellent and integrated overviews of infrastructural needs but without locating these in the detail of the economy, the anticipated changes in the composition of the output of goods and services, and in employment, the changing territorial distribution of economic activity and the effects on productivity – or poverty – of alternative infrastructural packages. Or again, the five year old collaborative Urban Management Programme of the United Nations Development Programme (UNDP), the World Bank and the United Nations Centre for Human Settlements (UNCHS), concentrates on the important issues of urban land management, environmental management, infrastructure and municipal finance, apparently without directly confronting the issues of what "urban managers" can or ought to do about urban productivity or the poor. If we measure the apparent agenda of issues by the published output of the programme up to November 1990, land management is easily in the leading position with 11 background papers, 21 case studies, 3 position papers and 5 "tools". Infrastructure comes second (with 7, 7, 1 and 3), followed by municipal finance (2, 6, 1 and 3) and urban environmental management (7, 1, 1, 0)[64]. Judgements of relative importance derived from this rating are, of course, quite arbitrary, but nonetheless one searches in vain for an examination of the real city economy and existing social conditions, an assessment of the

---

evils of substandard housing, even though the other problems may be much more severe"
– Leland S. Burns & Leo Grebber, *The housing of nations: analysis and policy in a comparative framework*, Macmillan, London, 1977, p.214.
We might note also that in a politically charged environment, visible change is at a premium for both local political leaders and aid donors.
63 *Brazil: medium-term strategy paper*, Infrastructure Division, Brazil Department, World Bank, Washington DC, Oct. 31st 1990, and *Indonesia: a strategy for infrastructure development*, Country Dept. V, Asia Region, World Bank, Washington DC, May 23rd, 1991.
64 Derived from Appendix III, List of UMP papers prepared under Phase 1, *Urban management programme: capacity for building for urban management in the 1990s: Phase 2*, UNDP, Nov. 1990, pp.25–9.

sources of urban productivity and poverty, and of the desirability and practicability of different responses by urban managers.

Consider, as a further illustration, the distribution of World Bank projects and programmes in 1990[65]. The 74 loans discussed are distributed between infrastructure, housing, municipal development, land (although work here, the author of the review notes, is only "timidly starting") and the urban environment. No doubt elements of these loans explicitly affect employment and output, and in general, they affect to some degree both productivity and poverty. Research at the Bank itself has excellently shown the high opportunity cost of neglecting the supply of infrastructure to industry in Nigeria[66]; the link between poor or nonexistent infrastructure and the health status and vulnerability of the poor is also well attested. Housing no doubt influences the capacity of workers to work at given levels of productivity and affects the capacity of the poor both to work[67] and to maintain their households. Strengthened municipal government, we presume, ought to improve the provision of services and so also affect economic efficiency and poverty. Land issues are of obvious importance here, although exactly how important in the sum of urban economic and poverty priorities is not self-evident. The urban environment is, with productivity and poverty, a priority issue in the Bank's agenda[68], and all three have important interrelationships.

---

65 *FY90 Sector Review: Urban Development*, UDD, Infrastructure and Urban Development Dept, World Bank, Washington DC, Jan. 1991. The discussion in the text concerns World Bank projects, not because the Bank is peculiarly guilty of the "errors" criticized, but because it provides publicly much greater material and openness on its activities and it has had a significant urban lending programme for longer than most donor agencies.

66 Lee Kyu Sik & Alex Anas, *Manufacturers' responses to infrastructure deficiencies in Nigeria: private alternatives and policy options*, INU Discussion Paper 50, World Bank, Washington DC, 1989.

67 The current *World development report 1991* (World Bank, Washington DC, 1991) includes figures on the costs of poor health for economic development – cf. pp.54–5.

68 *Urban policy and economic development: an agenda for the 1990s*, World Bank, Washington DC, 1991.

However, are improvements in these areas on their own enough to affect urban productivity and poverty significantly? If we started directly from the issues of productivity and poverty rather than seeking to rationalize existing concerns in terms of them, would the existing lending pattern exhibit the right priorities? The Bank – or, indeed, other donor agencies – might reply that the "urban" as construed here, that is, including the "real economy", is the concern of many other departments and divisions – finance, industry, transport, energy, education, etc. There are notorious problems in reconciling the sectoral preoccupations of line ministries and the multisectoral concerns of territorial areas, cities and regions (furthermore, there are other specialist reports that cover topics on a national rather than urban scale[69]). If this is so then the Bank's new agenda document promises more than it can deliver, for it cannot summarize the priorities for Bank lending in general as it affects urban areas, but may be driven back to precisely the traditional concerns. For those that manage cities, this is very troublesome ; they are urged to pay attention to productivity and poverty without having access to the key sectors for productivity growth or poverty reduction. What they *can* do appears only slightly relevant to what they are supposedly responsible for.

If the general perspective does not provide clear directions for effective action on the priorities, the more specific the programme, the greater the gap between general aims and immediate action. Indeed, some of those formulating the programmes may be unaware of the gap. Thus, an urban development policy for Vietnam[70] summarizes the authors' preoccupations as "not confined only to shelter or housing, but extending to such issues as water supply, sanitation and waste disposal, social infrastructure (schools, hospitals, etc.), energy supply, transportation and the protection of the environment".

---

69 Thus, the reports for different countries on poverty, for example: World Bank, *Nepal: policies for improving growth and relieving poverty*, Asia Country Dept., no.7178, NEP, Washington DC, Oct. 14th, 1988.
70 UNCHS, *Human settlements review: Socialist Republic of Vietnam*, Nairobi, July 1989, para. 1.1.

It is of great interest to discover how the issue of the environment succeeded so quickly – and rightly – in thrusting itself on to the world's urban agenda, but the economy did not!

The failure to locate urban lending in the context of the real urban economy is particularly surprising for the Bank since it itself has in the past undertaken so much of the basic research to identify the dynamics of the city economy, not least in the major study of Bogota. Furthermore, many Bank documents down the years have developed important policy prescriptions linking urban development programmes and the economy. For example, Kahnert's 1987 paper[71] contains a useful overview of many of the issues which are by no means restricted to the priorities listed earlier, but include directly also education and health, technical innovation, the operation of capital markets, etc.

Reconciling the priorities of raising urban productivity and the choice of urban lending programmes was, no doubt, not helped by the agencies with which the Bank and other donors dealt in recipient countries. At the city level, it is rare that there are people who perceive with any precision the economic rôle of the city and its changing contribution to the national and international economies, and therefore what the key priorities for urban borrowing should be if programmes are to have the greatest effect on the economy. City officials are almost invariably completely preoccupied with routine administration, the provision of services and political survival in a system dominated by the national government. Problems are made very much worse by inadequate and unstable resources flows, and in some cases, administrations are burdened with servicing debts from past rounds of investment. Talk of the need for them to relate what they do to the enhancement of urban productivity is likely to produce a glazed look in their eyes, an incomprehension as to what it is, what could be done about it and how this could be institutionalized in the context of so many other apparently

---

[71] Friedrich Kahnert, *Improving urban employment and labour productivity*, discussion paper 10, World Bank, Washington DC, 1987.

much more pressing priorities; the political rewards for improving productivity must appear very slight. Like the case for improved operations and maintenance of city infrastructure, the arguments are obviously sound and important but there is no powerful constituency which would gain significantly from paying attention to the issue. In any case, the routine budget will not stretch to maintenance, and it is sometimes far easier (as well as being politically more rewarding) to build new out of a capital budget replenished from the centre. Furthermore, local officials almost certainly see the local economy as being a primarily national concern; indeed, the national policy framework may be seen, rightly or wrongly, as so powerful, nothing effective is possible at the local level.

City planning agencies usually originate in the traditions of physical planning, and planners often find it exceedingly difficult to conceive of the city in terms other than this tradition. Furthermore, the legislative framework and the funding basis often does not allow the planners to innovate, to develop new approaches. The agencies may acquire new names, "Development Authorities", but the "development" equivocates between a concern to develop land and buildings, where the physical planners more often feel at home, and economic development. The terms of reference of the agency may emphasize ameliorating the condition of the poor, strengthening the informal sector, etc., but usually very little is done since the planners and the agency are not equipped to be effective on these aims. It is hardly surprising that national aims of economic development or relieving the conditions of poverty should become locally translated to the terrain most familiar to the planning agency: the organisation of land, distribution and density of population, the provision of infrastructure. In such a context, it is understandable that, for example, migrants become, not key contributors to the growth of city and national output, but problems, iron filings (reacting to magnets and countermagnets), or flows, floods and fluxes, blind tides that must be obstructed or deflected if the city is to avoid being swamped, saturated or drowned[72].

Are there serious prospects that the relative lack of power of local authorities may be reversed? There is much talk of decentralization, but the forces of centralization – particularly stemming from military or financial insecurity – remain very strong. However, the picture is very mixed, and some countries appear to have the potential for more active local governments than others, particularly where dispersed high economic growth occurs. Furthermore, there are suggestions that more open economies require more flexible government structures. Financial constraints impel national governments to seek ways of off-loading responsibilities, and they are obliged to permit local authorities to strengthen their financial position to cover these responsibilities. Thus, it would be wrong to be too pessimistic on the prospects of national governments relinquishing power (particularly the power of patronage which cements the political alliances underpinning government) for there are signs of possible change. Nonetheless, for the foreseeable future, national policy is likely to remain decisive for the local economy.

Politics

In the absence of dealing with what we have called the real city economy, the emphasis of urban action tends to fall upon "removing constraints" to the growth of productivity or the capacity of the poor for what used to be called self-improvement. This approach suggests that economic growth, the enhancement of productivity and the amelioration of poverty are always and everywhere possible if constraints are removed. However, while

---

72 The critique of the traditions of physical planning has been frequently made; for a summary, cf. my *Urbanization, economic development and policy in developing countries*, Working Paper no.19, DPU, London, Jan. 1990, pp.25–7; or *Economic development, cities and planning: the case of Bombay*, Oxford University Press, Bombay, 1978, pp.64–76.

there may indeed be constraints – and the Bank has excellently identified some of these in the urban context – it is not enough. There are recessions and slumps, and while the impact of these varies between localities, the brute impact may be far greater than anything that can be counteracted by variations in management reactions.

In a recession, there are still some sectors which grow even as others are declining. National and city managers and policy makers with a preoccupation to improve the mix of local output to offset downward fluctuations may be effective, but that requires a positive approach to shaping the city, not restricting matters to the contextual services or the regulatory regime. The emphasis on "constraints" suggests that poor growth is more often the result of positive government. It follows in this approach that if the government can be persuaded to adopt a more passive rôle so far as the real economy is concerned – at an extreme, to become the gatekeeper, or a referee in applying rules laid down in the world at large – then growth will automatically follow. The history of industrial society can only encourage scepticism on this diagnosis, particularly the dichotomy between a purely accommodating public authority, and private agencies with a monopoly of economic initiative.

Of course, aid agencies may feel obliged to adopt the stress on the need to remove "constraints" in order to protect an image of political neutrality.

The last observation highlights the importance of the political context of urban development, both the politics in the recipient country and in the aid agency and in its wider international context. For aid donors, projects and programmes have to be presented as technical improvements even though they must affect the standing and advantage of different interests, particularly political and social forces. Urban development programmes, like national policy issues, are therefore inevitably highly political, but unlike many national policy issues (for example, general macroeconomic assistance) they are implemented within a highly visible political arena, the city. Programme managers must be continually concerned with how their operations are seen by a wider public in the city and beyond, and, if they are to be successful, with aligning what they do with important political interests, with interests which stand to gain if the programme is successful. The exposure to critical public scrutiny is enhanced in regimes subject to periodic re-election, so that moves towards greater democratization must inevitably increase the politicization of programmes and projects. Inevitably, the need to ensure the success of programmes aligns aid donors with those in power rather than those outside power or in opposition (although the recent donor interest in NGOs may to some degree qualify this). As a Bank review of one urban development programme recently noted in a different connection:

"political considerations are the dominant variable in determining the outcome of institutional building efforts. Further, technical considerations are captured by the political process when these considerations may be used to support political objectives, and rejected when they appear to thwart these objectives"[73].

The need to appear not to be intervening in the domestic political affairs of a recipient country when inevitably all aid programmes are implicitly interfering – by strengthening some political interests rather than others – imposes upon donors a kind of technocratic naïvety. As the last commentator notes on the Bank's rôle in Recife,

"There is a tendency in Bank documents for the description 'political' to be used as though it were synonymous with 'irrational' . . . Wherever a conflict or issue is labelled political in a supervisory report, no further attempt appeared [in Recife, NH] to be made by the Bank to apply analytical tools to the issue"[74].

This is most regrettable since we do need to know what have been the political preconditions for successful urban development. In what contexts has it become favourable for

---

[73] J. Fitz Ford, *Review of the institutional development subproject of the Recife Metropolitan Regional Development Project*, UDD Discussion Paper, World Bank, Washington DC, Oct. 17 1990, para. 1.6, p.2.
[74] Ibid, para. 9.22, p.43.

dominant political interests to extend water supply or sewage services, to take the environment seriously, to pursue effective action to reduce poverty, let alone pay attention to the underlying economy.

The key to successful implementation lies in going with the political grain; without this, programmes are unlikely to succeed.

In summary then, the issues emerging from the preceding discussion are to identify what urban managers can or should do about the real economy to improve productivity – what is the urban economic agenda? – and to ameliorate poverty, and identify how any such programme could attain serious political dynamic. Such questions can only ultimately be answered in the context of one city and one polity, but at least we can try to explore some of the relevant considerations.

Factors shaping the city economy

The key elements which generally determine the economy of the city are reasonably well known, even if rather unknown for particular cities. First and foremost is the nature of the demand for the peculiar and changing package of goods and services the city produces, particularly markets external to the city. Within a national context and, even more, an open international one, cities should seek to exploit static and dynamic comparative advantages, producing changing forms of territorial specialization.

This specialization and change is concealed in the customary method of classifying cities by size of population. This can give a spurious homogeneity to classes of cities (for example, secondary and intermediate cities), when, in economic terms, they ought to be grouped by types of output. Of course, size classes may serve other functions by indicating status, service standards and powers.

Frequently the basic data to identify the specialized patterns of output of the city are lacking, or are collected on a different areal basis (regions, provinces or the national), even though these are precisely what are needed to begin to explore the determinants of changes in productivity. Even some of the larger cities fail to produce – or even sometimes see the need for – annual statistical yearbooks.

As is well known, national policies can play a powerful rôle in the development of city specialization. Those prices which are subject to government influence or determination – including interest and exchange rates – are particularly important here, affecting transactions, capital and credit flows, external exchanges (imports and exports), as well as sometimes energy, infrastructure supply, etc. Even given these prices, variations in macroeconomic policy, in credit and fiscal policy, industrial, export, energy, transport policies, etc. can have powerful effects at the level of a city (depending upon the composition of its output).

However, the overall effect of this diversity of policies is not at all clear and allows almost complete freedom to speculate. For example, a traditional economic case maintains that "over-urbanization" results from the complex of national policies grouped under the phrase import substitution industrialization, a case reflected in the original arguments for structural adjustment reform programmes in sub-Saharan Africa[75]. On the other hand, another case argues that the opening of a formerly closed national economy tends to encourage increased urbanization and concentration of population in the largest cities[76].

It is this lack of a clear perception of the sum total of implicit effects of national policies which leads some to argue that it is

---

75 The original argument was presented in I. M. D. Little, Tibor Skitovsky, Maurice Scott, *Industry and trade in some developing countries*, The Development Centre, OECD, Oxford University Press, London, 1970.
76 Sergio Boisier & Ivan Silva Lira, "Politica comercial y desarrollo regional: el impacto de la apertura externa de Chile sobre la estructura industrial regional", *Revista Latino Americana de Estudios Urbanos y Regionales*, EURE, 12/4, Dec. 1985, pp.65–92.

impossible to have an effective and coherent national urban policy which goes much beyond the attempt to programme urban infrastructure and ensure a neutrality in pricing between different localities (particularly between rural and urban areas). Thus, a recent report on the urban economy in developing countries identifies structural adjustment reform programmes as "de facto urban policy" since they seek to ensure this neutrality[77].

What is meant by a national urban policy, however, frequently confuses two aims: to ensure the urban sector works efficiently, and to seek to change the existing distribution of the urban population. While many governments have attempted to do the second, particularly through population decentralization schemes, there is little sound evidence that in general governments possess the power to achieve such aims at acceptable economic and political cost. That does not mean, of course, that government action cannot have strong effects in creating the conditions for some cities to grow economically quickly.

Some planners have seen the distribution of new infrastructural investment as a mechanism to achieve population redistribution[78]. The approach may often be valid at the local level, but the evidence does not support the idea on the national plain. Furthermore, there are grave dangers of wasting investment through the pursuit of population distribution policies which bear little relationship to the territorial economy. Infrastructural provision has to follow changing territorial activity rather than lead it, so that its rôle in shaping the distribution of population is passive.

---

[77] George E. Peterson, G. Thomas Kingsley, Jeffrey P. Telgarsky (the Urban Institute, Washington DC), *Urban economies and national development*, Office of Housing and Urban Programs, US Agency for International Development, Washington DC, Feb. 1991.

[78] As did, for example, the Indian National Commission on Urbanisation; cf. its *Report*, Government of India, New Delhi, August 1988.

Productivity at the city-wide level

In terms of the current agenda to improve productivity, the broadened scope of concerns is an important step forward. The old programme covered land, housing and services. The new spreads outwards to social infrastructure. Thus, for example, so far as workers are concerned, enhanced productivity requires a given level of health, a level which is rarely achieved in the poorer districts of cities in developing countries. Such a health standard derives both from the quality and quantity of basic diets (itself related closely to incomes and educational levels), environmental conditions (access to safe water and waste disposal, adequate shelter, work conditions, etc.), and protection from the hazards of large cities (including long distance movement in very crowded conditions with great delays). In poorer localities, a set of factors are often cumulatively damaging to the capacity to lead alert and energetic lives – low body weight and poor nourishment as infants, produce a poor ability to concentrate and hence an incapacity to benefit from education, made worse by the employment of children in work or fulltime household duties and persistent childhood sickness, all affecting adult capacities to work effectively when the children are fully grown. As adults, excessively long working and travelling hours lead to exhaustion, made worse by the time required to obtain basic services – thus poor water supplies oblige people to spend great time and often money in obtaining alternative supplies, to minimize use and so increase the dangers of contamination, particularly where safe waste disposal systems are lacking. It is often the women of poor households who are most exposed to many of these strains, and they are simultaneously exposed to the exhaustion of multiple childbirths. Indeed, if it were feasible to employ the methods of environmental economics to price this mass of unrequited labour inputs to household maintenance and thus to the output of goods and services of the cities, it is possible that urban productivity levels would be very much lower than currently assumed.

Education and training – the achievement of functional literacy, some measure of numeracy as well as vocational skills – are very important for improved productivity. But it makes little sense to discuss the question in isolation from the way of life which makes the absorption of education so difficult. The problems are most extreme in poorer districts for here children are frequently too important in the maintenance of household incomes (either directly or through assuming household care in order to free older household members to work) to be released for education.

This complex of issues directly affects the productivity of workers and hence both household incomes (and thus the consumption levels which sustain low productivity) and the efficiency of firms, the labour cost per unit of output. In addition, mention has already been made of the high costs of poor infrastructure to firms, of erratic power supplies, poor telephones, water supply and waste disposal system, congestion at docks, airports and in streets that delay the delivery of inputs, losses from pilfering because security services are poor, etc. Indeed, in sum, one must presume that the underlying profitability of urban activities must be very high to offset the extraordinarily high level of cumulative costs.

City authorities which came to be concerned about such issues could, with a self-sustaining financial basis, do much to make elementary improvements. A radical strengthening and regularization of operation and maintenance in urban services would make considerable savings. Waste reducing measures tend to reduce environmental damage, and can also be profitable; privatization of service provision also offers methods to secure financial replicability. Extending the coverage of the serviced area with the funds generated by proper financial recovery in the already serviced areas would then become possible, and full coverage could be achieved if standards of service were varied to come closer to existing household income levels in poor areas. Re-examining the appropriateness of the existing regulatory regime, insofar as it is really implemented, would be part of reconsidering the standards of provision.

Vocational education, city polytechnics and technical colleges, adult evening classes, etc. are well known mechanisms for improving the existing skills of the workforces. Varying standards in transport provision, without reducing environmental regulations, so that cheaper forms of transport become possible could extend the job market facing poorer households, reduce part of the daily attrition of the journey to work which exhausts workers, etc. In collaboration with the educational authorities, school children and non-governmental organisations, much greater efforts could go into providing education and skill acquisition to both women and children which acknowledge their inability to conform to the conventional timing and location of classes. Health education for women is a key priority in this respect since it is closely associated with the health status of poor households. Some city authorities might, in time, be able to emulate those countries which have been able to introduce school medical services to monitor and advise on the health of children, and school meals as a clear means to improve the standard of dietary intake. Lima's experience in providing free milk to poorer households may be an important initiative in this respect. Of course, what precise combination of these and other initiatives is appropriate depends upon the city, its administrative and financial basis, and a precise assessment of the effects of each initiative in order to choose those likely to yield the greatest returns in terms of their effects on productivity.

However, this agenda is directed to making the city work better as it is at the moment. There are a different set of issues involved in economic development, in continually seeking to change the structure of the city's output, to upgrade the long term productivity of the city and thus the incomes of its people.

Productivity in the real economy

In economic terms, a city is a spatially distributed system of producing a unique bundle of goods and services and of employing the labour force. The territorial distribution of activity implies the specialization of urban localities and interactions between them, just as the national territory supports interdependent specialized urban and rural localities. In the case of larger cities, the production of goods is possibly becoming of less importance than the rôle of cities as junctions in flows of goods, people, finance and information. Mobility, including communications, rather than fixed locations for production, thus becomes the key characteristic of urban activity.

Production and flows are determined in general by factors external to the city, and these external demands are continually reshaping urban activity. Those who manage cities should thus be concerned to react creatively to these primarily market forces which reshape the city's output, by seeking to improve the efficiency of the use of the factors of production in a context of competitive cities. The concept of an entrepreneurial local authority is far removed from the urban administrations of most developing countries today, but a more open world economy is perhaps going to make such ideas of increasing importance.

The spatial distribution of economic activity in larger cities falls into specialized districts which are well known. They include:

- the central business district (covering financial transactions, insurance, wholesale trading and brokering, exchanges, business services and communications);
- the "downtown" areas (of high income shopping, hotels, restaurants, clubs, agencies, etc.);
- the main transport junctions (sea, air, rail, road, with the elaborate means to secure swift transition from one to the other, and associated activities such as bus and railway stations, airports, warehousing, repair and servicing facilities, etc.);
- the main wholesale and retail markets and exchanges, which are major employers of labour, particularly poorly paid labour in developing countries, and closely linked to transport junctions and the large scale movement of goods;
- the main industrial areas, also tending to high degrees of specialization in the particular forms of urban manufacture; medium and large scale factories are now increasingly located on and beyond the periphery of the urban area, leaving small and petty manufacture closely interwoven with central

commercial and residential areas, but also specialized by locality.

The specific composition of the output of goods and services in these spatial configurations varies between cities, but in sum they constitute the main and the dynamic part of the city economy. The activities are interdependent so location is an important factor in the costs of transfer between localities. For example, steel arrives in the port, is traded in the wholesale market, financed by the credit services of the central business district, transferred to the warehouses of the transport junctions and then the steel stockholders, and thence moved to the minority of large and medium-size engineering firms on the outskirts of the city and, through many brokers, to the thousands of tiny metal users in the central urban areas. The efficiency of movement is thus a key component in creating the productivity of the metal using trades.

The participants in each specialized component of the urban economy know it with great thoroughness, but in many cities almost nobody can put the whole picture together. Thus, the capacity to anticipate emerging needs or bottlenecks is very limited, although less limited than the capacity to evaluate realistically innovations to capture important future economic activities.

Sometimes, fashions sweep through city authorities – to create a conference centre, to develop a leisure complex for tourists, or for smaller towns, to create a paved market, an abattoir or a cinema, and so on – with surprisingly little prior assessment as to whether this innovation simultaneously links the city's capacities to a known existing or realistically anticipated demand. Indeed, outside the Chamber of Commerce, there are usually very few bodies with much interest in such questions.

It is here that a strengthened local authority could be important. In many countries, local government is little more than an executing arm for central government of certain limited local functions, lacking any capacity to determine its own activities or finance or to vary its activities to suit local circumstances. "Success", as Ken Davey writes, "is measured by the ability to manipulate higher powers rather than to manage one's own destiny"[79]. The often very poor record in operating and maintaining the existing capacity of public services in the city, let alone extending them to unserviced areas, is adequate comment on the weakness and poverty of much local government. In essence, there is often no effective body which simultaneously links the provision, or facilitation of the provision, of public services to the needs of economic growth, and has a powerful incentive to promote economic development, such that it extends its purview from the traditional items of concern to all the other elements underpinning the growth of productivity, from the promotion of training, of health and education facilities in poor areas, of credit to small enterprises, to the issues involved in promoting the establishment of standardized quality control mechanisms and market research for small and petty enterprises, etc.

For such an agenda, the "urban managers", composed of the local authority, the chambers of commerce and the relevant industrial, commercial, financial and professional associations, require a much more extended and accurate view of the strengths and weaknesses of the city economy in its regional, national and ultimately international markets, its competitive advantages and disadvantages. As some recent commentators note:

"Typically, local officials possess no information regarding the way local economic activity fits into the national picture – i.e. what is produced in the local region, where it is shipped and to what users, what the current cost competitiveness of local production is and how it has changed in recent years, in what subsectors of the economy national demand is likely to grow fastest in coming years, who the locality's chief competitors (national and international) are and what cost structures these competitors have"[80].

---

[79] *Strengthening municipal government: the Turkish case*, INURD, Working Paper 6, World Bank, Washington DC, May 1989, p.iii.
[80] Peterson et al., op. cit., p.49.

The vacuum in terms of information is one of the reasons that city administrations are so often taken by surprise by the patterns of development and by urbanization itself. If aid donors are frequently taken unawares by political realities in developing countries, administrations are often similarly disarmed by swift changes in economic realities.

Thus, any serious effort to seek to change the structure of city output and anticipate emerging bottlenecks in order to sustain and enhance productivity must begin with attempts to identify economic activity and monitor its change. This needs a fund of relevant and regularly updated statistics on the key elements of the city economy, focused upon their territorial distribution and interaction . In larger cities, the focus of this work might be the production, where it is not already produced, of an annual statistical yearbook for the city (a useful publication, but particularly for the promotion of the city to outside investors).

In larger cities, where there are universities and research institutes, the city authorities might usefully seek to make up for their own shortage of appropriate skills by engaging the research capacities of such bodies in co-operation with themselves. Academic staff might be induced to work on secondment for the city in establishing the data base and the policy and briefing documents that flow from it.

On the basis of this data source, and in collaboration with the relevant business organisations, it becomes possible to prepare studies of the key sectors of city economic activity and their changing markets in order to identify opportunities of future growth potential, infrastructural requirements, labour skills and capital needs, current weaknesses and proposals for action either by the businesses concerned, the local authority or through pressure on the national government. Indeed, cities increasingly need to be able to act as a pressure group for changes at the national level which will improve the economic capacity of the city (for example, by persuading the government to change import duties or export constraints).

The analysis of the changing composition of the output of goods and services and their changing location would then, in conjunction with the earlier programme of efforts to improve the existing economy, provide appropriate criteria for the planning of future infrastructural services, the appropriate regulatory regime, the needs for land etc., but now linked directly to the attempt to enhance productivity.

The rôle of private firms is crucial to any such joint endeavour, since local authorities can never be in a position to best guess what market opportunities exist or what the emerging weaknesses are. The rôle of the local authority should not be to create a mini-command economy but to increase awareness, to provide city-wide leadership, and to facilitate appropriate action[81].

Aid donors can probably be most effective in helping in the upgrading of information and advice available to city managers. They can insist on an adequate data base and provide the technical assistance to achieve this.

This programme is fairly Utopian in many developing countries today, although there are important examples of local economic initiatives in cities in developed countries. In fact, the picture in developing countries is less uniform than often supposed. The USAID Report mentioned earlier documents two successful cases – the redevelopment of inner Kingston, Jamaica, and the medium sized city of Toledo, in Parana, Brazil[82]. In Mexico, initiatives shown in many cities along the border with the United States by *municipios* and local business groups created an environment to exploit changes in Mexican and United States' import regulations for a remarkable expansion in manufacturing employment. In Guangdong province, in south China, local authorities appear to have played a crucial rôle in facilitating and promoting an extraordinary rate of industrialization and urbanization in the eighties.

Neither case can be seen separately from the peculiar geographical position of the areas concerned, the extraordinary

---

81 These ideas are explored in more detail in my MMDA: *an economic advisory unit*, The British Council, TETOC, London (mimeo), April 1986, and "Metropolitan planning in the developing countries", *Habitat International*, 7, no.3/4, pp.5–17, 1983.
82 Peterson et al., op. cit., pp.50–52.

opportunities for high growth of manufactured exports and governments willing to facilitate expansion, or at least not obstruct it. Both cases relate closely to the continuing relocation of sectors of world manufacturing capacity to developing countries. In the eighties, this has also had important effects in Bangladesh, Thailand, Malaysia, Mauritius, Indonesia, Jamaica, Dominican Republic and other countries. Much of this new capacity is located in and around cities, and often closely linked to urban facilities and suppliers. Since the relocation process seems set to continue, local authorities are likely to become increasingly important in facilitating the process. Just as coping with urbanisation and the urban environment can no longer be left safely in the hands of national governments – hence the current fashion for administrative decentralization – the same may be true of industrialization.

Financial and administrative decentralization to the city level could also be the source of creating a strong incentive to local government to take the city economy seriously. If decentralization goes with greater democracy, some measure of local accountability is introduced, and just as the economic performance of national governments becomes an important element in their political standing and survival, so also this could come about for city governments. In a more open world economy, city authorities would thus come to take on more of the attributes hitherto associated with national governments.

In keeping with this rôle, city authorities would require much greater inputs of sophisticated policy advice and monitoring. At the moment, they have almost none. So far as the city economy is concerned, this would need the creation of economic advisory or intelligence units, linking the local administration, business associations, educational and infrastructure agencies etc. Ideally this might also include greater participation by the citizens at large in deciding which economic scenarios the city should pursue[83].

---

83 For details on the role of an economic advisory unit, see the works cited in footnote 80.

The argument of this paper has been that hitherto "urban development" has tended to exclude a concern for the underlying urban economy, making it impossible for city authorities to consider directly measures to enhance urban productivity. The agenda has been broadened from the immediate issues of maintaining order and providing services, to a concern with the environment of the poor. It needs now to consider the economy proper, particularly because increased administrative decentralization and a more open world economy are likely to make the rôle of city managers much more important (however these are identified). This will require considerable inputs of technical assistance, particularly to identify the city-specific agenda of issues and continuing mechanisms to monitor the changing economy. Hitherto, local authorities have had little incentive to trouble themselves about the economy within their administration. However, decentralization with greater democracy could enforce on local authorities an increasing interest in the sources of the city's revenues as well as the citizens' income.

APPENDICES

APPENDIX ONE
Summary

Urban policy and economic development: an agenda for the 1990s
World Bank Policy Paper, 1991

Executive summary

Rapid demographic growth will add 600 million people to cities and towns in developing countries during the 1990s, about two-thirds of the expected total population increase. Of the world's 21 megacities, which will expand to have more than 10 million people, 17 will be in developing countries. With urban economic activities making up an increasing share of GDP in all countries, the productivity of the urban economy will heavily influence economic growth.

This paper analyzes the fiscal, financial, and real sector linkages between urban economic activities and macroeconomic performance. It builds on this analysis to propose a policy framework and strategy that will redefine the urban challenge in developing countries:
- First, the developing countries, the international community, and the World Bank should move toward a broader view of urban issues, a view that moves beyond housing and residential infrastructure, and that emphasizes the productivity of the urban economy and the need to alleviate the constraints on productivity.
- Secondly, with urban poverty increasing, the productivity of the

urban poor should be enhanced by increasing the demand for labour and improving access to basic infrastructure and social services.
- Thirdly, more attention should be devoted to reversing the deterioration of the urban environment, an issue receiving short shrift in the face of global environmental problems.
- Fourthly, the serious gap in understanding urban issues must be closed. With the decline in urban research during the 1980s, few countries have a sound analytical basis for urban policy.

How are the World Bank and the international community responding to these challenges? Past urban operations focused on neighbourhood interventions, such as sites and services and slum upgrading during the 1970s and municipal development and housing finance during the 1980s. Assessments of this assistance conclude that city-wide impacts have been rare and that the pace of urban growth far exceeded the scale of the urban program. Today, there is a need to focus urban operations on city-wide policy reform, institutional development, and high-priority investments, and to put the development assistance in the urban sector in the context of broader objectives of economic development and macroeconomic performance.

The challenge of urban growth

Since 1950 the world's urban population has grown from under 300 million to 1.3 billion persons, with unrelenting annual growth of 4 per cent, adding 45–50 million persons a year. Growth rates of smaller towns have been even higher as non-farm employment has supported agricultural growth. While urban settlement patterns have varied across countries, in no country have efforts to restrain migration or urban growth been successful. Secondly, cities such as Kano, Surabaya, or Guadalajara have become metropolitan areas. Today, natural increase has replaced migration as the major source of urban growth in most continents except Africa.

The forces contributing to urban growth are strong. Higher urban wages reflect the higher productivity of labour in cities where economies of scale and agglomeration have made households and enterprises more productive. This productivity growth, although beneficial, has not solved the massive urban problems of the developing world, and serious issues of urban poverty and a deteriorating urban environment remain. Many households have not found employment and income-generating activities, and many live in squatter areas unserved by essential infrastructure. In 1988 some 330 million urban residents – about a quarter of the total urban population – lived in poverty. Even if poverty is still largely rural in many countries, as the 1990 *World development report* concludes, urban poverty will become the most significant and politically explosive problem in the next century.

Past government efforts and donor assistance

Since 1972 government efforts, particularly those supported by donors, have addressed urban growth and urban poverty through low-cost investment projects in shelter, water supply, sanitation, and urban transport. Sites-and-services and slum-upgrading projects were intended to demonstrate replicable approaches that could provide benefits to the poor while recovering costs and reducing the financial burden on the public sector. Many of these projects were reasonably successful in meeting their physical project objectives; this required devoting attention to physical implementation rather than sustaining policy change and strengthening institutions. As a result, they have not had major impact on the policies of national and local governments and the broader issues of managing the urban economy. In only a few cases, such as the Kampung Improvement Program in Jakarta, have citywide impacts been achieved. Most important, because many urban programmes did not achieve sustainable policy reform and institutional development, they were not replicable. Government and donor programmes tended to divide a city into projects, improving specific neighbourhoods without improving the urban policy and institutional framework such as the functioning of citywide markets for land and housing. Government efforts have not mobilized the private sector and community initiative, but in many cases have increased the cost of private solutions through over-regulation and the rationing of scarce capital for investment.

From a broader perspective, several additional conclusions come from assessing past efforts. First, it is apparent that neither governments nor donors have sought to understand the impacts of macroeconomic policy on urban economic activities. Second, those institutions and experts working within the urban sector have not appreciated the impact of their activities on macroeconomic performance. A third dimension of this narrow perspective on the relationships between the macroeconomic and urban levels is the absence of discussion of short- versus long-term impacts of policies at one level on the other. Finally, one of the most glaring deficiencies of previous efforts has been the insufficient attention given to the issue of productivity within the urban economy. The policy framework presented in this paper seeks to address these weaknesses of previous urban policy. It also seeks to incorporate the issues of increasing urban poverty and a growing urban environmental crisis within this broader perspective.

A new policy framework:
the urban economy and macroeconomic performance

The policy framework developed in this paper distinguishes between macroeconomic policies that are managed at the national level and urban policies that are largely, though not exclusively, managed at the city level. Macroeconomic policies establish the broad economic environment for urban economic activities. They affect interest rates, direct and indirect taxes, incentives for manufacturing and trade, and the pricing of key inputs such as energy and water. The financing of national fiscal deficits absorbs credit needed for productive investment, while also increasing interest rates and contributing to inflation. Trade incentives have direct impacts on urban production, concentrating industrial investment and adding to the growth of port cities. Similarly, national strategies for education and health have direct consequences for the quality of the urban labour force. Achieving the long-term objective of improving the productivity of the urban economy thus depends heavily on the successful balancing of the many parts of macroeconomic policy.

The performance of the urban economy also affects macroeconomic performance. Three linkages – financial, fiscal, and real sector – produce significant urban impacts at the macroeconomic level. The weak condition of the financial sector in most developing countries, and particularly its difficulty in mobilizing private savings, has left most of the financing of urban investments to the public sector. Since the spending of local and provincial governments, coupled with residential capital investment by households, accounts for 10–15 per cent of GDP and 30–40 per cent of fixed capital formation in the urbanized countries of Latin America, the financing of these investments can contribute to the widespread financial distress in these countries. The fiscal linkage between the urban economy and the macroeconomy is equally important: poor local government revenue performance contributes to the consolidated budget deficit at the national level. Similarly, the absence of means to mobilize private savings for housing has resulted in large public subsidies for housing. Local government expenditures can also destabilize fragile fiscal balances. In the real sector, constraints on productivity at the city level such as infrastructure deficiencies reduce the productivity of firms and households and thus reduce the aggregate productivity of the economy.

Within this perspective, better macroeconomic management over the long term is needed to establish the parameters for urban economic growth. At the same time, the short-term disruptions in orderly macroeconomic growth have important consequences for cities. Structural adjustment policies at the macro-level are intended over the longer term to create an enabling policy environment for more productive urban economies. Such an environment would increase the efficiency of firms and households and would thus support the economy-wide adjustment and the resumption of growth. For many countries, however, these policy changes require a corresponding urban adjustment to support national economic adjustment goals. Such a process should result in more flexible institutional and regulatory regimes at the city level to adjust to new macroeconomic realities. It would affect the production of goods and services and the broad context for investment, savings, resource mobilization, and capital formation in urban areas.

Improving urban productivity

The increased importance of the urban economic activities in national production requires greater effort to improve their productivity. But improved macroeconomic management is only a necessary but not sufficient condition to improve productivity at the city level. Macroeconomic policy must also take into account the spatial dimensions of the urban economy. Economies of scale and agglomeration economies are the benefits of the concentration of urban population and economic activities; however, these economies also have costs. Key constraints such as infrastructure deficiencies, the regulatory framework governing urban markets for land and housing, weak municipal institutions, and inadequate financial services for urban development all affect these spatial dimensions and limit the productivity of firms and households in producing goods and services. The cumulative effect of these constraints is to reduce the productivity of the urban economy and its contribution to macroeconomic performance.

Infrastructure deficiencies seriously constrain the productivity of private investment in most cities in developing countries. Firms must invest significant shares of their capital in private electric power generation. Traffic congestion impedes the movement of goods and services and thus reduces the economies of agglomeration of urban markets. Some cities have more cars than telephones, while the unreliable water supplies in other urban areas constrain manufacturing. Inadequate public collection and disposal of vast quantities of solid waste add to the deterioration of air, water, and land. These public infrastructure services constitute needed *intermediate* inputs to economic activities. If such services are unavailable, private enterprises are forced to provide them on their own. That increases their total investment requirements and constrains the productivity of that investment, reducing the growth of profits, incomes, and employment, and raising prices.

A second major constraint is the heavy cost of inappropriate urban regulatory policies. Regulations affecting the establishment of productive activities significantly hinder the speed and efficiency of investment. Lengthy procedures to obtain construction permits impose heavy additional costs. Other regulations, such as those governing the markets for land and housing have less direct, but nevertheless significant impacts on productivity by decreasing the costs of industrial and commercial investment and inputs needed for production.

A third constraint on urban productivity is the weakness of municipal institutions, both financial and technical. The dominant rôle of central government in planning and financing urban infrastructure has starved local governments of financial resources. The recent financial crisis has made this situation worse, especially in Latin America where previously well established municipal institutions have withered in the absence of central government financial transfers. In a 1984 survey of 86 developing countries, property taxes averaged less than 1 per cent of total revenue. And in 19 countries between 1978 and 1986, the deficits of subnational governments (provincial and municipal) accounted on average for half the consolidated government deficit, and thus a significant percentage of GDP.

Financial dependency on central governments also affects the operation of local governments. Central control over the public investment process has undermined local commitment and capacities to operate and maintain public infrastructure and services, directly affecting the efficiency of resource use. The failure to maintain infrastructure has reached crisis proportions, and maintenance has become a developmental priority.

A fourth constraint on urban productivity is the inadequacy of financial services for urban development. Poorly developed financial sectors constrain investment in infrastructure, housing, and other urban economic activities. Week financial systems are unable to mobilize private savings and lead governments to use public resources to finance housing. The links between the financial sector and the urban economy go in both directions, as pressure for financial subsidies in housing can have macro-financial effects.

These constraints on urban productivity matter more as urban economic activities have made up a growing share of GDP in developing countries. In the short term, the resumption of economic growth will depend in part on alleviating these constraints. In the long term, the economic future of urbanized countries will be closely linked to the level and growth of the productivity of their urban economies. While the stakes are of national significance, reducing these constraints will depend heavily on local policies and institutions, such as those for managing local fiscal deficits.

To increase the productivity of the urban economy and ensure its contribution to macroeconomic performance requires actions at the national and city levels to reduce these constraints on urban productivity. Achieving this objective will require sustained policy reform and increased efforts to strengthen urban institutions. It will involve a shift in the rôle of central governments from direct providers of urban services and infrastructure to "enablers", creating a regulatory and financial environment in which private enterprises, households, and community groups can play an increasing rôle in meeting their own needs. It will also require some measure of decentralization of responsibility to municipalities for urban finance and the management of infrastructure, with adequate safeguards to ensure accountability. This will be a complex and politically difficult process, requiring the establishment of a productive and sustainable balance between local autonomy and central control.

The strategy for loosening the constraints on urban productivity has four elements which apply to regional cities of different sizes as well as the capital city:
- Strengthening the management of urban infrastructure at the city level by improving the level and composition of investment, reinforcing the institutional capacity for operation and maintenance, and seeking opportunities for greater private sector involvement.
- Improving the citywide regulatory framework to increase market efficiency and to enhance the private sector's provision of shelter and infrastructure.
- Improving the financial and technical capacity of municipal institutions through more effective division of resources and responsibilities between central and local governments.
- Strengthening financial services for urban development.

Alleviating urban poverty

Despite the efforts of governments and donors, the numbers of urban poor continue to increase as a result of demographic growth and constraints on productivity, and therefore on the growth of employment and incomes, and constrained access to services. The physical manifestations of urban poverty are evident in all cities in developing countries: vast neighbourhoods of squatters – *barriadas, bidonvilles,* and *bustees* – living outside the legal framework of the city, lacking water, sanitation, urban transport, and adequate shelter, and unserved by social services such as health and education. Poor quality of life is worsened further amidst a deteriorating local environment.

Although serious in all countries, urban poverty has become particularly problematic in countries undergoing macroeconomic adjustment. Reduced subsidies to food, water, transport, and energy in urban areas, coupled with the shifting demand for labour and transitional unemployment, have reduced urban real incomes. Lower-middle class groups have been affected most, pushed into the lower-income category until the resumption of growth leads to improved opportunities for employment, higher productivity, and increased wages. These social costs of adjustment have been particularly visible in the political arena.

These broad channels link adjustment to the incidence of poverty:
- *Wages*. Since the urban poor are especially dependent on their labour, rather than asset ownership, they bear the greatest risk when unemployment rises. Restrictive monetary and fiscal policies affect the urban poor by shrinking labour demand.
- *Prices*. Wages adjust much more slowly than the prices of goods and services as adjustment reduces absorption, and as currency devaluations impose upward pressure on import prices. Whereas the rural poor might derive some benefit from exchange devaluation, the urban poor are net losers. In addition, fiscal reform usually involves real increases in tariffs, which again tend to affect the urban poor disproportionately.
- *Public services*. Cuts in public expenditure are usually a necessary component of adjustment programmes, including reductions in public health or education which tend to have disproportionate impacts on the poor.

Managing these links between macroeconomic developments and impacts on the urban poor are important on both equity and efficiency grounds. Supporting the productive contribution of the urban poor to the urban economy will require an appropriate strategy to stimulate the demand for labour while ensuring, through provision of adequate social services and infrastructure, that the poor can take advantage of the opportunities provided. It also requires a safety net for the most vulnerable.

The challenge of urban management in the economic environment of the 1990s is to improve productivity while directly alleviating the growing incidence of urban poverty, and thereby also improving equity. As *World development report 1990* spells out, this does not require a trade-off between strategies to promote economic growth and to reduce poverty; poverty reduction is possible in part through improving productivity at the individual, household, firm, and urban levels. This approach involves directly increasing the labour intensity of productive investment and improving the human capital of the poor through better education, health, and nutrition.

To alleviate urban poverty – due to the short-term impacts of macroeconomic adjustment and the longer-term structural problems of demographic growth, low productivity, and constrained access to urban services – requires:

Managing the economic aspects of poverty, through
- Increasing the demand for the labour of the poor through government policies to encourage labour-intensive activities.
- Alleviating the structural constraints inhibiting the productivity and growth of the informal sector by reforming regulations and codes that limit the access of the poor to urban services infrastructure, credit and markets.
- Increasing the labour productivity of the poor by reducing constraints preventing labour-force participants, such as constraints on women's time, including childcare and other family responsibilities.

Managing the social aspects of poverty, through
- Increasing social-sector expenditure for human-resource development of the urban poor by providing basic services in education, health, nutrition, family planning, and vocational training.
- Increasing the access of the poor to infrastructure and housing to meet their basic needs.
- Recognizing and supporting the efforts of the poor to meet their own needs through community initiatives and local, nongovernmental organizations.

Targeting "safety net" assistance to those most vulnerable to short-term shocks, such as women who head households, through
- Directing transfers in food assistance, health care, employment, and provision of other basic needs on a short-term basis.
- Introducing measures to moderate the decline in private consumption.

Protecting the urban environment

The third area requiring attention is the emerging environmental crisis in towns and cities, a problem receiving far less attention than that going to such global environmental issues as global warming or the scarcity of water resources. Urban environmental problems add much to these global problems because of the intensity of energy and resource use and the concentration of wastes and emissions. However, while the impacts of global problems are long-term, the impacts of urban environmental problems are also short-term. These impacts on the health and productivity of individuals, households, and communities are immediate – from congestion, air and water pollution, inadequate sanitation, erratic waste collection and disposal, and the destruction of marginal lands. In 1987, less than 60 per cent of the urban population had access to adequate sanitation, and only one-third was connected to sewer systems. The impacts on local environments are visible and dangerous.

The main health risks from environmental degradation are those from pathogens in the environment, indoor air pollution, substandard housing, and industrialization. Deaths and illnesses from gastroenteric and respiratory diseases are closely linked to substandard housing and infrastructure. Diarrhoea and respiratory infections are leading killers of infants in the least developed countries. Acute respiratory infections in children and chronic bronchitis in women are closely linked to inadequate housing and especially smoke exposure. Air pollution and exposure to toxic chemicals also exact a heavy health toll.

Environmental degradation also has long-term effects on resources, threatening not only human health and ecosystems but also the sustainability of development. Groundwater depletion or contamination can be serious, as can the loss of land resources when the development of wetlands, coastal zones, or erosion prone areas is not controlled. Hazardous industrial wastes are another major concern, since it is difficult to monitor discharges and ensure that they are not put into sewers or landfills, and since few developing countries have the facilities needed to treat and dispose of hazardous wastes. Many environmental problems with national and international implications – such as emissions of carbon dioxide, sulphur dioxide, and nitrous oxide – have their origin in urban industry and transport.

Despite these local problems, they are poorly understood in developing countries and require a major research and development effort to identify effective approaches to their solution. To develop sustainable approaches to the management of the urban environment requires:
- Raising global awareness of the urban environment crisis, in order to develop the political support for action.
- Improving the information base and understanding of the dynamics

of environmental deterioration in urban areas.
- Developing city-specific urban environmental strategies that respond to the circumstances of individual cities.
- Identifying programmes of curative action for cities to redress the most serious environmental consequences of past public policies and private behaviour.
- Formulating effective national and urban policies and incentives to prevent further environmental deterioration.

Increasing understanding of urban issues

After extensive investments in urban research during the 1970s, the quantity of urban research fell sharply in developed and developing countries in the 1980s. The scarcity of public resources for universities and independent research institutes, coupled with increasing interest in such other subjects as debt and adjustment, has led to a decline in urban research capacity just when many urban policy questions are becoming increasingly important. The need is thus great for increasing research on urban issues. The priority areas for research include the linkages between the urban economy and macroeconomic aggregates, the internal efficiencies of cities and urban productivity, the urban poor and the informal sector, the financing of urban investments, the rôle of government in the urban development process, and the urban environment. In response to this situation, the Ford Foundation is undertaking an assessment of urban research in the developed and developing countries during 1991-92. This assessment will be the basis for discussion in 1992 of international support for urban research.

Implementing the new agenda

While the World Bank and the international community cannot be expected to fully satisfy the enormous demands from developing countries for assistance in the urban sector, a major external effort should be made to increase local capacity in the 1990s to address these needs. The proposed agenda, with much greater emphasis on national and city-wide policies and institutional development is going to be much more costly, especially in terms of up-front policy analysis and institutional development. These types of activities have been funded increasingly by the bilateral agencies and UNDP-financed, Bank-executed programmes such as the Urban Management Program. This programme and other bilateral and multilateral initiatives should help meet technical assistance needs.

In response to the requests of member countries and heightened appreciation of urban problems in the regions, the World Bank's urban activities are expected to grow. Increased assistance will be accompanied by an intensified effort to improve the impact of lending by explicitly reorienting its emphasis through policy and institutional development in most countries. Bank urban lending will shift from provision of neighbourhood investments in shelter infrastructure to national and city level policy reform, institutional development, and infrastructure investments to support a country's overall development. These operations will focus on improving the national and city level policy and institutional frameworks and will involve increased policy content, for example, reform of central–local financial relations as part of strengthening municipal institutions or regulatory reform as an integral part of lending for housing finance. Public sector investments in infrastructure will continue but will include support for operations and maintenance at the city level, as well as rehabilitation where needed to maintain the reliability of services. The analytical foundations of urban assistance will also be strengthened, including assessments of land and housing markets, regulatory audits, and analysis of central–local financial relations.

An appreciation of the economic and political significance of urbanization in the developing countries is emerging slowly in the private sector, the official donor community, and the Bank itself. This appreciation is reflected in growing lending programmes, increasing requests for urban assistance to bilateral agencies, and the proliferation of discussions in many forums on urban infrastructure, environment issues, and growing movements of citizen involvement in the solution of local problems.

Cities, people and poverty: urban development co-operation for the 1990s
UNDP Strategy Paper, 1991

Overview

The relentless growth of cities is inevitable and irreversible. Standing at 2.4 billion in 1990, the world's urban population will rise to 3.2 billion in 2000 and 5.5. billion in 2025. The developing countries' share in these totals – 63 per cent in 1990 – will rise to 71 per cent in 2000 and 80 per cent in 2025. By the end of the 1990s, Mexico City will have almost 25 million people, and Sao Paulo almost 22 million. Calcutta, Shanghai and Bombay will each have more than 15 million residents. And 13 other cities in developing countries will have more than 10 million: Seoul, Cairo, Dacca, Delhi, Lagos, Beijing, Bangkok, Manila, Jakarta, Karachi, Tianjin, Buenos Aires and Rio de Janeiro. In addition to the growth of these megacities, the growth of small and medium-sized cities will also continue.

For decades this growth was seen as inimical to human development. Cities already benefited disproportionately from national development efforts, urban development was more costly than rural development and the growth of cities merely added to unemployment; these were the prevailing views. So, government policy and international assistance gave greater attention to the countryside.

Today the growth of cities is seen increasingly as essential for human development. The GNP per capita numbers are much higher in countries with more of their people in cities. The economies of scale in large cities generate goods and services far in excess of their share of the total population. This higher productivity of urban labour means that wages are higher and employment opportunities greater, especially for women. Cities also give their residents the knowledge and skills to become more productive – a propitious cycle. Cities promote the modernization of agriculture, provide markets for farm goods and reduce pressure on the land.

Despite the obvious efficiency advantages of cities, the negative consequences of urbanization for low-income groups are overwhelming. Simply, many city dwellers in developing countries live in crushing poverty – more than 300 million, or a quarter of all those in urban areas. That number promises to swell. By 2000 more than half the developing countries' poor will be in cities and towns: 90 per cent in Latin America, 45 per cent in Asia and 40 per cent in Africa. Their living conditions are alarming, for their numbers far outstrip the supplies of water, waste removal, transport and clinics. Nor do they and their richer neighbours help the environment – using natural resources and discharging wastes in disturbing quantity, with all the predictable effects.

The paper is about the new urban agenda for the 1990s, which will extend beyond GNP growth in cities to focus on alleviating poverty, on strengthening local government and decentralizing power and resources to cities, on providing housing, infrastructure and essential services for the poor, on improving the urban environment and on promoting the private sector, nongovernmental organizations (NGOs), and gender concerns. It is about local initiatives, human development as a macro-policy concern and the behaviour of bureaucracies – factors often overlooked in the past when governments of developing countries and donors focused on economic growth as the main objective of human endeavour.

Responses so far

Government policies and international assistance packages have followed three successive (and overlapping) lines. First, they tried to control the pace and pattern of urban growth. To slow the pace, some governments tried requiring identification cards to dissuade migrants from coming to the cities. Others tried bussing urban dwellers back. Still others tried making villages more economically viable. With such efforts doing little or nothing to stem the urban tide, governments turned to the pattern of growth. Growth poles came into vogue, with frontier development, until it was obvious that few wanted to stay in artificially created settlements and business centres along large transport corridors. Rural industrialization efforts and locational incentives for industry met similar fates.

Secondly, governments and donors tried to provide low-cost shelter and services. When bulldozing squatter settlements did nothing to discourage people from scratching out a living in cities, governments tried providing public shelter. But with demand way ahead of supply, they had little choice but to accept slums and squatters, and to provide basic services. Then, as even these basic services began to break down, governments gave squatters and slum dwellers more responsibility for maintaining their settlements, along with tenure, to encourage improvements and investments. Of late, these efforts to provide shelter and services have turned to providing access to credit, ensuring that public housing is affordable, giving people a say in the programmes being developed and coming up with more suitable building materials and techniques.

Thirdly, efforts were focused on strengthening local government. The big national programmes of the 1960s and 1970s undercut the authority and capability of local government. Central public works agencies then gave up some of their control to metropolitan authorities, to run multi-sectoral projects. But these authorities, designed to co-ordinate and supervise the work of sectoral agencies and local government, soon took them over, to implement foreign-funded projects speedily. Almost everywhere in the developing world, local government remains unsurprisingly weak. That is why much international assistance in the past few years has begun to focus on upgrading the management of urban institutions and increasing the mobilization of local resources for urban development.

Since 1971 UNDP has invested more than $3 billion to support broad urban projects – for schools, clinics, power, telecommunications, and transport and regional planning. It has also provided nearly $250 million for targeted urban projects, for planning, for housing, for infrastructure and services and for activities to generate income. Many of these projects executed by the UN Centre for Human Settlements (Habitat or UNCHS) and other multilateral agencies were to be catalysts for programmes and projects funded by other international organizations, like the World Bank, regional development banks and bilateral donors. Those projects directed the public's attention to issues of urban development. They created new processes to deal with urban problems and helped solve some of them. But a close evaluation shows that they did far too little to strengthen the capabilities of institutions responsible for cities and towns.

Agenda for the 1990s

The relationship between the growth of cities and the economies has been close, and will remain so. Urban development is thus synonymous with economic development. But if it is also to be synonymous with human development, centred on people, we need to look beyond economic growth. We need to look to political realities, income generating opportunities and targeted assistance for the poor, and restructuring international aid and national budgets to focus on human priority areas. If cities are to contribute to human development, we need institutional mechanisms that promote equitable growth, encourage gender-sensitive, participatory development and improve the financial and managerial capacity of cities and towns.

Within the above framework for urban policy, five urban challenges stand out as the most pressing for governments and form the urban agenda for the 1990s:
- alleviate poverty;
- provide the poor with infrastructure, shelter and services;
- improve the urban environment;
- promote the private sector and NGOs.

Strategies for dealing with the five challenges are as follows:

First, urban poverty should be alleviated by promoting income-generating activities for the poor, by promoting the urban informal sector, by expanding jobs in smaller cities, by encouraging the organization of the poor at the community and neighbourhood levels and by promoting the participation of women.

Secondly, it will be essential to promote "enabling" strategies for infrastructure and services by improving the poor's access to land, finance and building materials, by formulating national strategies for shelter and by targeting the supply of basic urban services.

Thirdly, improvements to the urban environment will be achieved by improving the living conditions of the poor, by improving energy use, solid waste management and alternative transport and by enacting laws for environmental management and incorporating the environment in urban planning.

Fourthly, efforts to strengthen local government and administration should focus on decentralizing power and resources to municipalities and market towns by bolstering the capacity of local authorities (and communities) to plan, manage and finance urban programmes and by improving the systems for land management and information.

Fifthly, to draw on the full complement of human energy in cities, the ingenuity of the private sector and NGOs will be tapped by encouraging private provision of urban housing and infrastructure, by privatizing such urban services as transport and waste management and by involving NGOs in local projects to alleviate poverty and improve the environment.

UNDP's strategy for urban development assistance in the 1990s

To improve the effectiveness of assistance for urban development, UNDP will focus more on human development. Specifically, UNDP's urban assistance in the Fifth Programming Cycle 1992–6 will build and strengthen national and local capabilities in the five areas identified in the urban agenda for the 1990s.

The agendas of several multilateral organizations will complement the UNDP's approach to urban development as outlined above. UNCHS is promoting the rôle of cities in sustainable development, strengthening urban management, and implementing the Global Strategy for Shelter to the Year 2000. UNCHS promotes enabling strategies for mobilizing human, material and financial resources and marshals the input of local authorities, community groups and other NGOs in the development of housing sanitation and other projects. In its approach to urban development for the 1990s, the World Bank is spotlighting the need to improve urban productivity, develop effective responses to urban environmental problems, alleviate urban poverty and expand urban research. The Bank's urban lending is projected to grow significantly in fiscal 1991-93, with the bulk of lending for urban policy reform. The UN Children's Fund (UNICEF) focuses on community initiatives to improve the access of the urban poor (especially women and children) to basic urban services. The UN Fund for Population Activities (UNFPA) has two types of projects – national and global/inter-regional – focusing on NGOs, child survival, problems of aging and enabling strategies. The World Health Organization (WHO) recommends (1) promoting the collection and dissemination of data on health and urban development, (2) strengthening the Healthy Cities Project worldwide and (3) facilitating technical co-operation in developing countries. Rapidly increasing lending by regional development banks for urban housing and infrastructure is expected to continue.

The integrated character of UNDP's new urban policy framework will hinge on the links between the country programme and regional and global projects. The effective management of urban areas will, along with other human development concerns, be examined when the government and UNDP prepare the country programme, all in the context of the country's human development priorities and targets. If urban issues are part of the country programme, a programme approach (rather than a project approach) will be used to provide assistance.

Over the past 20 years, when the developing world's urban population more than doubled and more than a billion people were added to cities and towns, UNDP devoted only about 2 per cent of its spending to targeted urban development projects. In view of this modest impact, UNDP will in the Fifth Programming Cycle:

- increase its technical co-operation for dealing with urban problems;
- operationalize human development in the urban setting by acting in the five priority areas identified in the urban agenda for the 1990s;
- experiment with new approaches to improve the efficiency and effectiveness of UNDP's technical co-operation for urban development.

During the next cycle, programming missions to prepare five year programmes of assistance for urban development will become the norm in countries where the government has asked UNDP to provide technical assistance for dealing with its urban problems, or where several urban projects are already under way.

The basic thrust of UNDP support for regional and global projects will be to provide regional and global forums for examining innovative policies and tools for urban development, to strengthen regional institutions for operational research and technical co-operation, to build the regional, national and municipal capacity for urban management and human settlement through exchanges of innovative policies and practices, and to relate directly to national development objectives.

UNDP – in collaboration with UNCHS and the World Bank – has a crucial rôle in co-ordinating international development assistance. By facilitating a dialogue among multilateral agencies, bilateral donors and NGOs, UNDP can provide a forum for identifying critical issues of urban development and forming creative partnerships to address these issues at the regional and country levels.

During the Fifth Programming Cycle, the Bureau for Programme Policy and Evaluation (BPPE) of UNDP will use Special Programme Resources (SPR) to develop new products and modalities to improve UNDP technical co-operation. These products will include Programme Advisory Notes on the urban environment and the informal sector, regional seminars on private sector initiatives, regional networks of national training and research institutions and strategic approaches to promote the rôle of women in urban development programmes. The products will be mainstreamed into UNDP activities, especially at the country level.

Equipped with broader policies and programmes that integrate country, regional and global efforts, UNDP will play a catalytic rôle in national and local capacity-building and resource mobilization for urban development.

These efforts – all in the framework of the above strategy for the next programming cycle – will enable UNDP to be more effective in co-operating with governments of developing countries to cope with the enormous challenges and opportunities in the cities of the 1990s.

APPENDIX TWO
The urban agenda for the nineties and the experience of national urban policy

Workshop programme
Development Planning Unit
9 Endsleigh Gardens, London WC1H 0ED
Tel: (+44 71) 388 7581   Fax: (+44 71) 387 4541

Thursday, 21 November 1991

9.30am   Chairman: **Patrick Wakely**, Development Planning Unit

Opening address
Tim Lankester, Permanent Secretary, Overseas Development Administration, Foreign and Commonwealth Office

Urban policy and economic development: the agenda
Michael Cohen, Urban Development Division, World Bank

11.00am   Chairman: **Paul Ackroyd**
Overseas Development Administration

The challenge of urbanization
G. Shabbir Cheema, Principal Technical Adviser, Bureau for Programmes Policy and Evaluation, UNDP

Discussion

WORKSHOP PROGRAMME

2.00pm   Chairman: **Nigel Harris**, Development Planning Unit

Responses from selected representatives of countries which have undertaken or commissioned urban development strategies

3.45pm   Chairman: **Kenneth Watts**, Development Planning Unit

Discussion

Summing up and reply
Mark Hildebrand, Technical Co-operation Division, UNCHS

6.00pm   RECEPTION
Sir Robin Ibbs KBE
Chairman of Council, University College London

Friday, 22 November 1991

9.30am   Chairman: **PSA Sundaram**

National urban development strategies: experience from the past
Kenneth Watts, Development Planning Unit

Problems and issues of implementation
Nigel Harris, Development Planning Unit

11.00am   Chairman: **Hendropranoto Suselo**

Response
Dr Emiel Wegelin, Head, Department of Human Settlements Economics, NE

Discussion

2.00pm   Chairman: **Jaya Appalraju**

The issues of urban management
Mark Hildebrand, UNCHS

Discussion

3.45pm   Chairman: **Sherif Hassan Kamel**

Summing up and reply
Alfred Van Huyk

APPENDIX THREE
Participants

Paul Ackroyd	Economic Adviser, ODA, London
Ove Anderson	Director, Swedeplan, Sweden
Jaya Appalraju	Adviser, Swedeplan/DPU, Zimbabwe
Sarah Atkinson	London School of Hygiene and Tropical Medicine, London
Azizan Bin Hussain	Deputy Director General Sectoral, Economic Planning Unit, Prime Minister's Department, Malaysia
Henry Boldrick	Acting Chief, Infrastructure Division, World Bank
Shabbir Cheema	Principal Technical Adviser, Technical Advisory Division, UNDP
Michael Cohen	Chief, Urban Development Division, World Bank
Alan Coverdale	Head, Asia & Oceans Economic Department, ODA, London
Mahmoud Musa Elsadig	Chief, Infrastructure & Industry Development, Policy Division, African Development Bank, Côte d'Ivoire
Rosalind Eyben	Social Development Adviser, Overseas Development Administration, London
Luis Fernandez	Urban Planner, GTZ, Venezuela
Fitz Ford	Senior Economist, Urban Management Programme, Urban Development Division, World Bank

PARTICIPANTS

Michel Fouad	Former Chairman, General Organisation for Physical Planning, Egypt
Paul Garner	London School of Hygiene and Tropical Medicine, London
Kazumi Goto	Chief Representative, Japanese Overseas Economic Cooperation Fund, London
Tony Gregory	Natural Resources Institute, Chatham, England
Lawrence Hannah	Principal Economist, Urban Development Division, World Bank
Jorge Hardoy	President, IIED-America Latina, Argentina
Nigel Harris	Professor of Development Planning, Development Planning Unit, London
Arif Hasan	Representative, Asian Coalition for Housing Rights, Pakistan
Hendropranoto Suselo	Departemen Pekerjaan Umum, Indonesia
Mark Hildebrand	Chief, Technical Cooperation Division, UNCHS
William Housego-Woolgar	Overseas Development Administration
Laszlo Huszar	Development Planning Unit, London
Hidetoshi Irigaki	Representative, Japanese Overseas Economic Cooperation Fund, London
Sherif Hassan Kamel	Chairman, General Organisation for Physical Planning, Egypt
Atta Ullah Khan	Director, Environment Control, Faisalabad Development Authority, Pakistan
Theo Kolstee	Head, Spearhead on Combating Urban Poverty, Ministry of Foreign Affairs, Netherlands
Andrezj Krassowski	Principal Officer, UNOV, Austria
Kry Beng Hong	Vice President, Comité des Peuples de la Ville de Phnom Penh, Cambodia
André Lagrange	General Manager, Development Bank of Southern Africa, South Africa
Tim Lankester	Permanent Secretary, Overseas Development Administration, Foreign and Commonwealth Office, London
David Leibson	Assistant Director, Agency for International Development, USA
Timo Linkola	Chief Engineer, Physical Planning and Building Department, Ministry of

PARTICIPANTS

Patrick McAuslan	Environment, Finland Urban Management Programme, UNCHS, Kenya
Desmond McNeill	Adviser, NORAD, Norway
Steffan Mildner	GTZ, Germany
Peter Paproski	Senior Programme Officer, CIDA, Canada
Michael Parkes	Senior Architecture and Planning Adviser, ODA, London
Pervez Tahir	Chief, Policy & Planning, Ministry of Planning & Development, Government of Pakistan
Jonas Rabinovitch	Adviser, IPPUC, Brazil
Eduardo Rojas	Sanitation and Urban Development Division, Inter-American Development Bank, USA
Manuel Sevilla	FUPROVI, Costa Rica
K. C. Sivaramakrishnan	Former Secretary, Ministry of Urban Development, Government of India
P. S. A. Sundaram	Joint Secretary, Ministry of Urban Development, India
Dr Paul Syagga	Director, Housing Research Development Unit, Kenya
John Turner	Director, AHAS, London
Al Van Huyck	Asfield Management Group, USA
Patrick Wakely	Director, Development Planning Unit, University College London
Kenneth Watts	Senior Adviser, Development Planning Unit, University College London
Emiel Wegelin	Head, Department of Human Settlements Economics, Netherlands Economic Institute, Netherlands
Gu Wenxuan	Senior Urban Planner, Department of Urban Planning, Ministry of Construction, China
Jonathan Zamchiya	Director, Department of Physical Planning, Ministry of Local Government, Zimbabwe

INDEX

Abidjan xvi
Accra 102
adjustment, see structural adjustment
Africa
  sub-Saharan ix, xii, xviii–xix, 17, 20, 32, 68, 81, 94–5, 97, 107, 117, 184, 200, 213
  South, see South Africa
  West 16
agriculture xvii, xix, 10, 45, 54, 58, 64, 80, 135, 160, 161 n, 200, 212
  output xvii, 142
  policy 136
aid xix, xx, xxi
  agencies xx, xxii, 49, 181
  donors xx, xxi, xxii, 5, 36, 46, 79, 81, 174 n, 182, 192, 193
  programmes xxiii
Appalraju Jaya 54, 58, 103
Asia 20, 31, 33, 68, 82, 95, 213
  Southeast 97

Bangkok 16, 70, 136, 137, 139 n, 142, 143, 146, 152, 163, 212
Bangladesh 30, 61–2, 72, 157, 194
Beijing 212
Bogota 178
Bombay 48, 53, 71, 81, 82, 89, 180 n, 212
Brazil 15, 19, 20, 21, 64, 80, 104, 175 n, 193
Buenos Aires 212
building codes 13, 30 (see regulatory regimes)
bustee improvement 18

Cairo 46, 113, 141, 212
Calcutta xx, 18, 53, 107–8, 212
Cambodia 139
capital xvii, xx, xxi, 22, 23, 74, 91, 114, 117, 135, 145, 162, 165, 184, 192, 201, 203
  budget 179
  market 178
Casablanca xvi
Cd Juarez 80
centralization 76 ff., 80, 81, 90, 180
centralized 147
Cheema, Shabbir xxiv, 1, 24–32, 39–42, 60–62, 72, 110–12
China xii, xv, 20, 47, 81, 149 n, 193
cities, city vii, xi, xii, xiv ff., 1, 2, 10–13, 16 ff., 25 ff., 33, 35 ff., 39, 55, 58, 63–4, 65, 71 ff., 81, 83, 86, 91, 96, 98, 100 ff., 107, 109, 117 ff., 124 ff.; in Egypt 46, China 47, Pakistan 47, 53, Thailand 152, 159
  economy 183–6, 186 ff., 190, 191, 203 ff.
  government, see government
  secondary 53, 126, 183
  size 53
  Thai classification of 130
  capital 137, 138
Civic Associations, "Civics" (in

225

INDEX

South Africa) 55 ff.
Cohen, Michael (Mike) xxiv, 1, 9–24, 36–9, 44, 50–53, 57–9, 63, 72, 75, 79, 80, 87–9, 108–10, 113, 114
community-based organizations (CBOs) 55 ff., 57, 100, 101, 103, 104, 105–6, 107, 111
conditionality 14, 29, 82, 87
Congo xv
corruption xv, 84, 89, 111
Côte d'Ivoire xvi
country consultation 102 ff., 104
credit 184, 191
  allocation 58
  policies 135
Curitiba 59

Davey, Ken 148–9 n, 149 (and note), 159 n, 162 n, 163, 171, 190
debt xv, 178
  in Latin America, 15
decentralize, decentralization xiv, 14, 32, 34, 37, 38, 39–41, 45, 47, 49, 52, 55, 73, 76–7, 81 ff., 86 ff., 109 ff., 142 ff., 155, 159–62, 163, 170, 180, 185, 194–5, 206, 215 ff.
Delhi 14, 53, 212
developed countries xiv, xx, xxv, 36, 49, 60, 193
developing countries vii, xi, xii, xiii, xiv, xv, xvi, xx, xxii, xxv, 1, 4, 5, 21–2, 24, 26 ff., 36, 40, 45, 49, 51–2, 60, 62 ff., 67, 74, 91, 97, 102, 110, 115, 173 ff., 185, 192 ff., 199, 209
development vii, xviii, xx, 2, 4, 9, 16, 25, 60, 70, 75, 125, 131, 135, 138, 143, 152 ff., 156, 164, 169, 190, 191 n, 192
  assistance 9, 22

community 3–4
control 87
costs 55
human, *see* human
policy 10, 85
urban, *see* urban
DAC (OECD) 4
Development Planning Unit vii, xxii, 1, 2, 109, 113, 114, 119
Disraeli, Benjamin xiii
Dominican Republic 194

economic development xv, xvi, xvii, xx, xxi, 9, 29, 43, 75, 86, 87, 117, 137, 141, 147, 173–4, 179, 188, 191, 200; *see* development
Economic Intelligence Unit (city-level) 86, 194
Ecuador 149
education xv, xxiv, 3, 15, 16, 18, 25, 97, 110, 113, 114, 128, 158, 177, 178, 186–8, 191, 202, 207
efficiency, efficient 12, 33, 37, 57, 78, 83, 84, 87, 92, 109, 116, 119, 124, 125, 137, 140, 141, 143, 144, 153, 167, 176, 187, 189, 201, 204
Egypt 46–7, 118, 134, 137, 140–41, 159, 163, 171
electricity 13, 71, 115, 129. 142, 204; *see* energy, power
employment xiv, xvi ff., 25, 28, 54, 75, 134, 135, 171, 174, 176, 178, 186, 187, 188, 193, 200, 201, 204, 207
  in small enterprise 46
enabling xxi, 1, 3, 29, 30, 37, 76, 78, 89, 215 ff.; *see* facilitating
energy 10, 92, 104, 142, 177, 184, 202, 206
Engels, Friedrich xiii
environment xxi, xxii, 18–20, 25,

INDEX

26, 30–31, 51, 52, 53, 58, 62, 74, 77, 81, 83, 90, 92, 95, 107, 109, 112, 113, 124, 137, 145, 147, 176, 178, 183, 187, 188, 194, 195, 200 ff., 208–10, 212 ff.
  management of 9, 67, 175
  -al deterioration/degradation xii, 4, 143
  conditions 23, 186
  costs 139
  economics 77, 186
  health 101
  pollution 144
Environmental Impact Fund (Thailand) 138
Environmental Management Act, 1982 (Indonesia) 138
equitable 146, 154
equity 44, 52, 83, 109, 116–7, 145, 153
exports xviii, 48, 82, 89, 90, 135, 136, 184, 192–3
External Support Agencies 65, 66

facilitating 78, 111, 194, 195
  see enabling
finance 14–15, 78, 97, 100, 126, 164 ff., 177, 180, 187, 189, 190, 199, 202–3, 204–5
  development 163–4
  distribution of 153–4, 157
  system 14–15
  stability 148
Ford, J. Fitz 82, 89, 95, 108, 182 n
formal sector xvii, 34, 54, 57, 65
France xvi, 96
Frankfurt 79
functional urban areas 161

Ghana 102

governance 2, 64
government vii, xii ff., xxi ff., xxv, 1, 2, 10, 14, 15, 21, 25, 28 ff., 33–4, 36 ff., 43, 47 ff., 55, 60, 62, 63, 65 ff., 75, 76, 79 ff., 85, 88 ff., 94 ff., 99, 102, 104 ff., 111 ff., 123 ff., 154, 156–8, 162, 168 ff., 178, 185 ff., 212 ff.
  local (city) - (authority) 2, 14, 31–2, 40, 56, 64 ff., 72, 73, 76, 78, 80, 81, 86, 87, 90, 91, 98, 100, 102, 107, 111 ff., 116, 123, 126, 132, 142, 147, 148–50, 151 n, 154, 155–5, 158, 159–62, 163 ff., 167 ff., 170, 180 ff., 201 ff., 213 ff.
    in Pakistan 47, Indonesia 49, South Africa 55
  entrepreneurial 78–9, 81, 189
  municipal, *see* municipal
  relations, central–local 14, 37
growth xxi, 10, 15, 16, 20, 46, 52, 74, 81, 82, 89, 90, 97, 114, 125, 131, 137, 139, 141, 143, 144, 147, 152, 158, 168, 169, 170, 173, 179, 180, 203, 207
Guadalajara 200
Guangdong 81, 90, 193

Harare 94
Harris, Nigel xi–xxv, 73–82, 86, 87, 88, 89–92, 95, 112, 113, 138 n, 173–94
Hasan, Arif 33, 54, 64, 103, 107
health 3, 13, 15, 16, 18, 25, 83, 88, 97, 100, 108–9, 110, 128, 158, 159, 162 n, 176, 178, 186, 188, 191, 202, 207, 208, 209
Hendropranoto Suselo (Hendro) 43, 69, 82, 109
hierarchy, *see* urban hierarchy

INDEX

Hildebrand, Mark xxiv, 60, 62–8, 93–5, 103, 106–7, 108
Hoselitz, Bert xvi
housing xx, xxi, 17, 29, 35, 37, 50, 51, 52, 74, 83, 87, 88, 115, 116, 118, 134, 144, 175 n, 176, 177, 186, 199, 201, 203, 204, 208, 213, 214
   in South Africa 56–9
   finance 200
Howard, Ebenezer xiii
human development 25, 27, 41, 62, 110, 174, 215 ff.
   in Indonesia 44
Hungary 38
Huyk, Al Van 112–19

imbalances (population) xiv
import(s) xvii, 78, 135, 184, 192, 193
   substitution (strategy) xvii, xviii, 135, 136, 184
income(s) xvi, xviii, xix, 25, 28, 45, 84, 116, 134, 149 n, 150, 162, 186, 187, 201, 204, 206
   distribution 16, 125
India xv, xvi, 35, 47–9, 53, 54–5, 68, 97, 185 n
Indonesia xv, 18, 28, 29, 43–6, 49, 60, 85, 86, 129–30, 135, 137, 138, 141, 142, 145, 151–2, 158, 160, 164, 171, 175 n, 194
industrialization (strategies) xvii, xviii, 134, 194
   in Indonesia 45
industry xvii, xix, 10, 135, 137, 143, 145, 146, 153, 176, 177
informal sector xviii, xix, 26, 28, 34, 54, 57, 65, 75, 179, 208
infrastructure xx, 10, 20, 21, 29, 31, 34, 37, 48, 53, 54, 67, 72, 77–8, 83, 87 ff., 95, 100, 126, 129, 137, 138 n, 141, 145 ff., 150 ff., 154 n, 158 ff., 174, 175 ff., 186, 187, 192 ff., 199 ff., 213
   in Indonesia 44 ff., 49, 141, 166–7, India 55, Thailand 143, Malaysia 144
   deficiencies in 11–13, 17
   development policy 166 ff.
   World Bank review 175
inmigration xv
   in Egypt 46
Integrated Urban Infrastructure Development Programme(Indonesia) 49, 86, 151, 160, 161
IMF 10
institutions, institutional xxi, 19, 22, 23, 32, 37, 39, 46, 49, 50, 55, 59, 60, 61, 65, 67, 76, 84, 98, 99, 100, 102, 104, 110, 112, 115, 118, 135, 174, 179, 182, 200, 201
   in Indonesia 44 ff.
   assessment 23
   framework 19, 20, 39, 65, 79, 157, 161
investment 12, 15, 20, 21, 23, 37, 47, 72, 88, 91, 110, 114, 123, 126, 129, 130, 132, 135, 140, 141, 142, 143, 147, 150, 152, 153, 156, 162, 163 ff., 185, 200, 201, 202, 203, 204–5
Ivory Coast (Côte d'Ivoire) 51

Jakarta 139, 142, 201, 212
Jamaica 194
Java 141, 142

Kampong Improvement Program 18, 201
Kano 200
Karachi 86, 104, 113, 129, 141, 212

INDEX

Kenya ix, 155
Kingston, Jamaica 80, 193
Korea 69, 130, 138 n, 144, 154 n
see South Korea

labour xvi ff., xvii ff., 16, 17, 21, 37, 53, 62, 74, 77, 78, 117, 187, 188, 192, 200, 202, 206, 208, 212
   intensive 17, 37
   division of 37
Lagos 12, 212
land 19, 30, 46, 55, 67, 74, 75, 87, 95, 100, 102, 115, 144, 175, 176, 179, 186, 193, 201, 204, 209
   in Egypt 159
   -use (control) xiv, 75
Lankester, Tim xxiii, 1 ff., 12, 62, 69, 102
Latin America 14, 15, 20, 35, 68, 82, 84, 95, 203, 204, 213
less developed countries, *see* developing countries
liberalization 78
   in India 48
Lille xx
Lima 64, 139, 188
Lipton, Michael xvii
local government, *see* government, local
Lome 94
London xii, xxv, 74, 77, 79, 83
low income 16
low-income countries, *see* developing countries
Local Initiative Facility for Urban Environment 31

macroeconomic xix, 20, 45, 48, 77, 79, 80, 82, 147–8, 169, 174 n, 184, 199, 200, 202, 203 ff.
Madras 53, 74–5, 86, 174

Malaysia 81, 131, 136, 144, 152, 156, 167, 171, 194
management xxi, 26, 32, 61, 64, 83, 86, 93, 96, 97, 102, 112, 114, 117, 124, 125, 143, 149, 151 n, 152 n, 155, 156, 164, 169, 181
   environmental 19
   macroeconomic 9
   urban, *see* urban
Manila xv, 139, 212
manufacturing, manufactured xii, xvi, xvii, 77, 80, 82, 90, 130, 135, 189, 193–4, 202, 204
market(s) 17, 35, 36, 78, 83, 84, 91, 116, 117, 125, 128, 130, 131, 135, 143, 145, 159, 165, 167, 178, 183, 188, 189, 192, 193, 212
Mauritius 194
McAuslan, Patrick 33, 93, 95–103, 103, 107–108
megacities vii, 21, 22, 212
metropolitan (regions, cities) xii, 48, 55, 56, 116, 137, 144, 200
Mexico xix, 13, 15–16, 23, 51, 80–81, 89, 90, 193
Mexico City 212
migrants xii, xiv, xvi ff., 153, 179
migration xiv, xv, xvi ff., 134, 200
Mozambique 29, 30
municipal, municipalities 13, 32, 37, 40, 61, 64, 83, 86, 93, 96, 97, 102, 112, 114, 117, 124, 125, 143, 149, 155, 156, 164, 169, 181
   development 37, 65, 176, 200
   development fund 164–5
   finance 67, 83, 95, 98, 175
   government 148, 159, 167, 176, 204–5

229

INDEX

management 151 n, 152 n

National Urban Development Strategy 119, 123–72
national urban policy xxii, 43 ff., 107, 110, 108, 111, 119, 159, 182, 208, 213, 216
  in Egypt 46–7, 51, 128, 134
Nepal 177 n
Niger xv, 17
Nigeria xi, 12, 13, 37, 38, 71, 77, 97, 107, 176
non-governmental organizations (NGOs) xxi, xxiv, 31, 34, 35, 57, 64, 94, 100, 101, 103, 105–6, 107, 110, 111, 182, 208, 213, 216

output xx, 78, 125, 175, 176, 179, 181, 183, 184, 186, 187 ff., 192
ODA vii, viii, ix, xx, xxii, 1, 2, 3, 105
over-urbanization xvi ff., 54ff., 136 ff., 184

Pakistan 10, 14, 47, 85, 129, 132, 141, 150, 151 n, 166, 171
Paris xvi, 63, 79, 83, 93, 95
participation xxi, 18, 27, 32–4, 38, 84–5, 88, 159, 162
Peru 13, 89
policy vii, xii ff., xvii, xxi–iii, 3–5, 9, 16 ff., 21 ff., 29, 34, 35, 37, 43 ff., 59, 60, 63, 64, 66, 67, 69, 71, 99 ff., 104, 109–10, 111, 117, 130, 158, 159, 167, 169, 170, 174, 178 ff., 199 ff.
  development 10
  dialogue 4, 22, 30, 33, 41, 64, 67, 68, 82, 84
  formulation 70 ff.
  national urban 123–72

politics, political xxii, 14, 24, 35 ff., 39, 44, 55, 59, 60, 63, 72, 74 ff., 80 ff., 87, 89, 90, 91, 94, 103ff., 109–10, 111, 112 ff., 116, 117, 140, 146, 156 ff., 161, 174 n, 178 ff., 183, 185, 194, 201
poor xix, xx, 15 ff., 17, 26, 28, 30, 35, 45, 46, 48, 57, 58, 75, 80, 81, 83, 84, 115, 116, 118, 124, 128, 150, 174, 176, 179, 180, 188, 195, 200, 206 ff.; *see* poverty
poverty xiv, xvi, xxi, xxii, xxiv, 1, 3, 4, 49 ff., 51, 52, 54, 61, 67, 73, 74, 75, 77, 82, 88, 91, 92, 94, 112, 125, 128, 199 ff., 206–8, 212 ff.
  in Indonesia 43 ff., 45, in Egypt 46–7
  alleviation 9, 26, 28, 106, 110
  urban 15–18, 23, 29; *see* poor
power (supply) 12, 46, 92, 168, 187, 214
primacy, primate city 139–40, 141, 145, 159
private (sector) xxi, 12–13, 26, 32–3, 35, 36, 56, 64, 66, 100–101, 102, 143, 147, 158, 167–8, 201, 213, 216
privatization 16, 17, 38, 187
productivity xvi, xvii, xix, xxi, xxii, 3, 10, 27, 37, 47, 52, 53, 54, 55, 57, 58, 73–4, 75–6, 77, 78, 81, 88, 89, 99, 112, 113, 119, 169, 171, 173, 194, 199 ff.
  urban xx, 11–15
  of the poor 28
  in Indonesia 43 ff.
programme (approach) xxiv, 5, 44, 65, 104, 105, 106, 112, 140, 164, 174, 176, 177, 181–3, 214

INDEX

project (approach) xxiii, xxiv, 14, 15, 17, 19, 22, 23, 27, 32, 44, 53, 60, 61–2, 65, 75, 82, 88, 148, 151, 152, 154, 155, 158, 162, 164, 165 173–4, 176, 181–2
 cycle 49–50
 orientation 44
public sector 12, 13, 35, 36, 64, 66, 89, 100, 102, 134, 147, 168

regulatory framework, regime 13, 30, 77, 83, 135, 154, 167, 181, 187, 193, 204 ff.
Renaud, Bertrand 133, 137, 138, 139, 140 n, 172 (reference)
research xxii, 20–22, 45, 46, 47, 60–61, 67–8, 70, 79, 82, 104, 105, 119, 133, 169, 192, 200, 210
"resource pool" 165–7
rural xii, xiii–xv, xvi ff., xix, 2, 4, 54, 55, 62, 64, 113, 118, 136, 153, 185, 189, 213

safety nets 16, 17–18, 54
Sao Paulo 12, 20, 72, 212
Seoul 144, 212
sites and service (schemes) 15, 52, 109, 200
Sivaramakrishnan, K. C. (Sivaram) 31, 43, 57, 65, 81, 82
slum (upgrading) 12, 15, 31, 39, 200, 212
 dwellers 34
South Africa 55–7, 58–9, 105
South Korea xv (see Korea)
Soviet Union 36, 90, 111, 157
squatters, squatter settlements xii, xv, 20, 35, 201, 212, 213
structural adjustment (adjustment) xviii, 4, 15, 16, 17, 18, 21, 36, 61, 77, 184, 185, 203
subsidies, subsidization 58, 87, 115, 134, 135, 136, 167, 203
 in Bombay transport 48
Sundaram, P. S. A. 33, 54, 82, 91, 103, 107–8
sustainable, sustainability 18, 27, 31, 96, 98

Taiwan 69, 70–71, 134, 138 n
technical co-operation, assistance 26, 29, 30, 41, 45, 49, 62, 67, 73, 94, 105, 152 n, 193, 195
telecommunications, telephones 12, 52, 72, 88, 117, 118, 129, 168, 187, 204, 214
Thailand 16, 29, 30, 70, 85, 112, 137, 142, 143, 157, 167, 171, 194
Thai 73, 129, 130, 131, 132, 135, 137, 138, 145–6, 161, 163, 165, 166, 167
Todaro, Michael xvi–ii
trade xvii, xviii, 60, 128, 189, 202
 policy 17, 136, 142
 terms of xvii, 169
training xxiv, 23, 191
transport, transportation xx, 12, 18, 30, 48, 56, 58, 76, 78, 87, 88, 96, 117, 128, 144, 159, 162 n, 168, 177, 184, 188, 189, 206, 213, 214
Trinidad and Tobago 97
Turkey 10, 14
Turner, John 72, 103

UN xiv, xxi, xxiv, 25
 General Assembly xxiii
 Global Strategy for Shelter to the Year 2000 xxi, 1, 3, 30, 216
UNCED 19, 31
UNCHS x, xxi, xxii, xxiii, xxiv, 22, 65, 66, 119, 124, 159
UNDP x, xxi, xxii, xxiii, xxiv,

xxv, 1–3, 22–33, 44, 45, 48, 49, 57, 61, 62, 66, 72, 73, 75, 93, 96, 111, 112, 113, 124, 159, 175, 211, 212, 214, 216–18
unemployment xvi, xviii, 206–7
UNICEF xxiv, 104, 105, 216
United States of America 48, 63, 81, 90, 112, 116, 117, 193
AID xx, 51, 80, 193
urban areas vii, xi, xiv, xv, assistance xx, 28, 39, 108 xvi ff., xxv, 3, 4, 14, 18, 55, 65, 66, 73, 82, 83, 125 ff., 185
Basic Services Programme, 105
bias xv ff., 4
development vii, 2, 14, 27, 28, 30, 40, 43–5, 54, 55, 63, 69, 70–71, 81, 86, 89, 108, 110, 123 ff., 174, 177, 181, 182
Development Co-operation Development Authority 98, 179 Strategy 27
economy 169, 172, 178, 185, 199, 201, 202 ff.
growth 2, 69, 200, 213
hierarchy 129–30, 132, 141, 143, 144
issues xxiii, 9, 22, 66, 86, 90
lending 17, 22
localities 188–9
policy 2, 9, 14, 25, 69, 70–71, 86, 90, 114, 173 ff., 185
population 16, 24, 26, 27, 31, 36, 40, 47, 54, 113
sector xxi, 10, 23, 25, 36, 44 ff., 88, 170, 173, 185
management 3, 78, 83–5, 93 ff., 95, 96 ff., 107, 108 ff., 112, 173, 175, 176, 191, 207
rôles 129
–rural linkages 4, 64
services 17, 26, 59
strategy 11, 44 ff., 48 ff., 56–7,
85, 93, 94
studies 20, 70, 71, 123–72
Urban Management Programme xxii, 22, 32, 42, 48, 50, 62, 63, 66, 67, 93–103, 104, 105, 106, 112, 159, 163, 172, 175–6, 211
urbanization vii, ix,, xii, xiii, xv, xxiii, xxv, 1, 3–5, 14–15, 24, 25, 54, 65, 83, 95, 102, 111, 119, 124 ff., 151, 170, 173, 184, 192, 193, 194

Vietnam 177, 178 n

wages xvii, xviii, 21, 204 ff., 207
waste 12, 13, 18, 20, 30, 84, 96, 151, 177, 186, 187, 204, 209, 213
reducing 187
water (supply) 12, 18, 19, 20, 31, 46, 76, 77, 100, 104, 109, 115, 137, 138 n, 151, 159, 162 n, 183, 186, 187, 202, 204, 209, 213
Watts, Kenneth 54, 69–73, 74, 85
Wegelin, Emie 182, 147 n, 149, 150, 163, 172 (ref.)
women 3, 15, 21, 26, 34, 76, 77, 97, 112, 186, 188, 208, 212, 216
World Bank ("the Bank") xviii, xx, xxi–v, 1–3, 9, 10, 14, 16–19, 22–4, 29, 30, 35, 38, 39, 44, 45, 48, 49, 50 ff., 53, 55–8, 60–3, 71–7, 83, 88, 93, 96, 104, 107, 112, 113, 116, 118, 119, 124, 133, 138, 141, 147, 148 n, 149, 159, 164, 166, 167, 169–71, 174–76, 178, 181, 182, 199, 200, 206, 210–11, 214, 216

Zaire xi, xv
Zimbabwe 56, 94, 105
zoning xiv, 13